# Key Papers from the Journal of Child Psychotherapy

The practice of child psychotherapy builds upon the writings and contributions of earlier writers, such that it is not only the latest research and theory that are valuable. *Key Papers from the Journal of Child Psychotherapy* provides access to classic and important papers from the early years of the *Journal* – papers that have previously been difficult to obtain. The papers are grouped thematically to cover the entire range of work represented in the journal: theoretical, clinical, applied.

The papers, written by professionals at the forefront of their fields, cover areas including psychoanalytical metapsychology, work with deprived children, work with trauma, and how psychoanalytic thinking can be applied in the context of institutions for children. Chapters include:

- Anne Alvarez's *Problems in the Use of the Counter-Transference*
- Edna O'Shaughnessy's *The Absent Object*
- Gianna Henry's *Doubly Deprived*

*Key Papers from the Journal of Child Psychotherapy* presents, in one accessible volume, essential papers for all those training and practising in child psychotherapy. It will be of great benefit to all professionals involved in direct work with children.

**Paul S. Barrows** trained in both Child and Adolescent, and Adult Psychotherapy at the Tavistock Clinic, London. He is now Principal Child Psychotherapist with the United Bristol Healthcare (NHS) Trust, and is Joint Editor of the *Journal of Child Psychotherapy*. His main interests are in parent–infant work and the links between child and adult psychotherapy. He has published widely in these areas.

# Key Papers from the Journal of Child Psychotherapy

Edited by Paul S. Barrows

Brunner-Routledge
Taylor & Francis Group

HOVE AND NEW YORK

First published 2004 by Brunner-Routledge
27 Church Road, Hove, East Sussex BN3 2FA

Simultaneously published in the USA and Canada
by Brunner-Routledge
29 West 35th Street, New York, NY 10001

*Brunner-Routledge is an imprint of the Taylor & Francis Group*

Typeset in Times by Mayhew Typesetting, Rhayader, Powys
Printed and bound in Great Britain by MPG Books Ltd, Bodmin,
Cornwall
Paperback cover design by Sandra Heath

This publication has been produced with paper manufactured to strict
environmental standards and with pulp derived from sustainable
forests.

*British Library Cataloguing in Publication Data*
A catalogue record for this book is available from the British Library

*Library of Congress Cataloging-in-Publication Data*
Key papers from the Journal of child psychotherapy / edited by Paul S.
Barrows.
        p. cm.
Includes bibliographical references and index.
    ISBN 1-58391-208-8 – ISBN 1-58391-207-X
1. Child psychotherapy. I. Barrows, Paul. II. Journal of child
psychotherapy.

    RJ504.K49 2004
618.92'8914–dc21

                                                2003008639


ISBN 1-58391-207-X (hbk)
ISBN 1-58391-208-8 (pbk)

# Contents

# Foreword

I remember the excitement with which my fellow trainees and I in the late 1960s and early 1970s opened each issue of what was then, as Paul Barrows writes, a small in-house journal. Many of the papers were written by our teachers, who had themselves been among the first students at our training school. They conveyed the sense that fundamental issues related to the practice of child psychotherapy were being thought through for the first time. Successive editors welcomed contributions from all members of the profession, making us feel that we were part of a pioneering scientific venture. Today, the much-expanded *Journal of Child Psychotherapy* occupies a pre-eminent position in the field, is expertly produced by Taylor & Francis, and is available on-line; but the papers published in it still convey a pioneering spirit and the passion which the authors bring to their work.

Reading the papers collected in this volume gives the reader a sense of the intellectual roots of the profession. Some of the theoretical and practical issues addressed remain fully relevant today. Others repay thinking through again in the context of changed circumstances, new findings or fresh points of view. The section on applied work is particularly topical in the context of current debates in the public sector.

Inevitably, as Barrows indicates, readers may find that particular favourites have had to be omitted. Many Freudian and Jungian contributions were published in other journals, including Kut Rosenfeld and Sprince's pioneering work on borderline children. Constraints on space meant leaving out papers by Martha Harris and Frances Tustin which did first appear in the *Journal of Child Psychotherapy*. Barrows notes that Tustin's contribution was unique in leading to developments in the psychoanalysis of adults, whereas more generally child psychotherapists have been influenced by psychoanalytic theories derived from the treatment of adult patients. Although her books are readily available, her papers in the *Journal* contributed to its characteristic atmosphere. I hope that this volume may be followed by another including some of these papers and providing a picture of the *Journal* under later editors, including the time of Barrows' own editorship together with Hamish Canham.

Paul Barrows has performed an important service in collecting these articles from the first 20 years of the *Journal of Child Psychotherapy*. This book constitutes an invaluable resource for students, and indeed for anyone concerned with the development of the theory and technique of psychoanalytic work with children, adolescents and their families.

*Maria Rhode*
*Professor of Child and Adolescent Psychotherapy*
*Tavistock Clinic/University of East London*

# Preface

The *Journal of Child Psychotherapy* has consistently been at the forefront of developments in the field of psychoanalytic psychotherapy with children. Indeed, until very recently it was the only English language journal devoted to this subject area.

Many of the papers that have appeared in the *Journal* have become classics – frequently cited and an on-going source of inspiration – as well being essential teaching tools in the training of child psychotherapists. To date, however, access to these texts has been difficult for students, most of whom do not possess sets of back issues of the *Journal*. Moreover, several numbers are now out of print (although those wishing to purchase as full a set as possible should contact the Association of Child Psychotherapists, 120 West Heath Road, London, NW3 7TU).

It was with this in mind that it was decided that it would be timely to publish a collection of some of these classic papers. Needless to say, the hardest part of this endeavour has been the selection of which papers to include – or rather, which of the many really valuable contributions to have to regretfully leave out. I have been greatly assisted in the selection process by many colleagues: representatives of the training schools; former editors; overseas representatives of the *Journal*. No one, I am sure, will be satisfied with the final choice and there will be personal favourites that do not appear. However I think the selection arrived at does include the most seminal papers for the profession, as well as giving some impression of its range and depth. In several instances the authors have also contributed an additional brief postscript.

It should, however, be emphasised that this collection in no way seeks to be representative of the profession as a whole. It is not intended to provide an overview of its historical development, nor to provide a balanced representation of the full range of theoretical orientations (there is an absence of Jungian papers, for example), nor even to convey the full scope of the activities in which child psychotherapists have become involved. Other, larger collections of papers have already admirably addressed these issues (see in particular Daws and Boston, 1988; Szur and Miller, 1991; and Lanyado and Horne, 1999).

Rather, it is intended as a resource for all those involved in the profession of child psychotherapy, whether directly or more tangentially, to enable them to have access to some of the key child psychotherapy texts. The criteria that have been used in determining the choice of papers have therefore included: the number of those consulted citing a particular text as a valued teaching resource; the date of the paper (I have deliberately chosen papers published pre-1990 as likely to be more difficult to obtain) and in some, though not all, cases whether the papers have already been reprinted elsewhere.

I hope that this will prove a valuable and helpful collection to have readily available.

# Acknowledgements

There are many people to thank for their help in getting together this collection. First, I am grateful to those who found time to think through the selection of papers and to further comment on the preliminary draft choices. Then, of course, my thanks go to the authors for their kind permission to reprint their articles. I am also extremely grateful to Marie Fraser for her ever-helpful and efficient scanning in of the original texts. Joanne Forshaw at Taylor & Francis has also been very supportive, encouraging and, above all, patient!

Particular thanks to my family who have had to tolerate my preoccupation and absence whilst working on this project, and to Margaret Rustin for discussion of the Introductory sections.

Finally, I gratefully acknowledge the financial assistance of the Tavistock Institute for Medical Psychology for a research grant that helped me to find time to complete this work.

# General introduction

It was in December 1963 that the then Association of Child Psycho-therapists (non-medical) published volume 1(1) of the *Journal of Child Psychotherapy*. This collection of papers from the early years of the *Journal* therefore affords a wonderful opportunity to celebrate its 40th anniversary.

The Association of Child Psychotherapists is more than 10 years older than the *Journal of Child Psychotherapy*, and in the course of those 50-plus years, child psychotherapy has become firmly established as a profession within the National Health Service in the UK, although its status as a core discipline in some other parts of the world remains equivocal. This year (2003) has also seen the creation of the first Chair in Child and Adolescent Psychotherapy in the UK, at the University of East London. In parallel with these developments in the profession, the *Journal of Child Psychotherapy* has also evolved, from being a quite 'local', in-house affair with a circulation limited to the membership of the ACP to being a major international journal – the leader in its own field. Its more recent associ-ation with Taylor & Francis has greatly strengthened its international scope, in particular through its on-line presence which means that it is now accessed by many more than those who actually subscribe.

During the 40 years of its existence, the *Journal of Child Psychotherapy* has reflected the immense creativity of the profession. However, due in part to the nature of its initial restricted circulation, many of the most influential papers from the earlier numbers have remained hard to obtain. This volume aims to make them more readily available, both to the growing number of students of child psychotherapy as well as to those whose own history, and collection of journals, does not extend back quite that far! These papers represent the clinical and theoretical backdrop and roots of the profession, and they have had an important bearing on subsequent developments both in relation to metapsychological theorising and to technique in the con-sulting room.

Child psychotherapy remains a profession which – quite rightly – 'stands on the shoulders of giants' in the sense that it builds upon the creative work of its founders, many of them represented here. A good grasp and knowledge of the work of those thinkers is an essential resource for the next generations of child psychotherapists who can build upon those foundations without being constrained by them, and it is primarily for this reason that the collection has been compiled. The papers span some 25 years and whilst it is striking, in reading through them, to register the extent to which Freud's own original work remains so influential, it is also a testimony to the life of the profession to see the ways in which that original work has been extended and modified – and indeed continues to be so.

Whilst a knowledge of earlier theoretical views remains essential, exaggerated adherence to them can, of course, only be a major impediment to the development of new insights. It has always been the expectation that theory (and practice) should continue to develop through the detailed, and unprejudiced, observation of clinical facts. The theories to emerge are then tested through the monitoring of the patient's reactions to those new theoretical insights, as conveyed through the medium of interpretation. This is the basis on which psychoanalysis has claimed its scientific status.

In the papers presented here we can, then, trace the origins of some of the later developments that have proved so important for the profession. These developments have influenced and enriched both the theoretical grounding of child psychotherapy as well as pushing forward the boundaries and scope of the work. The range of patients treated, for example, has been hugely extended, to include autistic, deprived and borderline children who now regularly constitute a large proportion of the child psychotherapist's workload, rather than being 'research' cases as they once were. Child psychotherapists have also increasingly gone outside the consulting room to apply psychoanalytic insights in a whole range of new settings (see, for example, *Journal of Child Psychotherapy* 28(2) which was entirely devoted to applied work).

This volume does not, however, aim to describe those later developments, accounts of which are already easily accessible both in recent numbers of the *Journal of Child Psychotherapy* and in an increasing proliferation of books and collections of papers. What it does seek to do is to set them in context. The book is arranged in three sections, focusing first on those papers that have made a particular contribution to the theoretical framework within which child psychotherapy is practised, then (in so far as it is possible to draw this distinction) looking at papers which have rather more of a clinical emphasis. Finally there is a section highlighting some early contributions in the area of applied work. Each section has an introduction that seeks to draw out some key aspects of the papers and to indicate the direction of later developments.

First, however, two rather more general points.

It is striking – and somewhat disappointing – to note that, whilst the present texts represent such a valuable contribution to the field of *child* psychotherapy, it remains the case that, with rare exceptions, the major direction of influence has been for child work to be influenced by developments in psychoanalytic thinking originating in work with adult patients, rather than vice versa. Thus, for example, Bion's work has profoundly influenced many of those working analytically with children. This is particularly well illustrated by O'Shaughnessy (this volume and O'Shaughnessy, 1981) in her accounts of how his ideas can be utilised in the playroom. However, even though Bion's work has been concerned with the earliest mental processes, for example relating to the development of the infant's capacity to think, the insights are derived from work with adult patients *not* from work with young children or even mothers and babies themselves.

By contrast papers that *have* been grounded in work with young children have not, on the whole, had a comparable influence on psychoanalytic work with adults. The one noteworthy exception has been Frances Tustin's contribution. Her work has prompted considerable interest in the problem of autistic enclaves in adult patients (see particularly H.S. Klein, 1980) and, more generally, in the nature of primitive mental processes, exemplified most notably in Mitrani's work (Mitrani, 1996, 2001). But she has been the exception.

This imbalance seems all the more surprising given that the pioneers of child psychotherapy – Anna Freud and Melanie Klein – both worked with children as well as adults and indeed felt that their work with the former was immensely helpful and informative for their adult work. As Klein noted:

> my contributions to psycho-analytic theory as a whole, derive ultimately from the play technique evolved with young children . . . the insight I gained into early development, into unconscious processes . . . has been of far-reaching influence on the work I have done with older children and adults.
>
> (Klein, 1955b: 122)

She makes clear that the analysis of young children led to insights that it would have been extremely difficult to acquire in work with adults, yet which could subsequently be fruitfully applied to that work. However, there now seem to be almost no examples of the continuation of this line of approach. It is rare for those trained as adult analysts to go on to also work with children – although it must be said that this is nothing new. Some 60 years ago Bick (1941) discussed, and regretted, precisely this state of affairs. On the other hand, a considerable number of those trained as child psychotherapists do pursue further training in adult work, so that this might be one route whereby such an approach might re-emerge. To date, however, no such trend has been reflected in the literature.

The other general point has to do with the developments in child psychotherapy that have taken place over the last 40 years leading to extensions in both theory and practice. Whilst it might have been antici-pated that this broadening of approach could lead to a growing divergence of views, there has, on the contrary, been an increasing *convergence* in many areas. The papers in the present volume, from the early years of the profession, show some marked differences in approach, for example in relation to the relative weight given to reconstruction as opposed to work in the here-and-now. A reading of papers in more recent numbers of the *Journal of Child Psychotherapy* would, I believe, show much less marked distinctions, and reveal that what takes place in the consulting room now may give little away about the therapist's theoretical orientation or where she or he trained.

Two particular areas in which this convergence has perhaps become most apparent are, first, the importance now attached by clinicians of all schools of thought to the counter-transference as a source of clinically usefully information about the patient's mental state. Second, there has been a much greater emphasis on the importance of the concept of deficit and the need, in consequence, for a developmentally (as well as psychoanalytically) informed therapy. This has been exemplified both by Alvarez (1996) whose formative influences are the works of Klein and Bion, as well as Hurry (1998) whose theoretical formation was that of the Anna Freud Centre.

This is not, however, the place for a fuller discussion of these issues. With one exception, the papers gathered here span roughly the first 25 years of the *Journal of Child Psychotherapy*'s publication. They represent an impressive contribution to the development of psychoanalytic work with children of which the profession can feel proud – and to which the present generation continue to add.

# Part 1

# Mainly theory

# Introduction

This first section of papers concentrates on those of particular significance for their theoretical contribution, as opposed to those more immediately addressing clinical or technical issues. However, one of the most distinctive features of papers appearing in the *Journal of Child Psychotherapy* has always been the extent to which they have been firmly grounded in detailed clinical material, so that this kind of distinction is perhaps more than usually somewhat arbitrary. Nonetheless, with that caveat in mind, it remains the case that these articles focus primarily on explicating some key theoretical concepts.

It is, of course, impossible to divorce the developments that have taken place within the theoretical frame of reference of child psychotherapy from those that have occurred in the wider field of psychoanalysis. This introduction in no way sets out to provide an overview of those developments, either in relation to child or adult work, which is already available elsewhere (for one such review see Likierman and Urban, 1999; for a detailed account of developments within the Kleinian framework only see Spillius, 1994, and for a review from a Freudian perspective see Hurry, 1998). I shall therefore concentrate on highlighting a few points that seem to be of particular interest and relevance, as reflected in these articles, with some comment on subsequent developments to try to set them in context.

## The role of transference

The transference has perhaps always been one of the most central concepts in psychoanalysis, and Rosenbluth's paper gives an extremely clear account of the Kleinian approach to work in the transference with children. Whilst all schools of psychoanalytic thought would subscribe to its central importance, the details of how it is to be understood, in particular in relation to work with children, have provoked some of the most heated disagreements between Freudians and Kleinians. As Rosenbluth (1970, this volume) noted:

it was in child analysis in particular that different techniques were evolved by the two main pioneers in this field, Melanie Klein and Anna Freud.

There are two key points that Rosenbluth emphasises which, I believe, would still be seen as tenets of a more distinctively Kleinian approach. The first of these is the emphasis on the unique nature of the psychoanalytic relationship and the importance, in consequence, of ensuring that that uniqueness is preserved. Crucial to this is the focus on the transference:

> There are many others in the child's environment, parents, teachers, relations, who can reassure, give presents, educate, be kind or stern, but our role is fundamentally different from theirs. Children, just like adults, are in the end relieved if we do not allow ourselves to be sidetracked from our main goal, which for us is the interpretation of the transference.

This has obvious and major implications for how the child psychotherapist conducts himself or herself.

The second is the focus on the here-and-now experience (in contrast to something more by way of reconstruction):

> The most important thing, it seems to me, is to stress in one's inter- pretations the current anxieties and conflicts in relation to the therapist; the link with the parents and with the past can often be implicit in one's wording.

The value of this kind of focus is thought to be two-fold. First, that in capturing the repetition of the past in the present in all the emotional intensity of the relationship currently being experienced it is both more convincing and therefore more effective therapeutically. Second, the focus on the transference relationship has the effect (almost by definition) of drawing the child's conflicts into the transference thereby making it easier to address them in that context, and with the added bonus of freeing the child's life outside from being the target of these conflicts:

> If all transference feelings are consistently interpreted, more and more of the child's unconscious phantasies and impulses gradually become centred around the treatment, and the baby relationship then becomes fully transferred to the therapist. This also means that the situation at home usually becomes relieved, as the baby relationship needs no longer to interfere so much with the present relationship between the child and his parents.

Debate over this position has continued and Alvarez notes in her paper (this volume) how the Kleinian position is sometimes (mis-)represented:

> I think some critics of Kleinian work in the transference assume a very mechanical process of interpreting every tiny piece of material as referring directly to the person of the therapist. This would mean always interpreting the object to the neglect of the ego or the id. This type of 'me-me-me' interpretive work would be a bad mistake with any patient . . .

Since the publication of these papers the debate over the nature of the transference has continued. There has, for example, been an increasing emphasis on what Meltzer (1967) refers to as the 'gathering of the transference'. This involves more of an acknowledgement of the length of time that it takes to draw things in to the transference relationship and, closely linked to this, there has been much greater recognition of the value of containment, within the transference relationship, *over time*. Hopkins's postscript to her 1986 paper (this volume) makes this point explicit.

The debate about the nature of the transference is inextricably linked to another on-going issue, namely the question of what are the factors that effect change in this kind of work. Is it only mutative *transference* interpretations (Strachey, 1934) or are there other elements at work? It seems to me that it is in this arena that essentially the same debate is currently being pursued, as for example in relation to whether the therapist is to be seen only as a transference figure or whether s/he may also be seen as a *new (developmental) object* (see Hurry, 1998).

The clinical and technical implications of these differing theoretical positions are important and were further opened up in the discussions that took place at the Study Weekend of the Association of Child Psychotherapists in 1999 (see Lanyado, 2001 and related commentaries in the same number of the *Journal of Child Psychotherapy*). Whilst opinions remain divided, there would also seem to be some areas in which there is a certain coming together of these discrepant points of view, in particular perhaps in relation to work with new and particularly challenging groups of patients such as children with autism. For example, the emphasis in some of Alvarez's later papers (see Alvarez, 1996) on the importance of being aware of the element of deficit in a child's experience, and the possibility that the therapist may therefore need to be performing a new function for them (for example in relation to finding ways of making real emotional contact with the 'un-drawn' – as opposed to withdrawn – child), has parallels with the 'developmental therapy' described by Hurry (1998).

There have also been related developments in the conceptualisation of what exactly constitutes an 'interpretation'. Increasingly, there is a widely held view that it is not only *verbal* interpretations that are important but that interpretations may also be conveyed to the patient non-verbally or through the therapist's more concrete actions, with whatever they might imply. Indeed, interpretations might remain formulated within the therapist's mind but not be put into words if this would be felt to be premature. They would, nonetheless, influence the on-going transaction between therapist and patient. For example Reid writes of her work with a very young child:

> Although I made few interpretations my actions were informed by my countertransference, checked against what I could observe of my patient's behaviour and the atmosphere at the time. I think at this point my actions could be described as *demonstrations* of my understanding of what Georgie brought to the transference, via my countertransference responses.
>
> (Reid, 1990: 37, emphasis added)

## The role of the external object

Inherent to these debates is the question of the status of the external object. Developmentally there is the question of the role of actual experience, as against the infant's own contribution (its interpretation of that experience in the light of its own phantasies), in the construction of the individual's internal objects. Allied to this there is the question of the aims of the child psychotherapist and the extent to which their focus is, or should be, primarily on modifying the child's internal objects through emphasising the child's contribution to the state of those objects. Or, in other terms, stressing the need for them to assume responsibility for their psychic reality and to withdraw their projections.

This debate has tended to be rather polarised around the view that the Kleinian position has been overly preoccupied with the child's internal reality to the neglect of real experiences, and the counter charge that the more Freudian view has overly emphasised external experience to the neglect of the child's contribution.

Whatever the rights and wrongs of this debate historically, I think a reading of current contributions to the *Journal of Child Psychotherapy* would show that there has been a considerable coming together of views in this respect and that, for example, 'Kleinian' papers would now take far greater explicit cognisance of a child's history and real experiences. I suspect that the contributions of Bowlby and attachment theory have played an important role in this respect. At the same time, a careful reading of the present collection of papers would also show that this polarisation was always perhaps somewhat unjustified.

For example, the earliest of these papers from a Kleinian author (O'Shaughnessy, 1964, this volume) already underlines the importance of the external object and shows *why* this matters:

her [the mother's] external presence gives him [the infant] visible disproof of his internal state, and he can introject the external object to improve his internal object.

Almost 20 years later Alvarez (1983, this volume) makes a similar point:

The concept of the container is Bion's (1962), and Spillius suggests that through this concept, Bion has made the external object an integral part of the system. She says his formulation shows not just *that* the environment is important but *how* it is important. I would say: *one* of the ways in which it is important . . .

Thus it has always been the case that, as in Klein's own formulations, external reality has been seen to have an important role to play. However, it is equally true that the emphasis has been on how it interacts with internal reality, by modifying or disconfirming it, rather than on how it might play a primary role in creating that reality.

It is a logical consequence that any psychotherapy conducted within this paradigm will privilege the modification of internal reality. As Rosenbluth (1970, this volume) puts it:

Certainly past external reality difficulties played a part in the origin of her conflicts, but we can do nothing about them any more. External reality should not be denied, but I do not think it is particularly helpful to interpret in such a way as to encourage the patient to fasten on to it to justify her own hostility.

This approach is also seen as having the advantage of reducing the risk of acting out. She goes on to say:

. . . this way of interpreting [putting the blame on to the mother] might encourage the child to act out her hostile baby transference at home in relation to the mother, whereas our aim should be not only to keep the baby transference in the treatment, but to focus it there increasingly.

As an aside, it is interesting to note that both O'Shaughnessy and Hoxter nonetheless also refer to the important role that the external object might play through its active intervention to limit the activities of the more destructive aspects of the child's personality. For example O'Shaughnessy (1964, this volume) notes:

What may add further to [the child's] distress is the absence of external control over bad parts of the self. Particularly if the ego is weak and destructive impulses are strong, is there need for external restraint.

Here of course the author has in mind what factors might have been important in the child's development, rather than the role the therapist might take. By implication, however, it might be the case that, in the face of overwhelming id impulses, there is a need for the therapist to act as a kind of auxiliary ego. Henry would seem to be suggesting just this when she quotes Boston writing about the difficulties of working with very deprived children:

> Understanding the hostility and phantasies may not be sufficient. The new object, the therapist has to prove that he can contain the violence and reduce its omnipotence by withstanding it and surviving as the original object in the patient's phantasy did not.
>
> (Boston, 1972)

Here too attention is drawn to the need for the child to have an experience of a new kind of object.

## Projection/projective identification

The concept of projection, like the transference, also forms an integral part of psychoanalytic metapsychology. Whilst Klein's 'extension' of this concept to include the mental mechanism that she termed 'projective identification' (Klein, 1946; 1955a) has proved immensely rich and fertile, it has also led to considerable confusion and lack of clarity because of the variety of different meanings that have subsequently accrued to it. Authors have all too often not been explicit in how they have been using and defining the term. Lubbe has given one account of the development of these differing usages of the concept in the *Journal* (see Lubbe, 1998) and it has also been extensively discussed by Sandler and others (Sandler, 1989).

Some of the differences in points of view clearly relate to the age at which it is believed certain mental processes are possible. Klein refers to projection (and introjection) as taking place in the first three or four months of life (see Klein, 1952). For Novick and Hurry (1969, this volume) this would simply not be possible since it requires an awareness of the separateness of the object, and the attribution of a mental and emotional life to that object, beyond the capacity of the ego at that stage:

> Thus we would see the use of projection as becoming possible at a later stage than that of externalisation – at a stage, in fact, when the capacity to manipulate objects in fantasy has developed to the point where a drive-derivative originally directed at an object can be subjectively allocated to that object, while the self is experienced as the object of that drive-derivative.

In other words, the infant requires what we would now call a 'theory of mind'.

Their point of view is based upon a very careful and precise dissection and definition of the terminology involved. Thus, they propose that it would be helpful to use 'externalisation' as the more generic term for the processes under consideration:

> We believe it would be helpful if the term 'externalisation' were to be accepted as the general term under which would be subsumed all those processes which lead to the *subjective allocation of inner phenomena to the outer world*.

'Externalisation', however, is to be carefully distinguished from 'generalisation' which does not involve the allocation of inner phenomena, nor is it defensive in origin. For example:

> Thus as the child becomes aware of his own wishes towards the object, for example the wish to devour, he *naturally* ascribes similar wishes to the object. This process is not projection proper; the conscious awareness of his own wish continues to exist. We would term this process 'generalisation' [original italics].

This seems an important distinction and not one, I think, that Klein would have made, in part precisely because her use of the term projection as applying to the youngest infant also predates any idea of the infant having a 'conscious awareness of his own wish'.

They then go on to tease out two specific meanings that are subsumed under the portmanteau term 'externalisation'. In the one instance the process refers to the externalisation of a drive, in the other to the externalisation of a self-representation. They propose that the term 'projection' be reserved for the former:

> we will focus in particular on the differentiation between those processes by which a drive is externalised and those by which an aspect of the self-representation is externalised. We would suggest that the term 'projection' be reserved for the former process – i.e. *drive projection*.

This is not a mere matter of semantics, and their paper makes clear the clinical relevance of these distinctions with particular reference to how certain material might be taken up with a child. It is particularly interesting to juxtapose this paper with that by Alvarez in this volume, which is similarly concerned with some of the fine differentiations that need to be made in considering what is being communicated in a session, if we are to be able to make the most helpful interpretation.

Alvarez draws particular attention to the need to distinguish between what is, in her terminology (or rather, as she says, Money-Kyrle's), a desperate projective identification, and what is a destructive one. For example, she writes:

> If what may be brought into the transference and put on to the person of the therapist are not only projections of parts of the patient's self, but also the whole of his inner world, including his objects, split or in parts, past or current, how is one to make the correct choice? Suppose an adolescent patient says to us, 'You look tired today', or a younger child holds up the mother doll and says, 'She just can't sit up today'. Is this a realistic perception achieved by a child who is learning to see what he sees – we do look tired – or is this a direct projection of an exhausted drained aspect of the patient himself? Or is this a consequence of the patient's greedy demands on us earlier in the session? Or, alternatively, is this an attempt by him to elucidate and give form to a damaged drained internal object which is normally quite repressed?

In many ways her initial question highlights the difficulties that are raised by a rather more blanket and undifferentiated use of the term 'projection' and the need to clarify precisely what it is that is being externalised. This, as Novick and Hurry spell out, will inform how we then interpret:

> Once the differentiation has been made it follows that interpretation of externalisation of aspects of the self must focus upon the need to defend against narcissistic pain, whereas interpretations of projection must focus upon the need to defend against the anxiety related to drive expression.

There is, then, a common thread linking these papers albeit this finds expression in very different language, and that is the importance of the clinician's sensitivity to the precise nature of the child's communication.

## A note on language

Finally, a brief comment about the use of language in these papers. Many readers of Klein, and of other Kleinian authors, struggle with the part-object language that is sometimes used to patients (illustrated here in the 1964 paper by O'Shaughnessy but also still used by other authors, particularly those more influenced by Meltzer). Such language does not feature in papers from colleagues of a more Freudian persuasion.

Kleinians themselves will, of course, differ in this respect. As Alvarez notes in this volume:

there are considerable differences among Kleinian analysts and Kleinian psychotherapists today in the manner and pace with which they would introduce part-object language into an analysis.

Spillius, more recently, similarly notes:

> A number of analysts, perhaps especially Donald Meltzer, find it appropriate to interpret unconscious phantasy directly in part-object bodily language, but the general tendency now is to talk to the patient, especially the non psychotic patient, less in terms of anatomical structures (e.g., breast, penis) and more in terms of psychological functions (e.g., seeing, hearing, thinking, evacuating).
>
> (Spillius, 1994: 351)

Despite this acknowledgement of a change in practice, I am not aware of any papers (either in the *Journal of Child Psychotherapy* or elsewhere) that really seek to grapple with the implications of this major shift. There appears to be, both in the literature and in the training schools, surprisingly little open debate about the pros and cons of such different approaches. Given the care and thought taken about what to interpret, and how and when, this seems particularly surprising. It must surely make a considerable difference to our patients what language we use in speaking to them. It must likewise be confusing to students not to hear any debate about such a central issue.

It is not my intention to begin that debate here (space does not allow) but rather simply to flag up the fact of this striking reticence in the hope that this might stimulate some more open discussion of the issue.

# Chapter 1

# The absent object

*Edna O'Shaughnessy*

Originally published in the *Journal of Child Psychotherapy* (1964) 1(2): 34–43.

The subject of this paper is the absent sustaining object. This first intrudes on the life of the baby in the form of the absent breast. The absent breast is an essential part of the breast relationship, since it is of the logical essence of a relationship that there be times when the one person is with the other and times when he is apart from that other. The unborn infant – being permanently in union with his mother – does not yet have a relationship to her, or to her parts: he enters on the condition for a relationship at birth. A relationship, moreover, needs to be distinguished from a simple association, which ends as the partners part. The feeding infant does not have a feeding association with the breast, like a strictly business association. He has a relationship to it, which spans presence and absence, which goes beyond the physical presence of the breast to the breast in its absence.

The first point of interest is that the character of the absent object is opposite to the character of the object when there. The object when present is *prima facie* a good object. Whatever the difficulties, the feeding breast sustains life. As against this, the absent breast is first experienced in hunger, when it is needed and is not there; that is, the absent object is a bad object which is leaving the baby to starve and die. Nevertheless, the absent object is an integral part of his life, and in the course of his development the baby must come to terms with it. It will be a major difficulty in the way of establishing the good internal object, since hatred will be mobilised against it because of its absence, making it hard to keep the good gained in its presence. However, as well as constituting a difficulty for development, the absent object is also a spur to development. By its harshness it forces reality on the child, and breaks the hold of phantasies which protect him from the realisation of his vulnerability and dependence. It makes him know reality.

In particular, the absent object is a spur to the development of thought. It is not an accident that this is so, since there is a logical connection between thought and absence. You can be asked to think of something that is absent, a painting in a gallery (say), but you cannot be asked to think of a painting you are already looking at; perception shuts out thought, in this basic and simple sense. You can think about – in the sense of reflect upon –

anything, things present as well as absent, but before you can 'think about' you must develop the prior capacity to 'think of'. This latter is essentially linked to things absent; developmentally speaking, to the absent breast.

Psycho-analytical theory has, indeed, always posited that frustration leads to mental development. Freud remarks on 'the exigencies of life' to which 'the psychical apparatus owes the impetus to further development', and goes on to say: 'The exigencies of life confront it first in the form of the major somatic needs' (1900). Freud himself did not say much more about the conditions for mental development, his fundamental concern being regression rather than development. And since Freud, there has not been agreement about the way frustration acts in the psychical system. Now, the nub of the question is: How does a baby *experience* frustration? When he has 'major somatic needs' what is his state of mind? In other words, when a baby has 'major somatic needs' what phantasy possesses its mind?

In his book *Learning from Experience* W.R. Bion has investigated this experience of need in the baby and gives the following account of it. When the infant feels hungry and in need of the breast, he is aware of a need not satisfied. This frustration, the pain of his hunger, is what is present to him, and this, initially, is felt as a bad breast present. The infant has now to make a beginning on a critical advance. For the wanted breast is *in fact* not a bad breast present, but a good breast absent when needed. The infant has in the course of time to come to know this fact, which is a fact of both inner reality – his need, and outer reality – the missing good breast. That is the infant has to advance from experiencing the needed absent breast in the phantasy of a bad breast present, to being able to *think of* the real missing good breast. This crucial advance in his development is hard, since the bad breast, which in phantasy is present, is felt *au fond* to be starving him to death, and it is only by tolerating the pain and terrors of his frustration enough that he can put himself in the position of being able to think about them, to think, eventually, that what he needs is the missing good breast. Such knowledge, in thought, of the good breast will also help him to endure his state of need. Since tolerance of frustration is essential for thought to develop, the infant who predominantly avoids facing his frustrations and in phantasy simply gets rid of them, is employing methods actively antagonistic to thinking, so that the development of his mental powers will be, at the least, inhibited, and may be disturbed. Thus we may say that the absent object gives the child his first opportunity to know reality through thought, and also gives him the incentive, viz., to make frustration more tolerable.

The child in treatment re-experiences the early alternations of his objects as the presence and absence of his therapist succeed each other by turns. Therapy repeats life in this respect, and allows us to observe the child's feelings about his objects in presence and in absence. It can be observed that, from the start, the child reacts to any break which disrupts the accepted rhythms of treatment, as the Easter, summer and Christmas holidays do. Furthermore, from the start, the child is sensible of even the ending of a session; with several sessions a week his reaction is particularly sharp at the weekends. From the start of treatment, the presence and absence of his therapist is experienced as an underlying alternation of good and bad, the current recapitulation of his early feeling of the breast when present as, *prima facie*, good, and the absent breast as, *prima facie*, bad.

Further, since according to Dr Bion's findings, the way the infant deals with the absent breast is critical for the development of his powers of thinking, it will likewise be the case that the way in which a child deals with gaps in his treatment will be critical for its successful outcome. The question here becomes: Can he preserve, and use, under the strain of the absence of his therapist, the insight – the thoughts – he gains in her presence?

The oscillation between good and bad felt in the comings and goings, and the difficulty of bearing the pain of absence so as to be able to think about it to make it more tolerable, explain the phenomenon, familiar in treatment, of the heightened clinical picture before a longer than usual break. Strong defences disown strong feelings about the coming separation, and at the same time, there is increasing urgency of need, fear and hate in the infantile parts, which may burst the defences and make the child unsteady with their intensity. In more severe cases, where the child is not able to acknowledge the coming separation, he becomes increasingly impoverished as he splits off more and more of his awareness until his personality seems to dwindle away. The general nature of the primitive phantasies the child has about the absent object is well known. In phantasy the object is attacked by various methods for its hostility, neglect, or selfishness in being absent and attending on itself or enjoying itself with others who are preferred. More basic, however, than such envious and jealous perplexities, is the feeling that the absent breast has left him to die. Listen to a small boy in a session before the Easter holiday when he became frightened of me as a malignant absent object. He spoke to the frightened parts of himself to try to reassure them. 'Listen,' he addressed himself, 'the lady wants to say something. She says you'll be saved: she'll give you a drink. She's *not* glad you're dying.' The fear of dying emerges during treatment as the basic anxiety stirred by the absence of the object.

I should like now to give a clinical illustration of a child who is unable to tolerate the impact of the absent object. It shatters his defensive phantasy that baby and breast are one, and exposes the reality of his separateness. The absent object is then experienced as a threat of death, and instantly – in phantasy – exploded away. In the course of the session which is given in detail, we see how the child stops expelling the situation. Instead, he begins to face it. He starts on the struggle to think about it, which makes him attack the absent object, as well as become aware of his own aloneness.

The session took place the day after I told John, a 12-year-old boy, about his first holiday break. He had started his analysis five weeks before Easter, four times weekly. From the first, he was frightened in the playroom, and stood in one place looking apprehensively round at the items of furniture, the walls, and the air between things. It was as if the room were filled with particles. He could not move. At moments he also looked very sad. Only in the third session did he bring himself to the open drawer, and he did so in a curious way. He placed his coat, satchel and gloves on the table to make a wall in front of the drawer, and then he bent down and crawled along behind the wall to squat by his drawer and finger something. He then crept back, and stared round the room. The impression was of crawling into something in order to get to the drawer. This impression was confirmed two days later, when, literally, he stepped out of his own shoes, left them at the door, and then entered the playroom, in phantasy stepping out of himself and entering a new medium, denser, because interior: the interior of the object, that is, which he crawls into to get at its contents. The following day he suffered an acute claustrophobic attack in the room, screaming and struggling, feeling he was suffocating in the object in which he was imprisoned. The next few sessions were concerned with his claustrophobic anxieties. This brief account brings us to his 11th session when, so that there would be a little time left, I told him that we should be stopping for a fortnight at Easter. He had been standing by the window, looking out. When I made this announcement, he swung round to stare at me, his face wide with disbelief.

The next day he brought with him an exercise book. Nearly filling the first page a large drawing was in progress, and he sat down to continue it. It had an inner circle, and four surrounding circles which were finely subdivided. At the top, it was as if a shaft had sunk to the centre, leaving a gap in the first ring, and a bit of each successive ring in the one below it. I asked about his drawing. In his customary halting speech he said, 'It's of England and France who were once joined. Then a volcano came, and they got separated. The middle bit got sunk, and now they're like this,' and he showed me with his pencil how each of the four rings was mismatched at the sunken bit. I said, 'You feel you and I are like England and France, that we were once joined. You felt us to be joined till I told you we should be stopping for Easter. Those words sunk into you like a shaft in the middle. And then you simply stared at me. I think when you stared at me you were seeing me as a bad going away breast, and then, with a volcano from your eye, you felt you dispersed this bad breast out of your sight and into me.' ('Bad breast' is used in this interpretation rather than 'bad mother' because of the nature of his relationship to me, which I understood as being on an early part-object level.) I went on: 'Now you feel we're separated, and we don't fit each other.' John was shading the centre circle. He said, 'There's a fire burning in the middle, because it mustn't get out the other side.' He inspected the other side of his page to see if his drawing showed through. He started to pass wind. I said, 'Your drawing pictures your inside. You feel you've got me inside as a breast with your volcano in it – this is now burning you up in the middle. You feel you mustn't let these burning gases get out your other side – but all the same, you feel they are leaking out in the smells from your anus.'

On a new page he drew three heads in profile: the first had a low forehead, the second a higher forehead, and the third a still higher forehead. He labelled the first head '– 1,000', the second head 'Now', and the third '+ 1,000'. He said they were just people, and that – 1,000 meant a thousand years ago when they had no brains, and now, they've got more, and in a thousand years' time they would have still more brains. His own long hair gives him a low forehead, and I said, 'These people are you, really. You feel you've more brains now you understand what you did to me as an absent breast, and what breast you've got inside. This is unlike yesterday, when you didn't see anything of it, since you exploded it out of your sight. This volcano-method seems so far from understanding, that yesterday seems like a thousand years ago. This sense of long ago comes also from the fact that the volcano-method would be how you got rid of your mother's absent breast, when you were a baby long ago. I think, too, that your sense of having more brains now gives you hope of still more brains in the future.'

He had started another drawing. He drew a circle and said it was the moon. He drew four rockets round it. He said, 'The rockets are dropping darts of air into the moon. Then there will be enough air to live.' I said, 'When you erupted the absent breast out of your eye, you felt the volcano came from your eye and travelled the space between us until it reached me, where it entered, and made me a moon breast. Now you feel you've got to breathe life into me and the atmosphere round me, and then there will be enough air for you to live, too. I think you feel your words to me do this – they are the darts of air which give life to the analysis.' He turned the page over to see if his drawing was showing through. He looked worried and touched the marks that showed, and all the while he was making smells. I said, 'You are worried your smells, which are attacking me for going away, are undoing the work of reviving the dead breast and its atmosphere; you're afraid they are fouling it.'

He started a small drawing. He drew the earth and then a big moon. He put in the four rockets – not round the moon as before – but near the earth. In a despondent voice he said, 'They're going back now.' I said, 'The four rockets are the four days you come to me. And now, Easter, you must go back.' On the moon he drew some irregular shapes. He said, 'They're what you see in the evening, if you look up at the moon.' I asked him what these things on the moon were. After a long hesitation, he replied, 'I know what they are now. They're called craters,' and he turned back to the drawing of the three heads and made the third head bigger. He was in an uneasy state. I then said, 'You know now that you see in me the craters from yesterday's eye-volcano and today's smells. Perhaps when you speak of looking up at the moon, it's also a memory of the baby-you looking up at the breast, and seeing how you attack it and put craters or extinct volcanoes in it to rid yourself of what will otherwise extinguish you. Knowing this brings you despair, because you feel a cratered breast can't keep you alive. Indeed, you have become uneasy with me now as a dead moon breast giving out foul gas.'

He turned back to his first drawing. In its centre he wrote 'Fire.' In the top sunken bit he wrote 'Wet from Water', saying, 'The sea comes in.' I said, 'You go back to your first drawing, to yourself inside, because I, the outside breast, am felt as dead and foul, and as far away for Easter as the moon is; and you show me how you feel on fire inside with the volcanic breast, and that the baby-you feels left to get wet outside from the water of tears and urine coming in on you like a sea when I leave you.'

Much in this session is not emphasised or interpreted, because it seemed subsidiary to the content of his anxiety about the holiday and his mode of response to it. The words of the announcement had entered him concretely: they were felt to sink him in the middle. The 'volcano' that then came was not an attack of anger, as one might at first suppose. He did not get angry. His eyes opened wide, not in a glare, but in a shock of disbelief: he could not believe *this*. Then he continued staring at me vacantly for a long while. The unconscious phantasy occurring during these moments was that he could volcano this absent breast out of his sight.

He was having an experience which may lie behind the stare of a very young infant in similar circumstances. It is sometimes supposed that because an infant only stares when the breast has gone, that he does not mind its absence, but we may presume that, at times, he responds to the absent breast – which for him is a starvation breast – by staring it out of his eyes in the way John does when he hears in the session that I am going to leave him. We could put it that death stares John in the eye, and when he turns round to stare at me, he has the phantasy that he stares out the death breast, hurtling it into me. That is, he is using a primitive pre-thinking mode of response to evade the anxiety of his extinction.

We can see how difficult it is for him to think, to use his brains, rather than evade fear by 'volcano' methods. He manages to think a little in this session, and each step in thinking seems to him so huge that it is as if it takes a thousand years. It is of interest that twice in the session he feels he has more brains: once when he finds out something about his inner world, that it contains a volcanic object which is burning him up; and again, when he knows it is his craters he sees when he looks up at the moon, that is, when he finds out what he does to his object. This second bit of knowledge is harder for him to acquire because of the persecution and despair of being kept alive that goes with knowing the breast is cratered. We can see the coming Easter break will be an especial strain now he has, as it were, more brains. The fact that his analysis helps him to understand what, in his language, 1,000 years ago he couldn't means that the break carries, in addition to the strain of the object being absent, the strain of anxieties which before coming into treatment he had been unable to face, and now may dread facing alone. Indeed, it is a commonplace that patients may not be able to contain such anxieties during a break, and may break off treatment, or commit follies, or even crimes.

We see, too, in this session how his full aggressive powers mobilise themselves to get rid of the absent breast. He himself describes it so: 'A volcano came.' This means he is not only expelling extinction into the breast, but with such violence, that – to continue in his images – the volcano shatters and cracks the moon as it lands. This is an important happening. It means that the re-internalised absent breast is a breast in inner decline because destruction is felt now to lodge in it. Further, since the original situation of hunger in which the object is absent means starvation and death to the young infant, it is really this threatening extinction which is projected out, and which the re-internalised object will be felt to contain. The internal object is then felt to die from within, and the absent object, by projection, in its turn becomes a dead object. Furthermore, at an immature stage of development, any processes which make for improvement depend very greatly on the presence of the external object, so that in its continuing absence the child is given over to increasing fear and despair, like at the end of John's session when he turns back in on himself, feeling that his internal object is burning itself up, while he is in a sea of wetting and crying.

This fact, that the internal situation declines in the absence of the external object, poses a difficulty for development. The internal object must be kept alive, or else at each re-union so severe a setback has occurred as to make a continuous relationship impossible. Now, the task for the infant in the presence of the breast is different from his task when the breast is absent. In the presence of the breast, he has to take in the good, overcoming difficulties of temperament and circumstance. The task in the absence of the breast is to keep the good gained in its presence, the counterpart task for a child in treatment being to use and preserve his insight into himself, when he is away from his therapist. But often, he finds himself instead on his own in a declining situation. The pain of needing the object when it is absent may force him back to primitive mechanisms, like those illustrated by the case of John. Unable to face his situation, the child rids himself of those parts of himself which feel and know about his pain by expelling them into his object with a violence that is felt to damage it. He resorts, that is, to increasing use of projective identification. The result is, that the object is taken in again worse than before since it is felt to contain now these violent parts of himself, and he is further hindered from rallying because the external object is not there.

In her paper 'Mourning and its relation to manic depressive states' Melanie Klein shows how the external presence of the mother is necessary to overcome such internal anxieties. It is not merely that when the mother is away she cannot replenish her child's stocks of food and love, but also that she is not then able to reassure him by her presence. When her child attacks her for deserting him, he internalises a damaged mother, so that her external presence gives him visible disproof of his internal state, and he can introject the external object to improve his internal object. The delight in regaining the absent object comes partly from this. Indeed, an inability to separate from the object may be due to a fear of being alone with an internally damaged object without the reassurance of its external presence.

There is another of the object's qualities which is lost to the child when the object goes away: there is no one then to receive and care for his unwanted parts. This capacity of the mother, in her reverie with her child, as W.R. Bion calls it, to absorb from him what he does not want to go on containing, and to return it to him in better shape, is as important on the emotional plane as the giving of love, just as the removal of urine and faeces is as important as the provision of nourishment on the physical plane. When the child has no one there to take his emotionally unwanted parts, he is left with the alternative of containing them in an unchanged state, or exuding them and then living in a space contaminated by them. Children who suffer an unduly long separation may get a look beyond being in decline, a look of having declined to a standstill. Internally this means that the flow in and out has ceased because of the continuing absence of an external object which can nourish and reassure, as well as receive his state of mind, so that the child feels overwhelmed by his condition.

What may add further to his distress is the absence of external control over bad parts of the self. Particularly if the ego is weak and destructive impulses are strong, is there need for external restraint. In the absence of a restraining object, the child feels himself at the mercy of his jealousy and envy which are aroused by the absence of the object, which is often felt to be absent because it is occupied with something else, another baby, or the penis, or selfishly, even its own insides. For instance, as a holiday came close, a boy of eight played several times in the following sort of way. He made a breast by placing a bowl upside down with a small red object on top for a nipple. He put some cars underneath inside the bowl. Then he brought wild animals to stand around this representation of a breast, and taking another car he pushed his way in among the residents of the breast, and battered them. Here we see a child's primitive parts gather round the breast which is felt to house others while away from him, and in phantasy enter it and savage its inmates.

These assaults on the internal object make it difficult for the child to preserve it and use it when the external object is absent. However, despite these difficulties which it creates, the absence of the object is an essential condition for development. As a small instance: The absent object shatters John's phantasy of living in a breast, and spurs him, in the interval between the two sessions – though he had not drawn, let alone prepared a communication before – to set down his state of mind on paper and bring the drawing to his analysis.

It is now necessary to take up again the discussion of the connection between thinking and non-presence, where it is shown that the ability to think must start with thought of an absent object. The absent object has the character of offering a 'critical' choice, in Dr Bion's words 'between procedures designed to evade frustration and those designed to modify it' (*Learning from Experience*, p. 29). John's 'volcano' method is clearly an evasion of the situation. He does not deal with it, and this is reflected in his own account of what happened. 'A volcano came', he said, which conveys how he felt that there was an occurrence in him, rather than that he exercised his mental powers. The first rudimentary thoughts, however, necessitate that the child face his frustration and exercise his mind to deal with it.

In the beginning stages, he may attempt to modify his situation by thought of an omnipotent kind, to save him from fully realising his situation of dependence on an object which is not there. An example is the preparations made by a 12-year-old girl for the summer break, in which she imagines herself the omnipotent possessor of all she needs. She constructed a calendar for the month of August, and illustrated it with a drawing of a tea-garden. Most of the picture was taken up by a table in the foreground on which were two tall glasses, filled with round ice-creams. From her associations we could understand that she was denying the separation from me, felt to be her mother, during August, by making herself in phantasy the owner of the tea-garden, that is, making herself into her mother with all her possessions, notably the ice-creams, her breasts.

During the holiday, the reality situation of being without me intruded into this phantasy, breaking it down, and a few days before she resumed her analysis she had a dream which she told in her first session. She was standing on the edge of the beach, and she had been advised to go out into the sea for a bathe. As she looked at the sea, it seemed cold, and already dark, and uninviting. So she decided not to try it. This was a prologue to a change of scene in the dream. She was in a hip-bath, together with another girl, a school friend. Her tummy was very big, and she was pregnant. There was a big knob sticking out at one place in her tummy which she thought must be the baby's head. Her associations, plus the general position of the dream in the analysis (coming, as it does, in the context of work on whom – when the object is absent – the patient feels she is), allow the dream to be understood in the following way. In the second part of the dream, she makes herself all at once the pregnant mother, the parental couple – she and her school friend, and the unborn baby – in a hip-bath. She becomes, by omnipotent phantasy, all that she is not, to deny the pain of what she is. Were this the only part to the dream, it would be an example of a patient omnipotently denying the absence of the object. The prologue to the dream, however, shows that in the holidays the patient is beginning to have insight into her omnipotence and to understand its purpose: it is to save her from going out into the sea, that is, to spare her the pain of coming out of phantasies of tea-gardens into the uninviting sea of reality, where she has to acknowledge that during a break in treatment she has not got her sustaining object with her. In the dream this is a cold state, already dark, so uninviting that she decides not to try it and resorts to omnipotence instead. She also understands that her analysis is, as it were, 'advising' her to bathe in reality. This holiday dream in which she saw the purpose of omnipotent thinking to be a defence against an uninviting state, proved to be the moment from which her use of omnipotent methods was much lessened. It would seem that the interruption of the treatment had been a stimulus to progress to real, as opposed to omnipotent, thinking about the absent object.

It is of interest to see how the dreamer conceives of the absent mother. She feels she has been advised by her to go out and bathe in the sea, and it is apparent she feels she has been despatched to so uninviting, cold, dark and solitary an experience that she will not even try it. The mother who does this to her is bad. Indeed, the absent object, from the time when it is first met in a situation of painful need, is felt to be bad for withholding the benefits of its presence from the child. The child's natural greed for his object will make him further resent its absence and so will his jealous wish to prevent his object having a relationship to anyone but himself. There are also morbid functions for which the child may require the presence of his object, such as the continuous reassurance already mentioned. Also, in this morbid category, is the need for the presence of the object by children who have a chronic sense of something lost. A small boy, for instance, was described as always losing things, even minute things like a match-head, which he must then find. With this went a strong anxiety about separating from his parents. In his case, his need of his external objects as 'necessary adjuncts' – in R.E. Money-Kyrle's sense – was due to his feeling that they contained the lost parts of himself.

This raises the problem of how the absent object can cease to be a bad object. What follows is a brief sketch of what is really a most intricate and slow process. As against the forces of temperament, the requirements for normal development, and the excessive demands of a disturbed development – all of which drive the child to cling to his object – as against these, there is a need in the child for the absence of his object. Absence is a natural and essential condition of a relationship, which otherwise becomes a symbiosis detrimental to the separate identity of either person. Time away from the object is needed to get an emotional perspective on experience had with the object. Appreciation, too, is sharpened in absence. Indeed, the continuous presence of an object would be persecuting; the child would feel the object was intruding into his identity, and he would also be burdened by guilt for claiming the object for himself.

It is not that the child, grudgingly, in the end, tolerates the absent object, but that he has need of its absence. His own emotional growth will help him oppose the forces which make him cling to the object. Chiefly, it will be his concern for the object in its own right, rather than as an accessory to himself, which makes him give it freedom for a life of its own. A child always, in part, wants even to be weaned. Further, as he matures, and can better tolerate his guilt, his need to have a bad absent object lessens, and the object can be allowed to keep its good qualities when away. Also, if it is felt to be benevolent when absent, it can be trusted to return when needed. In other words, the history of the absent object is this: first, it is a bad breast present; second, it is thought of as a bad aspect of the breast; and third, it is thought of as a good breast missing.

In the third stage, the absence of the object is felt to be reasonable and desirable even while it is missed. It is allowed to rest, and follow its own interests, while the child himself goes on with his own life. Greed, jealousy, and envy will be less, and love more active in protecting the object against attack. This means that the object which the child re-internalises is not in decline, but is alive, and can sustain him from within in the absence of his external object. This stage is reached in treatment when, by himself, the child puts to use his understanding of himself.

## References

Bion, W.R. (1962) *Learning from Experience*. London: Heinemann.
Freud, S. (1900–1) 'The Interpretation of Dreams, II', SE 5.
Klein. M. (1942) 'Mourning and its relation to manic-depressive states'. In *Contributions to Psycho-Analysis 1921–1945*. London: Hogarth (1948).
Money-Kyrle, R.E. (1961) *Man's Picture of his World*. London: Duckworth.

Chapter 2

# Projection and externalisation[1]

*Jack Novick and Anne Hurry*

Originally published in the *Journal of Child Psychotherapy* (1969) 2(3): 5–20.

---

Projection is one of the more frequently used terms in psychoanalytic literature, especially in clinical presentations. It is seen by some authors as fundamental to all clinical work. Rapaport (1944) states that the fundamental psychoanalytic postulates of psychic determinism and continuity require a concept like that of projection.

Projection was one of the first concepts developed by Freud and a detailed analysis of the topic can be found as early as 1895. It is a measure of the complexity of the topic that despite the history of its usage there remains considerable confusion and disagreement as to the meaning and applicability of the term. Currently, the most widely accepted definition of projection is, 'viewing a mental image as objective reality' (Rycroft, 1968). This definition is one which pre-dates Freud (Feigenbaum, 1936). In the current literature projection is used as a portmanteau term encompassing such diverse processes as displacement, generalisation, externalisation and some processes of adaptive mastery. A host of phenomena is described as subject to the process of projection: drives, introjects, aspects of the self, affects, sensations and structures such as super-ego and id. Projection is said to be manifest in such varied areas as play, artistic creation, religion, projective tests and persecutory delusions. Used in this way the term lacks explanatory power and significant clinical distinctions are blurred. The lack of a proper terminology perpetuates the problem. In recent years there have been attempts to differentiate some of the processes heretofore subsumed

1 Presented at the Study Weekend of the Association of Child Psychotherapists, March 1969. This paper forms parts of a research project entitled, 'Childhood Pathology: Impact on Later Mental Health', which is conducted at the Hampstead Child-Therapy Course and Clinic, London. The project is financed by the National Institute of Mental Health, Washington, DC, Grant No. MH-5683-07.

Earlier versions of this paper were presented at the meetings of the Index and Clinical Concept Groups of the Hampstead Clinic. We would like to thank Miss Freud, Dr J. Sandler and the members of both groups for their many helpful suggestions. Acknowledgement is due to Kerry Kelly for her collaboration in the work which led up to this paper.

under projection. In particular the concept of externalisation has been the focus of increased attention (Brody, 1965; Rapaport, 1944, 1950, 1952; Weiss, 1947). This however has added a terminological difficulty since those who write about externalisation tend to use it synonymously with projection, and it is not clear whether externalisation is viewed as a sub-species of projection, as a process distinct from projection, or as a more general process with projection as a sub-species.

The current difficulties can be traced, in part, to the fact that many misconceptions exist concerning Freud's use of the term, and most writers are not aware that there is in his writings a theory of projection and related mechanisms which is further advanced than current thinking on these topics. Thus, it is commonly assumed that Freud saw projection as only a defence and that his major discussion of the topic was in 1911 in the Schreber case where projection was described as a paranoid defence against homosexuality. This assumption omits the greater part of Freud's thinking on these topics. In fact, projection was one of the first concepts developed by Freud and remained of major importance to him for many years (1895). Projection was an essential conceptual tool in Freud's examination of many areas in both clinical and applied psychoanalysis.

In 1895, in a letter to Fliess, he defined projection as a normal process which could be abused for the purpose of defence. As a normal process it was related to causal thinking.

> Whenever an internal change occurs we have the choice of assuming either an internal or an external cause. If something deters us from the internal derivation, we shall naturally seize upon the external one.
>
> (1895: 209)

During the next few years Freud extended the application of the term so that by 1911 it was used as a portmanteau word in a way which is strikingly similar to its current usage. However, from 1911 there were substantial developments in Freud's views on the phenomena he had hitherto subsumed under projection. The differentiations he was to make in the following years were such that, were they to be applied today, they would overcome many of the current difficulties and represent a significant advance in conceptualisation.

We can summarise the four main developments as follows:

## 1. Projection as a basic early mechanism leading to the development of the self

For some years Freud held that projection played a central part in the early development of the self and the differentiation of self and object: that, governed by the Pleasure Principle, the early ego projected unpleasurable affects and sensations into the external world. Those writers who refer to this view of Freud's fail to note that even in his earliest presentations (1911, 1915) it is assumed that some structuralisation must take place prior to the occurrence of projection. Furthermore most authors omit the fact that in his later writings Freud explicitly excluded these early processes of differentiation from the category of projection, describing them instead as the 'origin' of projection (1920) and later employing phrases such as 'ascribe to the outer world' in place of the term projection.

## 2. Projection as a mode of thought

One type of normal projection of particular interest to Freud was that employed by primitive man in building up his picture of the external world. From his first mention of this topic in 1901 Freud showed an increasing interest in primitive thinking. This idea is most fully developed in 'Totem and taboo' (1913) where he wrote of anthropomorphic thinking:

> Animism came to primitive man naturally and as a matter of course. He knew what things were like in the world, namely just as he felt himself to be.
>
> (1913: 91)

These views are further considered in 'The uncanny' (1919) where for the last time Freud uses the term projection to explain primitive thinking, even though this topic interested him to the end of his life. Indeed, in 1927, in 'The future of an illusion' he explicitly qualifies his former views, stating that projection can offer no more than a description of what occurs, and is of little explanatory value.

## 3. Externalisation of aspects of the self

The term 'externalisation' was first used by Freud in 1913 in reference to the creations of the artist. It was an infrequently used term, synonymous with projection. In his early writings cases involving what we would see as externalisation of aspects of the self were instanced as examples of projection. In the Schreber case Freud explicitly differentiated a type of projection, which he termed the 'change of subject', from drive projection proper. He wrote that the proposition '"I (a man) love him" could be contradicted by the formula, "It is not I who love the man – *she* loves him". By means of this change of subject the whole process was "thrown outside the self" and became "a matter of external perception"' (1911: 64). It is worth noting that he never subsumed under projection the processes involved in narcissistic object choice although his major paper 'On narcissism' (1914) was written at the point of his maximum interest in projection. Similarly, in all his writings on homosexual object choice, or on the role reversal involved in some types of passive to active mastery, he did not once use the term projection.

## 4. Projection as a defence against the drive

From 1911 onwards Freud's most consistent and major use of the term projection was to denote a reflexive defence against the drive. Thus in the Schreber case he described how in the paranoid defence against homosexuality the *unconscious hate* was projected. The unconscious proposition 'I hate him' became transformed into the conscious thought, 'He hates (persecutes) me' (1911: 63). In later writings, notably 'Totem and taboo' (1913) and 'Some neurotic mechanisms in jealousy, paranoia and homosexuality' (1922) Freud linked drive projection with defence against ambivalent conflicts. The final major use of the term projection occurs in 1931 when Freud explains the girl's fear of being killed by the mother as due to the projection of her own hostile wishes.

The main point we wish to emphasise concerning Freud's use of the term projection is that, when looked at historically, we can see a clear line of progressive limitation in the application of the term, the exclusion of phenomena which had initially been subsumed under projection and the differentiation among types of projection, in particular, those involving projection of an aspect of the self-representation and the projection of a drive. In our view these differentiations made by Freud should be incorporated into any attempt to conceptualise mechanisms involving the subjective allocation of inner phenomena to the outer world, for two reasons: first, we would thus achieve an historical consistency the lack of which adds to misunderstandings; second and, more importantly, the differentiations made by Freud are based upon clinical distinctions which are obscured when these phenomena are subsumed under a portmanteau heading. Our interest in this topic stemmed from the fact that clinically we were making distinctions which we were unable to encompass and clearly communicate within the current terminology.

We believe it would he helpful if the term 'externalisation' were to be accepted as the general term under which would be subsumed all those processes which lead to the *subjective allocation of inner phenomena to the outer world*. As a general term 'externalisation' would refer to processes which might be normal or pathological, adaptive or maladaptive. Further, such a usage of externalisation would parallel the current general usage of 'internalisation' under which we subsume a variety of processes: introjection, identification, etc. But terminology which would delineate the various different types of externalisation has yet to be found. Of the many processes of externalisation we will focus in particular on the differentiation between those processes by which a drive is externalised and those by which an aspect of the self-representation is externalised. We would suggest that the term 'projection' be reserved for the former process – i.e. *drive projection.*[2]

Although we are aware that the distinction between drive and self-representation is an arbitrary one, since these two elements are intimately interrelated – aspects of the self-representation are, for instance, 'coloured' by the drive – we still propose that on balance one can say whether a specific phenomenon is related preponderantly to the drive or to an aspect of the self-representation. For instance, there is a difference between the statements, 'I am an angry person' and 'I am angry at (I hate) you'. The former is an evaluation of the self-representation, the latter a drive expression.

We would see all forms of externalisation as serving a primarily defensive aim. We distinguish externalisation from processes which may result in apparently similar surface phenomena, but which actually relate to modes of functioning and are not primarily defensive. In particular, we are referring to some processes of early differentiation and to generalisation.

Neither of these modes of functioning are defensive in origin, nor do they involve the allocation of inner phenomena to the outer world. We would, therefore, exclude them from the general category of 'externalisation'.

We will discuss these various processes in the psychic development of the child from two points of view: that of the maturation of the individual and that of the effect upon the developing individual when he is used as a target for the externalisations of others.

## 1. From the viewpoint of the development of the individual

### A. Early differentiation of the self from the outer world

Any statement concerning the earliest stages of development must be seen as hypothetical. It is however generally accepted that among the major tasks faced by the developing organism are those of integration and differentiation. Specifically the child must gradually differentiate the self and the outer world.

Writers in the field of developmental psychoanalysis and psychology have put forward a number of suggestions concerning ways in which, at various stages, this differentiation might be made. There is for instance the action-

---

2 The subject of externalisation is one of great complexity and our focus on these two particular processes stems directly from our clinical interests. Examination of this topic clearly indicates that further differentiations and qualifications will have to be made. We hope to take up the additional issues in future reports. In particular we plan to discuss Freud's category of the attribution of cause to the external world.

oriented mode of differentiation: that which can be manipulated by a motor action initially becomes part of a motor schema. Freud describes differentiation on the basis of the pleasure principle (1915). Clearly such modes will lead to faulty, unrealistic differentiation of self and object. On the other hand modes of correct differentiation do exist, such as certain types of integration of disparate sensory experiences, as in the 'double-touch' phenomenon described by Hoffer (1950). Those differentiations which are faulty are normally corrected by experience.

From an adultomorphic viewpoint many of the initial differentiations made are faulty. Some writers refer to this initial faulty differentiation as a type of externalisation, most usually a projection. But in our view to speak of processes involving the subjective allocation of inner phenomena to the outer world *prior* to the development of the self and the differentiation of inner and outer worlds, is meaningless, and confuses cause and motivation (Rapaport, 1960).

(We recognise of course that some of these processes of differentiation may be grossly interfered with, and that persistence of or regression to faulty differentiation may be seen at later stages – as for instance in some borderline children. Even here one must distinguish between a defensive ego-regression and faulty differentiation as a function of structural defect.)

## B. Generalisation

With the differentiation of the self from the external world, the child's view of the external world, and especially of his objects, will be largely determined by what he knows about himself. Thus as the child becomes aware of his own wishes towards the object, for example the wish to devour, he *naturally* ascribes similar wishes to the object. This process is not projection proper; the conscious awareness of his own wish continues to exist. We would term this process 'generalisation'. The process of generalisation remains the child's major mode of apprehending the unknown and persists to some extent throughout life. Examples are legion: the infantile sexual theories, for instance, provide clear illustrations.

The differentiation between projection and generalisation is of theoretical importance in many areas. For example, it is often assumed that Freud saw projection as playing a central role in super-ego formation. This is not the case. Freud ascribed the severity of the super-ego not to the projection of aggressive wishes on to the subsequently introjected object, but to three other factors, one of which was the *natural assumption* on the part of the child that he and the father had similar aggressive wishes towards each other. This is spelled out most clearly in 'Civilisation and its discontents' (1930: 128–130).

But in our view the major importance of the distinction between projection and generalisation lies in its clinical and technical value. Projection is a defence against an object-directed drive derivative, and as such requires the usual defence analysis before the impulse itself can be approached. In contrast, an extensive manifestation of generalisation beyond a certain age usually reflects a weakness of the ego due to immaturity, to faulty development, or to deterioration. The technical approach to generalisation is therefore fundamentally different from the approach to externalisation of aspects of the self or to projection – as is intuitively recognised by most experienced clinicians.

For example, Kevin was an 11-year-old boy referred to a child guidance clinic for a variety of obsessive-compulsive rituals. He was diagnosed as a neurotic whose major conflict centred around aggression. In psychotherapy he very soon showed conscious fears of being attacked by his therapist. These were seen and interpreted as projections, i.e. as a further attempt to defend against the awareness of his own aggressive impulses towards the object. The child soon became totally unmanageable and was referred to the Hampstead Clinic for intensive treatment. Soon after the start of analysis it became clear that the fear of being killed by the therapist was not based upon a projection but upon a generalisation of his own conscious wishes towards all his male objects, i.e. wishing to kill an envied male object, he simply assumed that the object had the same wishes towards him.

Diagnostically this use of generalisation alerted the therapist to other signs of ego-deviation, and finally a diagnosis of 'borderline' was confirmed. This new perspective on the case led in itself to modifications of technique. Despite positive changes which occurred during the first year of analysis, the use of generalisation persisted. At a certain point it became possible to focus on this pathological mode of functioning. The therapist then helped the child to develop those structures necessary to inhibit generalisation. By using the therapist as an auxiliary ego Kevin could slowly come to accept that he could not know the object's thoughts or feelings (unless these were communicated to him in some way) and that the object was therefore not necessarily like himself, and might have thoughts or feelings different from his own. It should be noted that with the inhibition of generalisation Kevin remained conscious of his own aggressive wishes, but there was a significant change in the intensity and quality of his anxiety. Only much later in treatment, after considerable ego-development, did Kevin make use of projection proper to defend against the conscious awareness of his own aggressive impulses.

While in this example we have emphasised the contrast between a mode of functioning and a defence, generalisation and projection, we are of course aware that after structural inhibition of early modes has taken place, they may be re-employed for defensive purposes. For example when Kevin, at a later stage in his analysis, insisted that the therapist had the same wishes and thoughts as he did himself, it emerged that this insistence represented a fantasy defence against loneliness. Kevin could then say, 'Oh, I wish you did think the same, because then I wouldn't be alone'.

## C. Externalisation

### (i) Externalisation of aspects of the self

With the emergence of the self from the state of 'primal confusion' the child is faced with the extremely difficult task of integrating the various dissonant components of the developing self. When one considers the rapidity of the physical and mental changes which take place in the child between, for instance, 8 and 18 months, one realises that the demands made upon his relatively weak integrative function are far greater than at any other period of life. In addition to the integrative demands made by his own physical and mental growth, the object's expectations of the child also undergo rapid changes, and these expectations are transmitted to the child. (Only in adolescence is the individual faced with changes which make integrative demands of a magnitude even approximating to those of infancy.) The earliest conflicts faced by the child in his attempts at integration relate to the existence of dissonant, seemingly incompatible aspects of the self. These conflicts are intensified as some aspects become narcissistically valued through both the child's own pleasures and, more importantly, the parents' response to one or other aspect of himself. Those aspects which are not so valued may become dystonic. Their retention within the self-representation will lead to a narcissistic pain such as humiliation. The toddler who falls often cries not only because of the physical pain but also because of the humiliation of seeing himself as unable to walk. One solution is to externalise that aspect of himself, for instance to make the doll or the baby the one who is incapable of walking, thus avoiding the narcissistic humiliation. At this stage of development such externalisation is both normal and adaptive.

It is adaptive in that the intensity of the current conflict is decreased sufficiently to allow progressive development to occur. When the child's self-image is stabilised at a higher level (through the consolidation of ego skills, the reinforcement of pleasure in functioning, and a general decrease in the intensity of the earlier drive derivatives) he is then able without threat to adaptively integrate many of those aspects previously externalised. Thus the child who is fully capable of walking can again allow himself to crawl without humiliation.

Externalisation may also be adaptive in many other ways. It may, for example, be used as a stepping-stone on the way to identification. The self is constantly reshaped by changing ego-capacities and drive aims. New shapes of the self may be externalised on to contemporaries, in play, on to imaginary figures, on to fictional characters, etc. In addition to its defensive aspect this process allows for what may be termed a trial reality test in which, via the object of externalisation, the child can assess the effects of and reactions to this new shape of the self. In the light of these effects and reactions he may then be able to accept this new aspect of himself.

Thus, as a transitory phenomenon, externalisation is a normal defensive process and can be adaptive, particularly at certain phases. However, the extreme or persistent use of this defence at any period of life may have serious pathological effects. It may result in a very restricted personality with important aspects of the self permanently split off and unavailable.

It is a defence not *primarily* directed against the drives, nor against object-linked anxieties, but is aimed at avoiding the narcissistic pain consequent upon accepting devalued aspects of the self. Object relations are only secondarily involved in this process, and in fact externalisation can be used as a defence against object relationships.

### (ii) Projection proper

The defence of projection proper is fundamentally different. It is motivated by the sequence of fantasied dangers consequent upon drive expression. It is a defence against a specific drive derivative directed towards an object and thus considerable structural development must take place before it can or need be employed. Among other things there must have been a channelling of drive energies into a specific aim and the establishment of the capacity to relate to a whole object. In addition there must be sufficient ego development to allow for the integration of drive derivatives with ego capacities in the formation of fantasy expressions of object-directed wishes. Thus we would see the use of projection as becoming possible at a later stage than that of externalisation – at a stage, in fact, when the capacity to manipulate objects in fantasy has developed to the point where a drive-derivative originally directed at an object can be subjectively allocated to that object, while the self is experienced as the object of that drive-derivative.

As a transitory phenomenon the use of projection may be normal at certain phases of development, but in contrast to other processes of externalisation it has relatively little adaptive value. It may be seen as adaptive in so far as it represents an attempt to attain, retain or regain object-ties, albeit in distorted form, and thus may presage the emergence of an object relationship. As Freud (1911) noted, projection could represent, an attempt at re-cathexis of objects following upon a psychotic withdrawal. But from the point of view of the observer, projection as a defence is remarkably inefficient for the avoidance of anxiety, except in so far as it makes possible actual or fantasied flight from the apparent source of danger. In contrast to externalisation of aspects of the self, which can effectively do away with painful affect, projection may leave the subject a constant prey to anxiety. Whereas externalisation of aspects of the self can be seen as a *relatively* simple one-step defence, projection is often the last step in a series of defences, and may in itself occasion the use of further defences, such as reversal of affect.

### (iii) Clinical and technical implications

It was primarily for clinical and technical reasons that we made the distinction earlier between mode of functioning and defence. For similar reasons we believe it essential to distinguish between the two types of externalisation outlined above.[3] Extensive use of either defence relates to, and results in, serious ego pathology. However, externalisation is more closely bound up with impairment in the integrative function whereas projection relates to a weakness in the defence system *vis-à-vis* the drives. Extensive use of externalisation of aspects of the self would indicate severe narcissistic disturbance with a very early fixation point; extensive use of projection would indicate severe conflict over drive expression, with a later fixation point, possibly related to the anal phase.

A transitory use of both processes, however, is frequently seen in treatment. At times it may be difficult to differentiate, from the surface manifestation, which process may be at work. But the differentiation is usually possible on the lines of the distinctions we have made. Thus a child may say that the therapist is a messy, uncontrolled person. Given that this represents an externalisation rather than a generalisation, a displacement and so on, it is of value to ascertain whether it is predominantly the messy aspect of the self-representation which is being externalised, or whether a drive derivative, such as the wish to mess upon the therapist, is being projected. One can note whether the defence leads to anxiety or relief on the part of the child. The former would indicate the working of projection with the drive allocated to the therapist and the child experiencing himself as the object of the therapist's wish to mess. Here there would be no relief, but the anxiety-driven wish to flee from the situation. In contrast there is relief where the externalisation is the result of the child's need to rid himself of a narcissistically painful self-image, for here he will perceive the externalisation as unrelated to himself, as different from himself, and as something which may be ignored, derided, or treated with contempt.

We chose this example of the child's calling the therapist messy and uncontrolled to underline the difficulties which may arise in the course of differentiating between the processes which may be at work, and to point to

---

3 It should be emphasised that although we find it of value to differentiate the externalisation of aspects of the self from drive projection we do not see these processes as mutually exclusive; they frequently occur together.

the child's consequent feeling state and attitude as a valuable indicator. Very often, however, especially in child analysis, the processes can also be differentiated on the basis of the degree of fit between the externalisation and the reality. In the case of projection there is always some degree of fit – i.e. what is projected always has somewhere a basis in reality. There is, for instance, no relationship without ambivalence, so that the child's projection of hostile impulses will always touch upon a core of truth – and in fact the child will frequently hang the projection upon some real event such as a cancelled session. In contrast there may be a very small, or even no degree of fit between an externalised dystonic self-representation and the reality. Thus the pre-school child who claims that the therapist is stupid and cannot read or function independently is clearly denying the reality of the therapist and simply using him in order to chuck out an aspect of himself.

For reasons of space it is not possible to cover the great variety of ways in which the externalisation of an aspect of the self-representation may become manifest in treatment. Among the more important is the externalisation of one or more seemingly incompatible aspects of the self in play; there is externalisation of a dystonic aspect on to therapist or toy accompanied by identification with a more syntonic aspect; there is the use of externalisation on to other objects, such as animals or other children in order to test out the therapist's reaction before dystonic aspects can be brought in direct connection with the self. And all these various forms have in common the need to defend against narcissistic pain.

Once the differentiation has been made it follows that interpretation of externalisation of aspects of the self must focus upon the need to defend against narcissistic pain, whereas interpretations of projection must focus upon the need to defend against the anxiety related to drive expression.

Michael, a 16-year-old boy, spent much of the first phase of his analysis being extremely condescending, sarcastic and derisive towards his therapist. The material would be purposefully presented in a confusing manner so that the therapist was often left in the dark or made errors in relation to the factual material. This could have been taken as a direct expression of aggression by the patient, or an attempt to ward off anticipated attack from the therapist, an anticipation based on projection. However, Michael's affect and the subsequent material clearly indicated that he was identifying with the powerful, arrogant father and was externalising the 'Little Mike' who was often laughed at, ignored and left confused. The therapist successfully handled this defence by first verbalising the manner in which he was being viewed by the patient, how he was being seen as a stupid little boy and how painful it must be to be treated in this manner. Michael responded by saying, 'Like a silly eight year old' and could then recount the earlier narcissistically painful experiences at the hands of a condescending father who laughed at him for his ignorance. The therapist could take up the persistence of this image in his current self-representation and his

attempt to defend against a recurrence of humiliation by use of externalisation. The use of this mechanism then decreased significantly. Michael
could accept the fact that he could be ignorant of something without being
humiliated and, most important, he could begin to relate to the therapist as
a real object.

With the emergence of object-directed wishes towards the therapist we
had the manifestation of projection proper as a defence. His material and
especially his non-verbal behaviour (such as the sudden inability to walk in
front of the therapist) clearly indicated a fear of attack. It should be noted
that when Michael was externalising aspects of the self he reacted not with
anxiety, but with relief. 'You've got problems, not me', he would say and he
seemed to look forward to the sessions. However, when projection was used
to defend against his hostile wishes the analytic situation became one
fraught with anxiety and Michael would frequently flee from or miss his
sessions completely. During the hour he would focus on those reality
factors which could be interpreted as signs of hostility on the part of the
therapist, such as the cancellation of a session, the unwillingness to change
an hour or the seeming attack of an interpretation. The therapist did not
deny the patient's interpretations of these reality events accepting them as
within the realm of possibility but suggested that what was feared was more
than dislike or lack of consideration on the part of the therapist but an
actual wish to hurt, possibly kill, the patient. Michael readily agreed that
this was his fear and the therapist could take up the magical equating of
wish and deed as a major factor behind the intensity of the anxiety. This
work on the omnipotence of thought led to a significant decrease in the
patient's anxiety, the establishment once again of the therapeutic alliance
and the gradual emergence into consciousness of Michael's own aggressive
wishes. Subsequent focus on the emphasis on only one side of the therapist,
the hostile side, allowed for the uncovering of Michael's intense conflicts
over ambivalence and with this the projections themselves disappeared. The
homosexual wishes which lay behind the projected aggression then came to
the fore.

## 2. Impact of parental externalisations and projections upon the child

Externalisations and even at times projections are fairly common occurrences within families. It is the extensive and rigid use of these mechanisms
by the parents which indicates that pathological processes are at work, and
we will examine the impact upon the child of the pathological parental use
of either externalisation or projection. This is a subject of great complexity
and here we will illustrate only some of our main findings through selected
aspects of two cases:

## Tommy

Tommy's mother was a woman who could not integrate her castrated, damaged, messy view of herself. Throughout her life she searched for objects upon whom to externalise this dystonic aspect. Thus all her male objects including, finally, her husband, were extremely messy, damaged and inferior individuals. From the moment of Tommy's birth until he came into treatment at the age of 11 the mother perceived him only as a damaged, messy, stupid child. This view of Tommy was not dynamically related to the vicarious gratification of her own primitive impulses. On the contrary, she had little involvement with the child, distancing him from her as far as possible and at times forgetting or even losing him.

At the time of referral Tommy was a prime illustration of what is frequently referred to as 'the self-fulfilling prophecy'. There was an exact fit with the patterns of the mother's externalisation. Despite indications of normal intelligence on psychological testing, he was retarded in all school subjects. He was a regressed, soiling, snot-eating child with little control over drive expression. Most striking was the relative absence of anxiety or guilt in relation to drive expression. What clearly emerged was the presence of a severe narcissistic disturbance with mental pain and conflict rooted in the acceptance of the devalued self and the inability to integrate positive aspects with this conscious self-representation. Outside the immediate family environment he defended against the narcissistic pain almost exclusively by means of externalisations. Despite Tommy's evident relief after having externalised the devalued part of himself, he still could not see himself as clever, competent, etc. A fluctuating and relatively adequate level of functioning could be achieved only by means of a conscious imitation, a type of pseudo-identification with those contemporaries who could manifest the positive qualities he could not accept in himself. Thus, as he later verbalised, 'When I pretended I was John I was able to score a goal but when I was myself I fell in the mud'. Within the family there was little need to externalise the degraded self since the role of the devalued, damaged object was compatible with the needs of all members of the family, especially the mother. The main reason for accepting the mother's externalisation lay in the realisation, at some level, that despite the mother's distancing manoeuvres she needed such a devalued object and that failure to comply with her need would leave him prey to the primitive terror of abandonment.

The father played an important role in Tommy's pathological development by offering him no alternative solution. He constantly reinforced the effects of the mother's pathology by using the same mechanisms along parallel lines. The father viewed Tommy as stupid, girlish and damaged, and frequently said so to him. Psychiatric interviews with the father revealed the extent to which this view was based upon externalisations of dystonic aspects of himself.

As Tommy began to progress during the course of his treatment one could clearly see the extent to which his acceptance of the parental externalisations had been a vital factor in the maintenance of the family equilibrium. Slowly, Tommy became consciously aware of the fact that, in his words, 'They put the bad on to me and they feel good'. As he gradually overcame the primitive fear of abandonment and could begin to integrate positive aspects within his self-representation, his material centred mainly on the sadness of the mother, the chaos in the home, the madness of the family members, and related to this, his own intense feelings of guilt. It should be noted that he was not guilty about the newly attained level of functioning *per se*, but about having deprived the family of a needed vehicle for externalisation. To a certain extent this material related to Tommy's own feelings, fears and fantasies but to a marked degree it also reflected the reality. As Tommy's positive development became unavoidably apparent, the family was thrown into a state of dis-equilibrium and chaos. The father took to his bed in a state of panic and confusion saying he was going mad, dying of a brain haemorrhage and losing his manhood. The mother, now forced to take back the dystonic aspects previously externalised on to Tommy, became depressed, disorganised and totally dishevelled in appearance. She remained unable to integrate these aspects adaptively. Her self-image became swamped by the dystonic colouring and she consciously viewed herself as useless and unlovable. There was a desperate search for a new object upon whom she could re-externalise.

There was another child in the family, George, three years older than Tommy. Until the time when Tommy began making significant progress, George had seemed like a boy with a well-structured ego who functioned efficiently in many areas. In the eyes of the family, including Tommy, George was a near genius. It was George who was chosen as the mother's new target for externalisation of dystonic aspects and very soon the family equilibrium was restored on a reversed basis, with Tommy now seen as the near genius and George seen as the stupid, messy, damaged child.[4] Tommy, no longer fulfilling his mother's most pressing need, now had to cope with the fact that he was an outsider in his own family. As he said, 'I feel the odd man out. I feel good but nobody notices me.'

### Mary

Mary's mother was a woman who had never been able to tolerate her own aggression. From childhood on, projection had played a major part in her

---

4 The changing roles of the two brothers represent a highly complex phenomenon related to many factors additional to the family use of externalisation. A more detailed report on the two brothers can be found in a recent paper by Novick and Holder (unpublished).

battery of defences. Her response to all objects was one of fear, and she was obsessed by the thought that her parents would murder her. In relation to her own child she made use of projection even before the birth, being consciously afraid that the unborn baby was killing her and eating her up inside. She continued to project throughout the child's development. A most pathogenic feature in her projections was the extent to which they were hooked on to the reality of Mary's phase-adequate aggressive impulses; Mary's early development intensified the mother's phase-linked aggressive conflicts. Thus, when Mary was in the oral phase, mother feared that Mary wanted to devour her. When Mary reached the positive oedipal stage, the mother's continuing projection of death wishes now took the form of the fear that Mary wanted to kill her in order to possess the husband.

(In this paper we are focusing solely on the role of projection in the pathological mother–child relationship. It is evident that the relationship is one of great complexity involving other elements, such as the revival of the mother's past object relationships, especially the infantile relationship to her own mother. In general, it is important to differentiate phenomena related to the revival of past object-relationships from projection proper. In this case, however, projection was a major defence utilised both within and outside the framework of the revived object relationship.)

The extensive use of projection left the mother prey to the constant fear that Mary only hated and wanted to kill her. This image of the child acted as an additional stimulus to aggressive wishes thus further threatening the mother's defences. Secondary defences were, therefore, necessitated and these could be maintained only provided that the child utilised the same mechanisms, i.e. denied her anger, displaced the hate on to other objects and reactively stressed the 'loving' aspects of the relationship – and this Mary did. She and mother spent much of their time in mutual assurances of love, the frequent exchange of propitiatory gifts and the mutual denial of aggression on the part of either partner. Frequently they would discuss their dislike for a shared displacement object. Mother would constantly say to Mary, 'You and I are just alike. We think the same way and we feel the same way.'

Unlike Tommy's father, Mary's father did not, on the whole, reinforce the effects of the mother's pathology. Indeed, so close was the bond between mother and Mary that the father remained a relative outsider.

Mary was referred at the age of 11 because of an increasing failure in school attendance and for sleeping and eating difficulties of marked severity. These symptoms were primarily related to the intense fear of destroying and being destroyed by the mother. When Mary was seen diagnostically all observers were struck by the degree of identification with the mother's defences. The major conflict related to the aggression towards the mother; all aggressive manifestations were felt to be prohibited and minimal aggressive drive manifestations were followed by overwhelming guilt and anxiety. Despite the severity of the pathology, there were no indications of a primary ego or narcissistic defect.

Very soon after the start of treatment one could see how ineffective and brittle the defence system was. Primitive aggressive breakthroughs began to occur – followed each time by the intensification of the defences shared with the mother. It was only with the analysis of the shared defensive system that Mary could become aware of her fear of aggression; at this point the role of projection in her pathology became increasingly apparent. While Mary's own aggressive wishes remained relatively defended the fear of being destroyed by the mother intensified and with panic in her voice Mary would say, 'She hates me, she'll kill me, she'll eat me alive'. Further analysis clearly revealed the largely projective nature of these fears.

This case involves a paradox which can be understood by taking into account the pathological impact of the mother's projections. Mary's ego and super-ego development had been precocious, with for example, verbalisation (including complete phrases) occurring by 11 months of age. Despite such precocious development Mary's defences remained completely dependent upon the presence of the object and formed no more than a brittle super-structure overlaying primitive and peremptory aggressive wishes. But this could be seen as a direct consequence of the mother's extensive use of projection. By constantly projecting her aggressive wishes on to the child she constantly revived, intensified and drew the child's wishes into the child's consciousness. The normal, developmental evolution of drive expression from direct and primitive to more distanced and less conflictual forms was grossly interfered with. The development of auto-nomous and adaptive defences was impeded and the child was left with no alternative but to use primitive defences (such as projection itself) and to accept the defences forced upon her by the mother.

With the working through of pre-genital and oedipal hostility towards the mother Mary began to function independently. Mother reacted to the positive changes in her child by making repeated attempts to re-establish the old, shared defence system. When these failed she became extremely disturbed, continuing to project her hostile wishes on to the child but now becoming increasingly aware of her own aggression. She became terrified that she might act upon her wishes and kill the child. She became consumed with guilt, increasingly disturbed and made a number of suicidal attempts. A period of treatment reduced the intensity of the disturbance but she continued her basic pattern of projection on to Mary despite the changes in her child, unlike Tommy's mother who reacted to his positive changes by shifting the object of her externalisations. Furthermore, whereas Tommy's change affected the entire family equilibrium, Mary's affected the family only secondarily via the effect of the mother's increased disturbance.

Study of the treatment of these and similar cases has led us to the following general conclusions:

1.  Children who are the objects of parental externalisations, as in the case of Tommy, manifest relatively little anxiety or guilt over drive expression. Rather, they show a severe narcissistic disturbance with mental pain and conflict rooted in the acceptance of the devalued self and the inability to integrate positive aspects with this conscious self-representation. There is a primary impairment of the integrative function of the ego, the maintenance of self-esteem, and the development of an adequate self-representation.

    On the other hand, in children who are the object of projection, as in the case of Mary, ego functioning and narcissistic cathexis are only secondarily involved in the pathology. They are subject to intense anxiety and guilt in relation to drive expression. The drives are constantly reinforced by the parental projections, and the development of an autonomous and adaptive defence system is hindered. A brittle super-structure, based on an identification with the primitive super-ego and defence system of the projecting mother, is created.

2.  The extensive use of either projection or externalisation by these children can be seen as a 'generational' effect which goes beyond identification with the parental defences.

3.  The use of either of these mechanisms by the parents relates not only to severe pathology in the parents but also to differing patterns of family dynamics. The extensive use of externalisation relates to a pathological balance in the family, a closed system (Brody, 1965) in which all members of the family play interdependent roles. A change in any one member of the family directly affects each of the others, and produces a complete disruption of the family equilibrium. Projection, on the other hand, indicates an intense dyadic bond, usually between mother and child. A change in the child directly affects the mother, and has only secondary effects upon the other members of the family.

## Summary

Projection is currently used as a portmanteau term and as such obscures important clinical distinctions and results in difficulties in communication. An examination of Freud's views on the subject reveals that he went beyond an initial portmanteau usage of the term, finally using projection to denote mainly a defence against the drives.

It was suggested that externalisation be adopted as the general term covering all processes by which inner phenomena are subjectively allocated to the outer world. These processes are primarily defensive. We distinguish externalisation from other processes which may have similar surface manifestations but do not involve the subjective allocation of inner phenomena to the outer world, and which are modes of functioning, not defences.

In particular we discussed some early processes of differentiation and generalisation.

Within the general category of externalisation we focused particularly on the externalisation of aspects of the self-representation and externalisation of the drive, i.e. projection proper. It was proposed that these two processes are significantly different. The differences were examined from the point of view of the individual and the family. The clinical and technical implications were noted and discussed.

## References

Brody, W.M. (1965) 'On the dynamics of narcissism: 1. Externalisation and early ego development', *Psychoanaltic Study of the Child* 20: 165–193.

Feigenbaum, D. (1936) 'On projection', *Psychoanalytic Quarterly* 5: 303–319.

Freud, S. (1895) 'Draft H. Paranoia', SE 1: 206–212.

Freud, S. (1901) 'The psychopathology of everyday life', SE 6: 1–279.

Freud, S. (1911) 'Psycho-analytic notes upon an autobiographical account of a case of paranoia (dementia paranoides)', SE 12: 3–82.

Freud, S. (1913 [1912–1913]) 'Totem and taboo', SE 13: 1–161.

Freud, S. (1914) 'On narcissism: an introduction', SE 14: 69–102.

Freud, S. (1915) 'Instincts and their vicissitudes', SE 14: 117–140.

Freud, S. (1919) 'The uncanny', SE 17: 219–252.

Freud, S. (1920) 'Beyond the pleasure principle', SE 18: 3–64.

Freud, S. (1922) 'Some neurotic mechanisms in jealousy, paranoia and homosexuality', SE 18: 223–232.

Freud, S. (1927) 'The future of an illusion', SE 21: 5–56.

Freud, S. (1930 [1929]) 'Civilisation and its discontents', SE 21: 64–145.

Freud, S. (1931) 'Female sexuality', SE 21: 223–243.

Hoffer, W. (1950) 'Development of the body ego', *Psychoanalytic Study of the Child*, 5: 18–23.

Rapaport, D. (1944) 'The scientific methodology of psychoanalysis'. In Gill, M.M. (ed.) *The Collected Papers of David Rapaport*. New York: Basic Books (1967) 165–220.

Rapaport, D. (1950) 'The theoretical implications of diagnostic testing procedures'. In Gill, M.M. (ed.) *The Collected Papers of David Rapaport*. New York: Basic Books (1967) 334–356.

Rapaport, D. (1952) 'Projective techniques and the theory of thinking'. In Gill, M.M. (ed.) *The Collected Papers of David Rapaport*. New York: Basic Books (1967) 461–469.

Rapaport, D. (1960) 'On the psychoanalytic theory of motivation'. In Jones, M.R. (ed.) *Nebraska Symposium on Motivation*. Lincoln, NE: University of Nebraska Press 173–247.

Rycroft, C. (1968) *A Critical Dictionary of Psychoanalysis*. London: Nelson.

Weiss, E. (1947) 'Projection, extrajection and objectivation', *Psychoanalytic Quarterly*, 16: 357–377.

# Chapter 3

# Transference in child psychotherapy[1]

*Dina Rosenbluth*

Originally published in the *Journal of Child Psychotherapy* (1970) 2(4): 72–87.

## Freud's discovery of transference

Early in his work Freud discarded hypnosis in favour of the interpretation of unconscious conflicts, for in hypnosis the conscious, rational part of the patient, the ego, was not involved, whereas in free association and the assimilation of interpretations the ego had to take an active part in the treatment. But Freud was again disappointed when he found that even after the cause of his illness had been explained to the patient, the symptoms did not necessarily disappear. Intellectual understanding was not enough; and furthermore, patients invariably developed strong feelings of love or hate towards the analyst, which Freud at first felt to be nothing but a hindrance to the progress of their analysis.

Yet it was these strong feelings and impulses directed towards the analyst, and disproportionate as a response to his actual behaviour, which led Freud to discover that they were transferred from some earlier childhood relationship within the family to the present therapeutic relationship. Freud discovered then that patients not only remembered earlier situations of conflict and anxiety in their childhood, but always transferred these to the current situation in analysis, where they re-experienced and relived them. In fact he found that only in so far as they were thus emotionally re-experienced and understood could any real change in the patient be brought about. This necessarily involved a lengthy 'working through' of childhood conflicts and feelings towards the analyst, becoming fully aware of them and of their origin in relation to the parents, and gradually being able to find new solutions to these conflicts. All of this implied that a consistent interpretation of all transference manifestations had now become a central task for the analyst; far from being a hindrance to treatment Freud now came to regard transference and its interpretation as the analyst's main tool.

---

1 This paper is reprinted from the Bulletin No. 2, March 1961, of The Association of Child Psychotherapists, in response to requests by a number of therapists.

Freud described transference situations as follows (Freud, 1905):

> They are new editions and facsimiles of the impulses and phantasies which are aroused and made conscious during the progress of the analysis, but they have this peculiarity, which is characteristic of their species, that they replace some earlier person by the person of the physician. To put it another way: a whole series of psychological experiences are revived, not as belonging to the past, but as applying to the physician at the present moment.

Further (Freud, 1905):

> Transference is overcome by showing the patient that his feelings do not originate in the current situation, and do not really concern the person of the physician but that he is reproducing something that happened to him a long time ago. In this way we require him to transform his repetition into recollection.

There are elements of transference in all our relationships. As Freud said (1905): 'psychoanalytic treatment does not *create* transferences, it only brings them to light, like so many other hidden psychical factors.' Elements of transference, as Freud implied, are present from the beginning of treatment. But the therapist attempts to keep his own emotional reactions and phantasies out of his relationship with the patient who is thereby enabled to project his feelings and phantasies onto him. Thus the patient's transference tie to the therapist becomes stronger as treatment progresses.

Today there is no disagreement among Freudian psychoanalysts about the central role of transference in the treatment of adult neurotic patients. This is what distinguishes psychoanalysis, both as a scientific method of investigating the functions of the mind and as a form of treatment, from other forms of psychotherapy. Present-day conflicts and relationships are understood as determined by unresolved past childhood conflicts, and therefore the main focus in treatment is on the interpretation of these transferred phenomena in the current relationship between patient and therapist.

## Melanie Klein's development of concept of transference

Although all groups of Freudian analysts agree on the importance of transference in the treatment of adult neurotic patients, some differences in both theory and technique have emerged. I shall attempt in this paper to show how Mrs Klein's work, and in particular her theory of unconscious phantasy and early object relations, has deepened our understanding of the

phenomenon of transference itself, as well as helped us in our under-standing of *what* is transferred; that is, in our understanding of the anxieties and conflicts of the earliest period of life. I shall try to show how this affects our approach and technique in child therapy, because it was in child analysis in particular that different techniques were evolved by the two main pioneers in this field, Melanie Klein and Anna Freud.

Melanie Klein set out with the expectation that, because a young child's natural manner of free association was not purely verbal, the provision of small toys and play material might enable him to play as well as talk, and that in this way his impulses, phantasies and thoughts could be elucidated in a manner essentially similar to that used to elucidate the dreams and verbal free associations of adults. From her analyses of young children she soon became convinced that this was so, and that even in a young child the personality structure was sufficiently developed to enable him profitably to undergo psychoanalytic treatment, provided that he could understand verbal communication. For Mrs Klein's technique remained purely inter-pretative, discarding educational methods or the deliberate fostering of a positive transference which could interfere with the child's expression of his internal conflicts. In using this technique she found that the child did transfer situations and feelings for the parents from the earliest period of his life to the therapist, as adults do.

By first establishing a suitable setting, and then by observing all the young child's feelings and phantasies and understanding them in terms of transference of earlier relationships, in short by adhering to the essence of psychoanalytic technique, Mrs Klein made further discoveries about the depths of the mind from which the earliest period of life could be reconstructed.

In this paper there is space to discuss only some aspects of her discoveries and to try to relate the ways in which these can help in understanding our patient's behaviour, in understanding the transference relationship.

Mrs Klein found evidence that from the beginning of life the baby's instinctual drives and needs seek not only pleasure but also an object. Taking Freud's and Abraham's findings about part-object relations as a starting point, she found that the earliest relationship of the baby is to parts or aspects of the mother or person who cares for him, and that from this develop the later relations to whole people. The earliest relation, at first primarily to the breast, implies that an image of this part of the mother becomes established in the baby's mind. This is so not in conscious memory or thought, but in unconscious phantasy. To quote Susan Isaacs (1948):

Phantasy is, in the first instance, the mental corollary, the psychic representative of the instinct. There is no instinctual impulse, no instinctual urge or response, which is not experienced as unconscious phantasy.

It is an inchoate, feeling kind of mental activity, allied to bodily sensations, and must be clearly distinguished from later conscious fantasies or day-dreams. Unconscious phantasy is the original primary mental activity of the baby. It is in unconscious phantasy that the food, nipple or breast is taken inside, introjected, as the mental counterpart of the actual sucking at the breast and taking in of milk.

Freud had earlier discovered the importance of introjection and pro-jection in the oral stage of development, and the earliest 'primary identi-fication' with the breast; Mrs Klein has added to this the dynamic and continuing importance of the unconscious phantasy accompanying these early processes, and the importance of these early mechanisms in estab-lishing an inner world of objects, which help in forming the later integrated ego and super-ego.

Unconscious phantasy has been found to continue throughout life to operate in all mental spheres, underlying the most rational and adult mental activity. In the same way the constant interplay between introjection and projection which forms the first object relations continues throughout life to influence our relations to people, and is of the greatest importance in understanding the transference relationship. The discovery of unconscious phantasy accompanying all impulses is an enrichment of Freud's concept of transference, for transference is not then thought of as emanating from the repressed unconscious only, but from the continuous stream of unconscious phantasy accompanying all libidinal and destructive impulses, with the therapist now as their object.

Furthermore, as the baby's earliest relationships, anxieties and conflicts vitally influence later development, and as in the depth of the mind they continue throughout life to be worked through and are the foundation of character, they have far-reaching implications. For transference emanates from different depths of the unconscious, and Mrs Klein has helped us in understanding the early babyhood relationships and conflicts, both in relation to the feeding mother and in the pregenital oedipal stage, which underlie the later childhood relationships and conflicts.

## Early anxiety situation

I shall now attempt to describe briefly the two main kinds of anxiety situation in the baby's life, as these vitally affect the way we understand our patient's anxieties in relation to us in the transference.

A relationship is a two-way process from the start. So the picture of the mother, or of parts of the mother, that is taken inside the baby is highly distorted by his feelings and impulses. As the baby is endowed with both libidinal and destructive impulses, the initial relationship to the mother tends to be split into a wholly good and a wholly bad one. This results from the 'all or none' quality of the baby's emotions as well as from the lack of cohesion of the early ego. But there is also the need to split off in particular the destructive impulses and project them outside. And, as Mrs Klein put it (1960):

> . . . persecutory anxiety reinforces the need to keep separate the loved object from the dangerous one, and therefore to split love and hate. For the young infant's self preservation depends on his trust in a good mother. By splitting the two aspects and clinging to the good one he preserves his belief in a good object and his capacity to love it; and this is an essential condition for keeping alive. For without at least some of this feeling he would be exposed to an entirely hostile world which he fears would destroy him.

This anxiety was vividly shown by a patient of mine, Ronnie, aged five-and-a-half-years at the beginning of treatment. When he first came to me he lived in a world of terrors and could not separate from his mother. He was quite paralysed by his fears, which included among many other things children of all ages, trains, houses or cars in the street or any toy which was in the slightest way damaged. He clung to his mother's side to the extent of being virtually one-handed, the other having to clutch her skirt. Thus he was unable to go to school and was referred to the clinic.

For quite a time at the beginning of treatment the mother had to sit next to him in the playroom. There he was also terrified of innumerable things, but soon made a positive contact with me. He quickly became possessive, bossy and outstandingly greedy towards me, demanding more and more time, toys and drawing materials. One day during this early period he was playing with sand. He was still glued to his mother's side and unable to go across the room to the sandtray, so that I had to bring him a little bucketful of sand to play with on the floor. Here again he showed his greed by demanding more and more sand. When eventually I refused to bring him any more, he became suddenly frightened of me, turned his back to me, hid his head against his mother and whimpered. Then, quite suddenly, he actually vomited. In his eyes I had suddenly become the mother, or breast which was not under his omnipotent command and was then immediately hated and felt to be terrifying, not only externally so that he had to turn away from me to his mother, but also internally, so that he actually had to sick me up, as the bad mother or breast, and get rid of me that way too.

We can see then how the child comes to cling to the idealised mother, or the baby initially to the breast, as a defence against persecutory anxiety, that is the unconscious fear of being overwhelmed and destroyed by external or internal bad forces.

As the baby grows into a more integrated person and becomes able to differentiate between the inner and the outer world, he develops an increased feeling of responsibility for his own impulses. In his relationship to the mother and to the father, each now as a whole and separate person, a new anxiety appears. He realises that in one person there are both good and bad, loved and hated aspects. This marks the beginning of the true conflict of ambivalence and the resulting anxiety Mrs Klein has called the depressive anxiety. There now arise a wish to spare the mother, and feelings of remorse and guilt for the greedy way in which the idealised mother, or breast, was exploited, or in phantasy omnipotently controlled and not allowed to have any separate existence of its own. To quote Mrs Klein again (1960):

> It is my hypothesis that in the fifth or sixth month of life the baby becomes afraid of the harm his destructive impulses and his greed might do, or might have done, to his loved objects. For he cannot yet distinguish between his desires and impulses and their actual effects. He experiences feelings of guilt and the urge to preserve these objects and to make reparation to them for harm done. The anxiety now experienced is of a predominantly depressive nature; and the emotions accompanying it, as well as the defences evolved against them I recognised as part of normal development and termed the 'depressive position'.

To come back to the little boy Ronnie: after his greed had been shown to him, and the consequent fear had diminished that the mother, breast and therapist whom he had drained of their goodness would retaliate, he gradually began to change.

The feeling that he then had no good internal figure to support him against his destructiveness was modified, as was the need to have his real mother by his side constantly as a reassurance that she was unharmed and not persecuting. He was able to let the mother go to the social worker's room, at first for part of each session only. By then some of his acutest fears had lessened. The mother reported at this stage that he was then for the first time, occasionally openly aggressive to her. He frequently made such statements as 'I hate you, no I don't, I really love you' to his mother.

During this time he told me that sometimes 'when evening joins to night' as he put it, he felt unhappy in bed and called his mother. Last night he felt very sad about a song, but he could not remember what it was called. A little while later his mother left the room to go to the social worker. Ronnie was after her in a flash, urged her to come back to the playroom and when she would not do so hit her furiously, and tried to pull her away. Eventually, after she did return to the playroom, he attacked me and began to boss me mercilessly. Later he told me for the first time of a cat the family had got rid of many months previously because the doctor said it gave him colds, how sad he felt that she had gone and would never come back. When I interpreted his sadness at losing the cat and losing people he loves so

much, and linked this with his possessiveness, the greediness and attacks on me and mother just before and his consequent fear that he would lose us altogether because of it, just as he felt it was his fault that he lost the cat, he suddenly said 'that reminds me of the song that made me unhappy last night. It's called "losing the one you love"'.

To me this phase of Ronnie's treatment was striking; once his omnipotence and control had slightly diminished, and the acutest persecutory anxiety had abated so that he could allow himself to experience his feelings of ambivalence and openly to express some of his hostility, both in the transference and at home, it was clear how the depressive anxiety against which he had hitherto so strenuously defended himself came to the fore in full force. His tyrannical behaviour was now followed by remorse and sadness and fears of losing his loved objects, and no longer only that he would be attacked himself.

A distinction between the persecutory anxiety which initially arises in the acutely helpless stage of development and where the main concern is for the safety of the self, and the later depressive anxiety where the concern is for the object, is of immense value both in diagnosis and in treatment. As Freud (1937) pointed out, in normal development the final structure contains fragments of earlier libidinal fixations, for (1937) : 'all that has once lived clings tenaciously to life. Sometimes we are inclined to doubt whether the dragons of primaeval times are really extinct.' Thus the two kinds of anxiety are not envisaged as replacing the stages of libidinal development described by Freud and Abraham, but rather as anxieties and defences which operate in the oral stage and continue in all later stages of libidinal development to determine the manner in which each new situation is dealt with.


## Transference interpretations

What the child transfers and projects on to the therapist are his unconscious images of his internal parents or aspects of his parents, images which were created by a fusion of his own impulses and feelings, his own phantasies, and external experience. And what is re-experienced in the transference relationship are the feelings, impulses and anxieties not only from the oedipal but also from the earliest periods of life.

The central focus of technique should, in our view, be on the consistent interpretation of the child's relationship to the therapist, and on the transference nature of this relationship. Transference interpretations are not thought of as just part of treatment, but the whole treatment should be an analysis and interpretation of the transference. All the child's behaviour, the way he uses the playroom and the box of toys, and in particular the way he reacts to or makes use of interpretations, and not only his direct references to the therapist in his talk are seen as indications of his transference feelings. As Mrs Klein writes (1935):

> My conception of transference as rooted in the earliest stages of development and in deep layers of the unconscious is much wider and entails a technique by which, from the whole material presented the *unconscious elements* of the transference are deduced.

In what then should such transference interpretations consist? James Strachey (1934) says that an interpretation, to be effective, must be emotionally immediate, that is really in touch with the feelings or anxieties in activity at the very moment, and must also be specific, detailed and concrete. Strachey calls such an interpretation, which really effects a change in the patient, 'mutative', and states that it must include two phases. The first should enable the patient to become aware of his feelings and impulses towards the therapist, and the second should make him aware that this impulse is directed towards a 'phantasy object and not a real one.' By this Strachey means that, as the patient all the time projects internal phantasy figures on to the therapist in accordance with the feelings and impulses of the moment, so interpretation of this should help the patient to contrast phantasy with the reality of the therapist's behaviour. The timing of so called 'deep' interpretations must depend entirely on whether both phases of such a complete interpretation can be given, rather than on the stage of the treatment. What finally change the super-ego and, in Paula Heimann's (1956) words:

> divest it of its demoniacal or godlike character are processes in the ego: its conscious recognition of its impulses, its accepting responsibility for them and withdrawing projection from its external and introjected objects. This process of working through is experienced in the transference with the analyst in the role of the original and internalised objects, and includes the re-experience of infantile conflicts down to the levels which Melanie Klein has described as the paranoid and depressive positions. Alongside the modification of the ego the super-ego changes its character.

She adds:

> An introjection of the analyst as a benevolent permissive figure bypasses this development of the ego. The interpretation that such introjection is in progress is a vital part of the analyst's work.

We should constantly ask ourselves therefore, 'What is the child doing to me at the moment, feeling in relation to me now?' The answer to this is the transference interpretation. To give an example: a little girl starts off a session by silently picking out a little chicken and then a lion from her drawer and puts them beside her. She is here showing her feelings about our relationship. She feels herself to be the helpless chicken confronted by me as the dangerous lion. I can show her then that she is telling me about her fear of me, but the second phase of the interpretation, enabling her to become aware of the transference nature of her picture of me, showing her what role from the past and from her inner world she is putting me into, is missing. Later, with more detailed material, it became clear that the lion stood for aspects of the mother, and then the interpretation could be completed, could include both phases.

Giving a theoretical outline of what transference interpretations should do and consist of is not too difficult. In practice, however, and especially when treating children, one is constantly brought up against innumerable difficulties, and to adhere consistently to the interpretation of transference is in fact no easy task.[2]

## Establishing a suitable setting

In order to foster the child's communication of his unconscious phantasies the first task of technique is to establish a suitable setting within which this can take place. For this reason we avoid all non-analytic, non-interpretative methods such as the encouraging of positive attitudes towards us, reassurance, explanations or educational methods. We avoid giving any actual gratifications, presents or food, birthday or Christmas cards, as all this could force a 'good' therapist on to the child when we want him to be able to transfer his pictures of good or bad internal parents on to us. We also prefer a simple playroom, where there is the minimum need to make prohibitions. From this point of view it is helpful if each patient can have a small box or drawer of his own toys, so that with these at least he really can do what he likes, and we avoid expensive or communal toys which we

---

2  I should also make it clear that there are individual differences in theory and technique both among the analysts who trained and supervised the Tavistock Clinic child psychotherapists, and among the therapists themselves. But transference technique is an outcome of object relations theory, and although there are some individual differences regarding the particular theory of object relations held by psychoanalysts associated with the Tavistock Clinic, there is agreement in principle about the existence of early object relations. In this paper I am attempting to describe some of Mrs Klein's views as her contribution has been the most important one in emphasising the role of transference in child analysis. The therapists do not necessarily always deal in the same way with the various problems of technique I shall now enumerate. Ultimately, within the framework of the basic elements of technique, one has to find one's own way of interpreting and learn from one's own experience.

would need to protect from his destructiveness. These are some of the ways in which we can from the start avoid as much as possible acting either the 'good' gratifying or the 'bad' forbidding parent.

But even with the most foolproof playroom there are times when we have to set limits to what the child can be allowed to do; for instance we cannot let him play with electric fires or break windows or attack us physically. Here it seems to me we are forced to act as authority figures but as long as we also interpret the transference situation and reveal just why the child is forcing us into a role at that moment, we can usually soon get back to the more purely interpretative analytic relationship.

However, there are many other aspects in which decisions about technique are difficult. How far should we take part in games, or talk and act in assigned roles in dramatic play? There arises the problem of winning or losing the game in reality, or if we act in roles and talk, unprompted by the child in these roles, we are in danger of confusing the child with our own associations. In any case our ability to stand aside and understand the transference situation is lessened. If the child asks for help with reading or with a drawing, should we give it? In fact children often try to force us to help in some way other than by interpretation just in order forcibly to keep us a 'good' figure, as a reassurance or defence against their hostile impulses and projections, just as they sometimes force us into being a forbidding, authoritarian 'bad' figure, either as a reassurance against some worse unconscious fear or as a relief for their guilt about their own hostile feelings.

I have gradually come to prefer to keep out of playing games as far as possible, and if I do act in roles assigned to me I always ask the child to prompt me what to say. I also try to avoid giving active help in handling materials or with reading and writing, unless I know the child really cannot do it himself, and even then only for a little while until I feel I understand more about the problem and can interpret. Although this inconsistent behaviour naturally makes for difficulties at times, I found that children on the whole understand very well that my real task is not just to play but to help them find out more about themselves, and that I cannot do this as well when I am involved in a game. In fact children value it if we do not allow ourselves to be manipulated, just as we do not manipulate them. What distinguishes us, as the child's therapist, from others in his environment is solely our ability to interpret the unconscious and interpretation is our only tool. There are many others in the child's environment, parents, teachers, relations, who can reassure, give presents, educate, be kind or stern, but our role is fundamentally different from theirs. Children, just like adults, are in the end relieved if we do not allow ourselves to be sidetracked from our main goal, which for us is the interpretation of the transference. For ultimately the patient's co-operation is based on his wish to find out the truth about himself, and he values truthfulness and singleness of purpose on our part.

## Transference at the beginning of treatment

Children bring with them to any new relationship expectations and attitudes which are transferred from earlier expectations and attitudes in other situations, and ultimately from their relationship to their parents. Transference feelings are likely to be quite intense, however, in a child starting treatment, coming for help to a new person, whether he consciously understands the purpose of the treatment or only senses, by his parents' attitudes, that something important is in the wind. Usually one can quickly see in the first session what the expectations and attitudes are, hopeful or fearful, friendly or hostile, and we feel that it relieves the child and helps him to communicate further with us if these feelings are not only understood but put into words for him straight away. Sometimes the child may even make it quite clear soon, through his talk or play, from where these expectations and feelings are transferred, what the unconscious phantasy is, but at other times it is more difficult to understand quickly what role the child is putting us into. Then we need to wait for further association or further sessions before we can clarify the origin of the present relation to the therapist.

To go back to the example of the little three-year-old girl who started a session near the beginning of treatment by peering solemnly and silently into her drawer, then picked out a tiny chicken, and then the lion and placed him next to the chicken: I think it is clear that this was a communication of her feelings about the situation she found herself in. But how could she have this fear of me if she had never before had such fears and anxieties about anyone close to her? Whom exactly I stood for, mother or father, or what aspect of them, could of course not immediately be seen. By my acknowledging that I had understood how afraid she felt of me, she was enabled to unbend a bit, to talk and go on playing. Later, there were repeated sequences of play where she herself acted the growling, biting lion threatening to eat me up, followed by attacks of anxiety; the whole situation of greed, attack and fear of retaliation could then be shown to her, as well as the way these were repetitions of phantasies accompanying the early relation to the feeding mother. What we look for, then, before interpreting are not only the symbolic representations in play but all the signs of emotion accompanying it, any verbal associations or associations becoming clear through *sequences* of play.

This same little girl, also very early on in the treatment, dreamily looked out of the window one session and said to herself 'This is my *loveliest* room in all the world.' What she was expressing was obviously not an appraisal of the playroom which was far from lovely, but her feelings about me at that moment, feeling satisfied with the interpretations and in touch with an internal picture of a wonderful ideal mother who satisfied all her needs, which was projected on to me. Here we see again, then, the split between the wholly good, ideal mother figure and the wholly bad, persecutory one (in the shape of the lion), a split which appears to be characteristic of the earliest relationships.

## Example of ways of interpreting the transference

It is perhaps worth looking now in a little more detail at our method of interpreting the transference. A complete interpretation, as described earlier, should include two aspects: one where we make the child aware of his impulses and feelings towards us, and the other where we make him aware of the transference nature of these, that is of their origin in himself and in his relation to his parents.

Mary, a six-year-old patient, came back to the first session after the Christmas holidays with a big smile, scrutinised me, then the smile quickly vanished as she rushed into the playroom and proceeded to ignore me completely. I sat down in my chair while she quickly took her coat off and rushed to her drawer. There she sat on the floor, her back to me and in such a position that I could not see what she was doing, and she silently rummaged around in her drawer. After quite a time of silence I said that she was now shutting me out, making me feel left out by not taking any notice of me, and was in this way showing how very cross and angry she was with me, because I had left her over the holidays. At this she put something into her hand, came over to me, held out the closed hand and said triumphantly and tauntingly that I could not guess what was inside. She asked me to guess then, but knew already from past experience that I would not. I said that she was now the Mummy Miss Rosenbluth who had secrets during the holidays, and I was turned into the little girl Mary who feels left out and cross and doesn't know what Mummy is doing. I reminded her further how before the holidays she had wanted to know where I was going and what I was going to do, and how angry she was when I did not answer these questions, and how she had been so cross about my going away at all that she had not come to the last session before the holidays. (She had in fact herself contrived this.) Mary looked surprised at my reference to this missed session and said 'Didn't I come? Oh yes, I forgot about it, I got muddled.' I said she forgot about it because she did not want to come and say goodbye because she felt too angry about my going away, about the treatment Mummy not being there all the time, and that her anger was muddling her up now, too, so that she was trying to make me into the angry little girl who did not know what she, Mummy, had got inside. She now opened her hand and showed me its contents, the little baby doll from the family, and again gleefully triumphed over me that I had not been able to guess. I now said she was the Mummy Miss Rosenbluth who had a baby in the holidays, and I was the little girl Mary, so jealous and angry.

While I was interpreting she went back to the drawer and collected a number of toys. She proceeded to enact a game with the baby animals on the table and told me the story as she went along, saying that all the baby animals were running away from the bad farm lady and man, who were wicked and had not given the little animals enough food, 'didn't even *care* how much they squeaked.' A little girl featured in this story too, who tried to persuade the animals to go back to the farm, but they wouldn't go because the farmers were too cruel.

In this material she showed her ambivalent feelings towards me, on the one hand her pleasure at seeing me again, the smile, and her longing for me in the pouncing on the drawer; on the other hand she showed her anger with me for having left her over Christmas. Indeed in the beginning of the session, in her silence, her back to me and then her taunting me with *her* secrets this seemed to be the predominant feeling. The complexity of the unconscious phantasy is also evident: her interpretation of my deserting her was that I was felt to have had a baby over Christmas (the secret baby inside her hand, as well as the rummaging in the drawer to find what was there). I was felt to have been too preoccupied with my baby and husband to give her a thought, was cruelly neglectful and uncaring about her. She also dramatised the struggle within herself, the little animals representing the angry part of herself that wanted to run away from me again, just as she had in fact run away and missed the last session before Christmas, and the little girl urging the animals to go back representing the more friendly part. Furthermore one can see how the cruel farm lady was the therapist who had been internalised during the holiday as a result of Mary's own hostility which was expressed in missing the last session.

Here the deprivation experienced through the separation from the therapist increased her hostility, and in consequence her persecutory anxiety. The predominant feeling here was one of being starved, cruelly treated by a neglectful therapist mother, although some sadness at losing the good therapist and the wish to regain her was also present. All these feelings and phantasies were a repetition, a reliving of her experiences when her mother did have another baby, as well as of her own baby feelings about being kept waiting for her feeds. In this example I began by interpreting her hostility to me and relating it to the feeling of being deserted by me as a neglectful mother. When she then elaborated the phantasies, the first stage of the transference interpretation would be to show her the feeling that I had become the wicked farm lady who did not give her any food (treatment), during the holidays and did not care how hungry she was or how sad, but was only concerned about my own secrets my own private life. The second stage would relate this to its origin in her feelings about the mother, both in the present when the mother was not always available to her but concerned with father or baby sister, and in the past when the next baby was born, and further back in her own baby situation of the feeding mother not always being there straight away when she was hungry, when she felt her mother to be cruel and not caring how much she cried and longed for her.

The second stage of the interpretation could, however, also be implicitly stated, as the baby part of the child was at that moment dynamically operating in relation to the internal image of a cruelly neglectful mother, which was projected on to the therapist. One could therefore have worded the interpretation in some such way as: 'The baby part of you is so angry with me now, wants to run away from me, because you feel I am such a bad Mummy, bad farm lady therapist, who doesn't care about you, goes away for so long and doesn't give you any milk, treatment.' I think this way of putting the interpretation has some advantages in that it stresses the fact that the baby part is feeling this now, is tempting her to run away from the treatment in a 'cutting off her nose to spite her face' manner. This will enable her to become aware that this is not something of the past, over and done with, but a kind of reaction that currently makes for difficulties for her, both in relation to me and to her parents and in other present-day situations. The most important thing, it seems to me, is to stress in one's interpretations the current anxieties and conflicts in relation to the therapist; the link with the parents and with the past can often be implicit in one's wording.

Sometimes the child's conflicts and the material he brings about the parents at home are so clear that one is tempted to interpret outside the transference. An eight-year-old boy, living with his parents, could discuss and accept even the most painful oedipal wishes and hostile feelings in relation to his mother and father, but reacted with great resistance when I linked these to myself in transference. The mistake I made then was sometimes to talk immediately about his feelings about his parents at home, by-passing his relation to me. However I learnt that this way of interpreting was quite ineffectual. While he was with me the parents and the home seemed sufficiently far away for him to be able to think about his problems with them, past and present, in a detached and intellectual manner, but it did not really effect any change in him. He habitually used his intellect as a defence and I only colluded in this. Analysis became an interesting detective game, but his feelings were not really engaged. Here, as always, it was clearly very important to get the patient to recognise that it was in relation to the therapist at the moment that his conflicts were also played out, to show him over and over again that he was treating the therapist as the sexual mother he wanted for himself, or as the father he wanted to eliminate.

In all cases the links between the current transference relation and family relationships, present and past, have eventually to be made. But of most immediate importance is the current relationship with the therapist, and in particular the way the patient uses the interpretations, the treatment. Once this is really well analysed the links with the earlier relationships are usually not so difficult to make or accept.

## Importance of interpreting the negative transference

One of the problems in ourselves, making for difficulty in interpreting the transference is, I believe, the fear of alienating the child from the parents, a fear that if the child becomes too attached to us he will have a less good relation to his parents. This is not in fact the case if we are careful to interpret all negative feelings as well as the positive ones and their inter-relation, together with their transference nature. I think we also become less afraid of interpreting all the child's feelings and impulses towards us once we are fully convinced that they are in fact transferred, do not really belong to us in our own right, so to speak.

In this connection Ronnie, the little boy I mentioned in the beginning who could not leave his mother's side, was very interesting to me. As his mother was actually in the room, by his side, during the early part of treatment, I was at first in two minds how to interpret. I decided, however, to interpret in the usual way because his material was particularly clear. Thus I interpreted his possessive wishes to have me, as the treatment Mummy, all to himself; his greed in wanting to feed more and more from me, his anxieties about exhausting me and there being no treatment Mummy left for him, his behaving to his Mummy at home in the same way and therefore needing his real Mummy there all the time as a reassurance that she is all right, as against his picture inside of a worn-out Mummy, etc. I did all this with some trepidation, however, because of his mother's presence, and decided to have a talk with her privately one evening to try to explain both why I referred to myself as 'Mummy' so often, and why I made the link with the feeding situation. In the event the mother had no difficulty at all in understanding all this. She said she had been extremely surprised how quickly Ronnie had begun to treat me in just the same possessive, controlling manner in which hitherto he had behaved only towards her. As regards the links with the feeding situation, she said that Ronnie had quite soon at home started to count the time interval between sessions (he came twice a week) by the number of meals, so that he would say 'five more meals and then I see Miss Rosenbluth!'

The danger of alienating the child from the parents seems to me to be much more acute if we deliberately try to foster a positive relationship to us, by granting gratifications, giving promises or attempting by other means to make the child dependent on us, ignoring his hostile feelings as incon-venient. In that case, indeed, the child might be encouraged to split off his hostile feelings and direct them in renewed force against the parents at home.

Maybe another difficulty in interpreting the negative transference is the fear that this will only increase the child's hostility towards us. But in the session with Mary, it was after I had interpreted her negative feelings that she became able to show me more details of her phantasies, and what is more it was then the more positive co-operative part of her, in the shape of the little girl who wanted the animals to go back to the farm, could emerge. It is in fact often only after anxiety has been relieved as a result of interpreting the negative transference that genuine positive feelings can emerge.

The impetus to co-operate in treatment, the 'therapeutic alliance', is fostered most effectively when the child gains the conviction that we understand him and are not afraid to put into words even the most violently hostile impulses and phantasies. If he feels that, in contrast to his parents and to that part of himself that wants to deny or gloss over his aggressive feelings, we can understand and interpret and in that way make them more manageable for him, the impetus to co-operate fully in the treatment becomes thereby strengthened.

## Stress on psychic reality

My patient Mary, earlier on in the treatment, would sometimes tell me reproachfully and full of self pity, that she had been told she had in fact cried a lot as a baby because her mother did not have enough milk for her. She used this external reality situation, as we are of course all apt to do, to make her own hostile impulses more bearable and excusable. Certainly past external reality difficulties played a part in the origin of her conflicts, but we can do nothing about them any more. External reality should not be denied, but I do not think it is particularly helpful to interpret in such a way as to encourage the patient to fasten on to it to justify her own hostility. Mary's image of a cruelly neglectful mother was surely not solely or even predominantly created by external experience, because the mother in reality, though she had difficulties and was anxious about feeding, would never have left her to cry for long. One could say to Mary: 'You are angry with me now just as you were angry as a baby with your mummy when she *really* did not give you enough milk.' But this would seem to be putting the blame on to the mother and not help the patient in the least to grapple with the distortion of the mother into a cruelly neglectful figure, which is ultimately a consequence of the child's own hostility. Also this way of interpreting might encourage the child to act out her hostile baby transference at home in relation to the mother, whereas our aim should be not only to keep the baby transference in the treatment, but to focus it there increasingly.

It is after all only internal reality that we are able to influence in treatment, and this is what we feel needs to be stressed as the most effective way of creating a change in the child's personality. It seems to me preferable then to concentrate on the child's impulses and phantasies and on how these distort reality in the current transference situation.

Even in cases of severe deprivation, what we have to look for and interpret is the way it was or is experienced by the child. Some children will exaggerate past deprivations and nourish feelings of resentment, whereas others may deny them and need to pretend that their early experiences were idyllic. In fact one child, owing to the interplay and relative strength of his libidinal and destructive impulses, will experience the same traumatic situation differently from another. To quote Freud (1937): 'Only by the interaction and counteraction of the two primal instincts – Eros and the Death Instinct, never by one or the other alone, can the motley variety of vital phenomena be explained.' It is the internal situation, and ultimately the 'interaction and counteraction of the two primal instincts' which determines whether the deprivation is experienced predominantly in a persecutory or in a depressive manner, and it is therefore primarily the internal psychic reality that needs to be understood and interpreted.

## Conclusion

If all transference feelings are consistently interpreted, more and more of the child's unconscious phantasies and impulses gradually become centred around the treatment, and the baby relationship then becomes fully transferred to the therapist. This also means that the situation at home usually becomes relieved, as the baby relationship needs no longer to interfere so much with the present relationship between the child and his parents. But a deepening of the transference depends on the technique used, that is on a consistent interpretation of all transference phenomena, negative as well as positive, from the beginning of treatment. As Mrs Klein writes (1952):

> Transference originates in the same processes which in the earliest stages determine object relations. Therefore we have to go back again and again in analysis to the fluctuations between objects, loved and hated, external and internal which dominate early infancy.

Only when the child's earlier relationships and anxieties are fully re-experienced in the transference can they be worked through and a real change take place. For the aim of child treatment, as of that of adults, is essentially a re-integrative one, to take back and re-integrate parts of the self. The unacceptable impulses and parts of the self which had previously been split off and projected had led to distortions of the picture of the parents, both externally and internally. To effect a change (to quote Mrs Klein (1952) again):

> . . . our field of investigation covers *all* that lies between the current situation and the earliest experiences . . . It is only by linking again and again . . . later experiences with earlier ones and *vice versa*, it is only by consistently exploring their interplay, that present and past can come together in the patient's mind. This is one aspect of the process of integration which, as the analysis progresses, encompasses the whole of

the patient's mental life. When anxiety and guilt diminish and love and hate can be better synthesised, splitting processes – a fundamental defence against anxiety – as well as repressions lessen while the ego gains in strength and coherence; the cleavage between idealised and persecutory objects diminishes; the phantastic aspects of objects lose in strength; all of which implies that unconscious phantasy life . . . can be better utilised in ego activities, with a consequent general enrichment of the personality. I am touching here on the *differences* – as contrasted with the similarities – between transference and the first object relations. These differences are a measure of the curative effect of the analytic procedure.

(I am aware that I have not dealt at all with the problems of frequency of attendance for treatment, but I think I have made it clear that we are convinced that the interpretation of transference is of equal importance whether a child is seen once, twice or five times a week. Continuity of transference at deeper levels may, however, not be so easy to maintain in some children if they are seen only once a week, and the therapist's own skill plays an important part here.)

## Summary

I have tried to indicate that transference and its interpretation are the essence of child psychotherapy. I have also tried to show how this has many implications for technique: the importance of establishing a suitable setting within which the child's communication of his unconscious phantasies is encouraged; the importance of concentrating on the interpretation of the transference in both its negative and its positive aspects, and how, when this is consistently done, the child's earliest babyhood anxieties and conflicts are re-experienced and can be worked through in the transference relationship.

## References

Freud, S. (1905) 'Fragments of an analysis of a case of hysteria', SE 7.
Freud, S. (1912) 'The dynamics of transference' in 'Papers on technique', SE 12.
Freud, S. (1917) 'Introductory lectures on psycho-analysis', Ch. 27. SE 16.
Freud, S. (1937) 'Analysis terminable and interminable', *International Journal of Psycho-Analysis*, 18.
Heimann, P. (1956) 'Dynamics of transference interpretations', *International Journal of Psycho-Analysis*, 37.
Isaacs, S. (1948) 'The nature and function of phantasy', *International Journal of Psycho-Analysis*, 29.
Klein, M. (1927) 'Symposium on child analysis', *International Journal of Psycho-Analysis*, 8.

Klein, M. (1932) *Psycho-Analysis of Children. International Journal of Psycho-Analysis*, Library No. 22.

Klein, M. (1952) 'The origins of transference', *International Journal of Psycho-Analysis*, 33.

Klein, M. (1960) *Our Adult World and its Roots in Infancy*. Tavistock Pamphlet, No. 2.

Strachey, J. (1934) 'The nature of the therapeutic action of psycho-analysis', *International Journal of Psycho-Analysis*, 15.

# Chapter 4

# Problems in the use of the counter-transference: Getting it across[1]

*Anne Alvarez*

Originally published in the *Journal of Child Psychotherapy* (1983) 9(1): 7–23.

As work in the counter-transference is so closely linked with work in the transference, it may be useful to comment on some developments and difficulties in the notion of transference. In Freud's earliest thinking, in the *Studies on hysteria* and in the Dora case, the transference is seen mostly as an obstacle, a resistance, a symptom to be removed, decontaminated (1895, 1905). Gradually it changes. What starts, in the *Studies on hysteria*, as a transference of a woman's compulsive wish for a kiss, and is consistent with libido theory, changes by the time of the Wolf-Man to a transference on to Freud of the wish to have the love (frequently it is still only the sexual love) of a valued father (1918). The gradual humanisation of Freud's general conceptual structure was accompanied by a major change in his view of the source of the forces of repression. Thus, in *The Ego and the Id*, the controlling, restraining forces are no longer seen as issuing from external reality, as a sort of lid on the cooking pot, but as a conscience speaking with a human voice to the child in the patient (1923).

Melanie Klein pushed the humanising process even further in her study of the very primitive super-ego in paranoid and depressive psychotic patients and in very young children (1955). She found scattered human elements existing in piecemeal form in what appeared to be phantasies of the most inhuman forces and objects. In this light a fascination with fire or electricity, a sensual attachment to a velvety fabric, say, would be seen as representing not only sexual impulses of the patient, but also the imagined sexual and sensual qualities and powers of his parents, or parts or aspects of his parents. Object relations theory, and especially part-object relations theory, and even more especially, split-object relations theory, does extend the arena in which the transference can be seen to be played out. For example a psychotic patient of mine used to reach with his arms and his whole body towards me, or sometimes only with his gaze, in a manner that

1  This paper was presented at the Study Weekend of the Association of Child Psychotherapists in March 1983.

Frances Tustin has called 'entangling'. It was indeed very entangling. It felt loving, harmless, gentle, but unbelievably enveloping. It felt not human, not even animal, but more like the infinitely slow but inexorable growth of a plant. At times I felt he must be brain-damaged; this wasn't human – this was vegetable love. In fact, I came to see that he seemed to be using his whole body as a sort of giant tongue, and to sense that I was simply some giant object for licking – a sort of nipple-less breast, perhaps. He used his eyes in the same manner, for licking instead of looking.

There are two further developments following from the work of Mrs Klein to which I wish to draw attention. The first is her emphasis on the importance of the negative transference, and the second is her concept of projective identification. In her paper, *The Origins of Transference*, she concluded that transference arises from the same processes which originate early object relations, namely, the primal processes of projection and introjection directed towards their first object, the mother's breast. She declared that the introjection of the mother's breast is the beginning of super-ego formation (1952). The infant observation studies initiated by Mrs Bick (1964) and the recent flood of child development research would encourage us to add: the mother's smell, arms, lap, voice, touch as equally vital elements in the building up of this early introjected object (Macfarlane, 1977). The point, in any case, which Klein is making, concerns a theory of the origins of transference, its clinical history, as it were. There are considerable differences among Kleinian analysts and Kleinian psychotherapists today in the manner and pace with which they would introduce part-object language into an analysis. I happen to think myself that this is not only a technical issue, it's a theoretical one which connects with Bion's (1962) notion of alpha function, Segal's (1957) view of symbol formation, and Meltzer's (1981) view of reconstruction, but space does not permit discussion of this issue here (Alvarez, 1981).

Klein (1952) then goes on to make her rather revolutionary and still controversial technical point about the advances in technique which follow from the recognition – in work with young children, but also with schizophrenics – that we are unable to penetrate to what she called the deepest layers of the mind without analysing the negative transference alongside the positive. I want to stress the last three words, 'alongside the positive', because I think it's important to notice their presence. In a paper called 'Developments from the work of Melanie Klein', Elizabeth Spillius (1983) suggests that both Klein and her followers have often been accused of overemphasising the negative. Spillius says, and I quote,

> Certainly Klein was very much aware of destructiveness, of defences against it, and of the negative transference, but she also stressed, both in theory and in practice, the importance of love, the patient's concern for his object, of guilt and of reparation. Further, in her later work

especially she conveys a strong feeling of support to the patient when negative feelings were being uncovered.

Spillius says that it is her impression that Mrs Klein was experienced by her patients not as an adversary but as an ally in their struggles to accept feelings they hated in themselves and had had to deny and obliterate. She goes on: 'I think it is this attitude that gives the feeling of "balance" that Hanna Segal says was so important in her experience of Mrs Klein as an analyst'. In this respect, then, says Spillius, some of the authors of the early Institute of Psychoanalysis membership papers took a step backwards from the work of Klein herself. Spillius got hold of and studied a large number of membership papers at the Institute from the 1950s, 1960s and 1970s and found that in the 1970s destructiveness began to be interpreted in a more balanced way. She suggests that there has been a change, not in the emphasis on death instinct and destructiveness, but in the way it is analysed – with less confrontation – more fine differentiations. She thinks the change has developed from several sources: from Bion's emphasis on the normality of certain forms of projective identification, which has been further elaborated by Rosenfeld (1969) in his stress on projective identification as communication, and from Joseph's emphasis on the need for the analyst to avoid joining the patients in sadomasochistic and other forms of acting out, e.g. becoming a scold or a moralising judge. She suggests other sources as well. The change, I think, can also be seen in a quite urgent statement by Money-Kyrle (1977). He states in his paper, 'On being a psychoanalyst', that Bion's work has made it easier but very important for us to distinguish between a desperate projective identification and a destructive one, or, he says, as both forms may occur together, to see which was the predominant one. He adds, 'I believe (though not with certainty) it is both easy and terrible to mistake a desperate projection for a destructive one. For by this means, I think, the beginnings of a constructive link between patient and analyst may be destroyed'.

I think that a change away from the interpretation of destructiveness also arises from the work of Bick (1968), Meltzer (1975) and Tustin (1972; 1981) with autistic children. All of these writers in their different ways suggest a failure to achieve projective identification on the part of these children, and stress that lack of integration rather than destructive disintegrating processes plays a part in their psychopathology. All three also hint at possible failure in the containing aspects of the maternal object. The concept of the container is Bion's (1962), and Spillius suggests that through this concept, Bion has made the external object an integral part of the system. She says his formulation shows not just *that* the environment is important but *how* it is important. I would say: *one* of the ways in which it is important. I would suggest that the containing function is only one maternal function among many, and only one analytic function among many.

I want to say a little more about the transference before coming on to a second further development of Mrs Klein's, that is her concept of projective identification. But first, I want to point out that the Kleinian broadening of the theory of the transference to which I have referred does not make the work easier. If anyone, or anything in the patient's material, e.g. concerning his outside life, or anything in the room can be seen to be connected with earliest feelings and earliest objects, but also to be connected to the person of the therapist, then the job of selection is enormous. I think some critics of Kleinian work in the transference assume a very mechanical process of interpreting every tiny piece of material as referring directly to the person of the therapist. This would mean always interpreting the object to the neglect of the ego or the id. This type of 'me-me-me' interpretive work would be a bad mistake with any patient – a phantasy may need room and space to develop, to breathe, and take shape – but is especially dangerous with claustrophobic or confused patients who need help in finding themselves. Adolescents are a good example, because they are often *both* claustrophobic *and* confused, and so cannot take in a surfeit of interpretations about dependence on the maternal object, whereas they may respond when some of the interpretations refer to a more responsible bit of themselves or even a belief or a principle which they hold dear. A similar problem arises with autistic children who can become so easily overwhelmed by the power of the object when they are in an opened-up state, that they may retreat further if the need to be inviolate is not understood. Stress on work in the transference need not mean that every interpretation has to refer to the person of the therapist and it need not mean becoming a nag.

Yet even without this difficulty, the selection problem is still enormous. If what may be brought into the transference and put on to the person of the therapist are not only projections of parts of the patient's self, but also the whole of his inner world, including his objects, split or in parts, past or current, how is one to make the correct choice? Suppose an adolescent patient says to us, 'You look tired today', or a younger child holds up the mother doll and says, 'She just can't sit up today'. Is this a realistic perception achieved by a child who is learning to see what he sees – we do look tired – or is this a direct projection of an exhausted drained aspect of the patient himself? Or is this a consequence of the patient's greedy demands on us earlier in the session? Or, alternatively, is this an attempt by him to elucidate and give form to a damaged drained internal object which is normally quite repressed? Objects, not only impulses, can be repressed. Joseph's (1978) view is that in the latter case the patient may be just beginning to try to represent and explore a denied inner world, and so it would be premature to interpret and search out, or even to assume the existence of, attacks which may have led to such a drained object. She believes that one of the things Bion meant by analytic containment was not to push back this type of projection too quickly.

I've often thought it was interesting that Klein does not mention the counter-transference in her paper on transference. It was after all written in 1952, six years after 'Notes on some schizoid mechanisms', where she described the process of projective identification (Klein, 1946). Spillius says she did not envisage its use in the form in which it developed among her close colleagues. There was a lovely example of her caution and sanity in this area given by Dr Segal at the Memorial Meeting for her last July at the Tavistock and quoted by Spillius (1983). A young analyst told Mrs Klein in a seminar that he felt confused and therefore interpreted to his patient that the patient projected confusion into him – to which Mrs Klein replied, 'No dear, you *are* confused'.

Nonetheless, Bion's (1962) use of projective identification as a normal process, his idea of the analytic object as container, and Rosenfeld's (1965) concept of the transference psychosis, led inevitably to the view that the psychoanalyst may not only play the part of the patient's objects and selves in the patient's mind, *but in his own mind too*. The patient may project so skilfully that he may not only feel his therapist is depressed, he may make her become depressed.

Paula Heimann has written a good deal about the transference and counter-transference. In 1950 she wrote about the analytic ideal of the 'detached' analyst, and says that she found the literature 'does indeed contain descriptions of the analytic work which can give rise to the notion that a good analyst does not feel anything beyond a uniform and mild benevolence towards his patients, and that any ripple of emotional waves on this smooth surface represents a disturbance to be overcome'. Her thesis, on the contrary, is that the analyst's emotional response to his patient within the analytic situation represents one of the most important tools for his work. His counter-transference, she claims, is an instrument of research into the patient's unconscious. She thinks that the first view may derive from a reading of some of Freud's statements, such as his comparison with the surgeon's state of mind during an operation, or his simile of the mirror. But she makes the very interesting point that Freud himself used the counter-transference as an instrument of research. She says that psychoanalytic technique came into being when Freud abandoned hypnosis, and discovered resistance and repression. When he tried to elucidate the hysterical patients' forgotten memories he felt that a force from the patient opposed his attempts, and that he had to overcome this resistance by his own psychic work (Heimann, 1950). In a later paper (Heimann, 1960) she pointed out that the analytic situation is a relationship between two persons. I quote: 'What distinguishes this relationship from others, is not the presence of feelings in one partner, the patient, and their absence in the other, but the degree of feeling the analyst experiences and the use he makes of his feelings, these factors being interdependent'.

It may be important at this point to define the way in which I myself shall use the term counter-transference, and also the ways in which I shall not use it. I will use it to include all the feeling the therapist may have toward his patient. This might include his own unanalysed transference to the patient or a displacement on to the patient from outside, but it would also include feelings put into him by the patient. It would *not* include a perception of something going on in the patient which is not accompanied by a similar or related feeling in the therapist. For example, I would not say that 'my counter-transference told me that the patient was depressed', unless for no apparent personal reason I suddenly felt depressed myself when with him. I would prefer to call the former situation empathic perception. Such perceptions are just as important for picking up previously unrecognised bits of the patient as is the counter-transference.

I wish now to say a little about Bion's (1962) concept of containment. His notion seems to be that if the mother is capable of something he calls reverie, the baby may project his frustrations, rages and fears into her and get them back in a modified form. The second half of the process – the getting back – he later called transformation (Bion, 1965). He likened this to the activity of the artist, and also to the interpretive activity of the analyst. I would like to suggest that in fact the process can really be seen to be made up of three phases; the receptive or containing stage when the material first makes its impact, the transforming work which goes on inside the therapist, and the third phase, the interpretive work. It may seem artificial to divide them up, particularly phases two and three, in this manner, but I find it helpful when thinking about how the process varies so greatly with different kinds of patients. Otherwise, I believe the notion of containment can colour and interfere with, and even prevent the effective operation of, the other two functions. Grotstein (1981a) appears to be thinking along these lines in his book *Splitting and Projective Identification*. He says it is very important to differentiate Bion's conception of containment from the mirroring mother as denoted by Lacan, Winnicott and Kohut. He believes that containment for Bion was a very active process which involved feeling, thinking and acting. I would suggest that the notion of containment is after all a *metaphor* with spatial connotations. It makes one think of a bowl, a lap, the mother's encircling arms, something essentially concave. Grotstein (1981b), in his introduction to the Bion Festschrift book, says it is often thought of as a sort of 'flexible rubber bag, which expands with the impact of the infant's projections' (p.19), but he adds that Bion's theory includes a second step, interpretive transformation. The first more concave receptive function is to my mind only *one* analytic function. The danger is that the spatial metaphor may take over and interfere with the functions of transformation and interpretation. The therapist may then become, not tolerant, but denying, not flexible, but passive.

The God Hermes is the patron of thieves, merchants, travellers, heralds and of messengers. Kermode (1979) points out in a book on biblical narrative that Hermes is the patron of all interpreters. Thus hermeneutics is the study of the interpretation of texts. Kermode suggests that Hermes must therefore also be the patron of psychoanalysis. 'For he is the God of going between: between the dead and the living but also between the latent and the manifest'. He is also the guardian of boundaries and the guide of departed souls to Hades. I invoke him today not just for fun but because, to my mind, Hermes exemplifies a vital part of our work: he is the message or herald whose job is not only to contain in the counter-transference, but also to transform the messages from the patient, and then, thirdly, to get something back across to him in order to help him to feel *known*.

I would like now to give three clinical examples of some problems in the use of, that is, the communication of, the counter-transference. The first, a very brief one, is a fairly classic example of a patient making use of what I think was a desperate type of projective identification both to evacuate and communicate terrible hopelessness. Here I will stress that the containing function is most important.

In the second and third examples less containment and receptivity is required but the message is all important. Hermes is invoked.

The first and third cases are my own and the second is Mrs Laporte-Steuerman's.

The first case is a 12-year-old boy named Richard who was referred to me 16 years ago as a borderline schizophrenic with learning and social problems. I saw him for three years, twice weekly. Richard complained to me that there seemed to be a cogwheel in his brain going round and round. He hallucinated at times, and one of the things he saw was a clock with all its works falling out. He had had a pretty terrible infancy. His mother was manic-depressive, and used to fly into rages and beat him. She became pregnant again when he was five months old, and then ran off with another man, leaving behind his father, the new baby, and Richard when he was 18 months old. He was moved back and forth several times after that between the home of his aunt, and that of his paternal grandmother. After a guarded paranoid start with me this very persecuted and despairing boy began to open up a little. He told me on one occasion how mother goose was sobbing and went mad. She died of grief from having produced a rotten egg. He began a frenzy of destructiveness unleashed mostly on the room and furniture, only rarely on me. Gradually the hallucinations and cogwheels left him, the aggression towards the room diminished and he began to concentrate his destructive efforts more on me and my person. But the cruelty and torture were not physical, they were mental. I had to watch him pry faeces out of his bottom and shove them up his nose. He glared into my face as he did this, and I did watch. I felt appalled, disgusted and sometimes absolutely hopeless. Once when I was thinking to myself, 'There is no hope for you, Richard' but not knowing what to say, he sang, 'Cape of No Hope – Cape of No Hope'. I think he was projecting hopelessness into me but mostly out of what Money-Kyrle calls a desperate motive rather than a destructive one. I had not sorted out those differentiations in those years, but I did make myself watch him, and so perhaps to an extent he did feel I contained some of his hopelessness for him. Where I think I failed to contain it enough, is in the frequent interpretations I made that it was his *own* hopelessness which he was projecting into me. I suspect Bion (1962) and Joseph (1978) would claim that I was pushing it back too prematurely. Richard may well have needed to let me have it all for a long while before he could take it back. His family were extremely kind but excessively genteel and there had probably been simply nowhere for the heartbreak, persecution, guilt and murderous fury to go. Later, as he improved and began to verbalise more feelings, he sometimes said 'If I could only make you *bleed*'.

Rosenfeld (1981) is clearly another writer who has strong views on the needs for containment through time with psychotic patients. He writes in the Bion Festschrift book:

> In the treatment of psychotic patients the patient tests again and again the analyst's capacity to bear his frustrating experience, his anxieties, confusion, his helplessness and hopelessness which he projects into him . . . Any slight disturbance in the patient/analyst relationship can lead to serious misunderstandings; for example, when the analyst reacts too quickly before he has had any chance to experience fully what the patient is communicating to him, the patient feels rejected, as he experiences the analyst's quick response as a refusal to accept his projection and he feels that his projects are thrown back at him. (p. 176)

The second case is a boy named Alexander who was a patient of Monica Laporte-Steuerman's. She had been treating him once weekly for four months. He was 10 years of age, a twin, and he and his twin brother are the oldest siblings in a large family. The twins were confined to their darkened room for most of their life until age four, when they were fostered for the first time. They were fed there, the dog was kept in there and was allowed to defaecate there. They were fed mostly scraps of food, and later used to cry whenever they saw other people's food. When they were fostered for the third time at age six, they seemed to have little idea of space or time, and did not even know how to make their own way down a street. The mother was negligent and psychopathic and sometimes violent but was not seriously abusive physically towards them, and was sometimes affectionate, but usually to the other, stronger twin. Alexander was extremely thin, like a reed, and seemed all mouth with protruding teeth. He had rubbery octopus's hands. He was a very adhesive child, who giggled a lot in a silly manner and made strange primitive sounds much of the time. His insidious quality did not, however, seem sinister or evil to Mrs Laporte-Steuerman. His foster mother, who had helped to socialise the twins and to make them educable, was aware both of Alexander's insidiousness and also of his intelligence.

Mrs S. began to feel that this boy was beginning to irritate her terribly. She knew he had been deprived; she knew he was all over the place and clumsy – how could he be otherwise? He was ugly with strange teeth and a silly false placating grin – how could he be otherwise? But yet she began to mind all this very much. She minded his awkwardness and clumsiness far more than she would have minded these qualities in other chaotic and deprived children. She had previously tried to be containing, understanding, receptive, but in the first session presented here we shall hear how she changes tack. I think we shall see that the new tack is much more than simply a question of setting limits. Setting limits is a helpful concept for dealing with management problems, but is inadequate as a description for situations where the management problem is not of the patient's wild behaviour, but of the therapist's strong reaction *to* the patient's often quite tame behaviour.

Here is the session.

Alexander came in with a sort of 'net briefcase' containing six balls.

He throws balls under the sofa making quite a lot of noise (as the balls are heavy). He moves a lot, all over the place.

He stops the play with the balls and goes to the big heavy desk. He starts pushing it very slowly. The friction of the desk legs against the ceramic tiled floor makes a very piercing noise. A. laughs at it and each time it happens he giggles, looking at me to see the effect. He wants to move it into a corner between the cupboards and the sink which is almost the size of a bath. This corner is exactly the same size as the desk.

A. pushes the desk into the corner but it gets stuck by the cupboards' handles. A. pulls and pushes impatiently and noisily. I am not sure if he is being clumsy or careless. He giggles a lot when he looks at me. Finally, dodging the desk, he manages to overcome one of the obstacles (there are three handles). While this has been happening I am silent, feeling quite disturbed and irritated. I can see the water stains at the back of the desk. Has he made them through his countless 'washings'? Is he going to scratch the desk with the handles?

I am trying to sort my feelings out, trying to think of what is happening between us when he goes to the taps and turns them on, letting a strong flow of water fall. It falls while he goes back to the desk, struggling to push it further into the corner.

After some water play he goes to the cupboard, getting some pencils, a ruler, scissors and Sellotape. He steps on the easy chair and stands on the low table beside me. He sticks pieces of Sellotape on the venetian blind rail.

A pencil falls on the table right beside me, making a rattling noise that at this moment I feel to be quite disturbing. I look up and see A., pencils under his left arm, making a slight, disguised movement, letting another pencil fall and finally all of them. He giggles.

I say, 'You're doing this on purpose.' He says, 'No I'm not'. I reply, 'You know very well you are'. I continue, saying that he comes into my room to move things around, spoil them, waste and drop them, making me feel spoilt, wasted and dropped.

He gets embarrassed and serious. I feel he became real.

I say he is embarrassed because he felt that I got to see a side of him and I am not going to let him get away with it.

He starts moving the little table beside me. He moves it slowly and clumsily, making faces and giving me the impression he knows he is getting under my skin. Many times he lets the table fall on the floor which makes a big 'bang' and he restrains a giggle when looking at me to see the effect of the noise.

I say to him that he thinks I am stupid as I don't hit him or do awful things to him. So he uses this and enjoys seeing me getting upset and on edge that he might break something in my room (I was afraid he might let the table fall against the window glass, breaking it).

'You think people who are nice to you are also stupid.'

'Some are'.

It is time. We start tidying up. He pulls down the Sellotape, with the risk of making the rail fall. I show this to him. He does it properly.

I show him that he knows how to do it properly but that he has to try me and see if I'll let him get away with it. I also say that I have got in touch with a side of him that is clever and I am not going to let him forget about it. He leaves the room, returning to ask me if he should go to the waiting room.

I see him out.

I want to make two points about this material. The first is that if we decide to assume that Mrs S. is right and that there was a subtly provocative element in this boy's clumsiness, this would in no way account for the original cause of his clumsiness, or even all of his clumsiness now, but it would account for a way in which he now *uses* his clumsiness. I think this is something that occurs with many patients who have been ill since infancy. As they improve, some of the earlier defensive motives for the original madness recede and the symptom is used for much milder motives. It's often hard to see the mischievousness of a relatively normal child in a particularly ghastly symptom.

I should also point out that there is no doubt that there was a certain hard edge to Mrs S.'s voice when she described this session that is not normally there. I think this is probably almost a universal phenomenon: the first time we become conscious of a piece of counter-transference of which we have been previously unaware, our initial response is often quite strong. It's important, I think, to note that she must, however, have done a considerable amount of transforming work within herself, because she did not really act out in the counter-transference. She didn't shout, or end the session, or get into a scuffle. A common experience, I think, when the provocation has been subtle, is to find oneself acting out with sudden bursts of unreasonable, forcible restraint, or acting out verbally with an interpretation about the child's fear of loss, say, which somehow carries a veiled threat. I think we should not guiltily set aside this type of acting out as simply an aberration, but rather as *the first sign* that something very important in the counter-transference may have been neglected by us. Only when it is finally confronted and examined, can it be transformed. There is a very fine line between acting out in the counter-transference, and making the interpretation in such a way that the patient hears and feels its meaning. But it is a line that I believe can be drawn, and should be drawn. Fluctuations close to and sometimes over the line are probably inevitable. In fact, Mrs S. learned later that fostering had nearly broken down precisely because Alexander's foster mother had begun to find his subtle teasing unbearable.

At this early stage, however, it was not yet possible to understand Alexander's wider motives for the provocation. Was he identified with the stupid ugly near-animal that his own mother may have felt he was? Did he feel provocation had become his only way of attracting her attention? He and Mrs S. did not know yet. Remember that he did give Mrs S. an embarrassed, serious, *real* look. I think sometimes for the child the experience of being known is so precious that the whys really can wait until later. They should never be a substitute for the whats. Getting those across is our first task. One can never be sure of anything in this work, but I think Hermes was with them that day.

Here is part of a session three weeks later.

A. came along the corridor praising my shoes. It was in fact the first time he had seen them although they are plain, old, laced shoes.

A. was carrying a black umbrella, closed.

As soon as we get into the room he praises my shoes and asks me, what do I think about his umbrella. 'Do you like it?' 'It is nice, isn't it?'

I tell him that it seems that we should begin today's session praising one another, making sure one finds the other nice.

It is an automatic umbrella that when closed can have its size reduced. He opens it and closes it, makes it big and small. He does this many times, asking me if I think it is nice and saying my shoes are nice.

I try to inquire what does he see in my shoes to feel they are so nice. He is unable to tell me. I say to him that I believe he wants us praising one another to do away with the fear he has of me.

In a frightened way he denies it. I tell him that he is frightened now, the moment I talk about his fear. He denies it again, going to the desk and starting to move it. He leaves the umbrella on the easy chair and now gets the low table beside me and giggling starts moving it around. He puts it lengthways up, holding the top legs with his hands and the bottom legs with his feet. The table legs are T-shaped and A. starts playing a dangerous play which he calls 'dodgy'.

I get on edge for fear that he might fall and say he knows very well he's not supposed to play that way.

He jumps, slides and almost falls backwards with the table on top of him. I jump from my chair in a worried state to help him but he manages to balance and nothing happens.

He looks at my face and giggles, saying, 'See, nothing's happened.' I say, 'This is not true, something has happened, you've managed to see me jump and get worried about you.'

He wants to play 'dodgy' again. I stop him and he conforms.

He gets chairs and starts sliding around. He stops and starts moving the desk into a corner between the cupboards and the sink.

I say that this moving the furniture around makes me feel like he is moving parts of my body around, like moving my eyes to my ears, my mouth to my forehead. He'd like to change me all round.

He agrees, saying 'Yeah! I would like to change you into the Incredible Hulk.'

I say to him that I think he is so frightened I may suddenly change into the Incredible Hulk that he prefers to feel he changes me before.

I try to understand what is the Incredible Hulk for him. He says it's a green man that smashes everything up. I say he would like to turn me into this green Hulk man smashing everything up (he is still moving the furniture around).

He says, 'I am not the Hulk, you are. You are in green trousers'. I say perhaps he thinks what I really am is the green Hulk disguised into a lady psychotherapist.

He agrees with satisfaction.

I say, 'So you're frightened that at any moment I may show you this Hulk me'.

He, in a frightened way, 'No!' I say that he gets frightened even when I only speak about it. 'You're frightened now', I say.

Two things are interesting about this ensuing session: first, Mrs S. no longer feels annoyed by Alexander's furniture-moving; second, they have begun to explore together some of the motivations and anxieties behind his behaviour. This of course accords much more with the ideal of the psychotherapist's function. Yet the question remains: could this fruitful second session have occurred with this particular child without the irritations of the first? Could the second stage have been achieved in any real way without at least *some* of the counter-transference elements which obtained in the first? If the analytic process is like other living processes, then it too may have its expansions and contractions, its wave formations and rhythms.

The third case is a boy patient of mine named Cyrus. He is eight years old and was referred at age five for various phobic fears and separation difficulties. His family had come from abroad when he was aged two years from a country which has had major political upheavals for some years now. They belong to a small, somewhat threatened, religious minority within that country. The parents and an older sister of 15 continue to suffer much depression, anxiety and concern for friends and relatives at home.

I have chosen his material because I think it illustrates, in a way similar to Mrs S.'s Alexander, some problems for the therapist in the communication of understanding. My patient is a child I feel I've come to know well. He comes five times a week and he has been coming for three years. Analysing his destructiveness and apparent destructiveness is difficult because he seems to be a very tricky patient. He is no longer phobic – that part was fairly easy; he seems well able to enjoy his life, can separate from his parents fairly well and has many friends. He is still very much an underachiever at school. A major problem has been a continuing repetitive destructive play, and a total refusal to let me speak, which *at times* seems based on genuine rage: he is a terribly possessive controlling child and reacts passionately and exorbitantly to things like breaks. Sometimes he has feigned rage and felt nothing. At other times, he has feigned rage but felt real fury underneath. He is an actor and also a juggler with his own emotions.

A further problem has arisen, however. It is partly a problem in my understanding, but, even more, a problem in the communication of whatever understanding I am able to achieve. The problem is this: I began to feel that this child's destructiveness – constantly destroying play materials, constantly beginning to shout, sing or swear the moment I began to speak – had become quite motiveless. That seems a defeatist, unthinking thing for a psychotherapist to say, since we are supposed to be in the business of trying to understand motives. What I mean by it is that he had become stuck and addicted to a mode of being with me that had begun from defensive motivations and acquired destructive controlling motivations along the way, but had somehow gradually lost its heat. The heat, however, was not completely gone. His behaviour was, for example, still fed by his narcissism. That was clear, and yet the interpretation of this didn't change much. There are patients who do exploit and misuse and do not seem to benefit from the non-retributive, tolerant qualities of child psychotherapy. I set limits on physical damage to me or the room but nothing seemed to limit his other more subtle but powerful forms of destructiveness. The timing of his interruptions whenever I began to speak was impeccable and wonderfully effective. There were times when this was clearly defensive – he is a passionate, easily hurt child. There were also times when it was very sadistic. But the more difficult problem concerned the times when even real sadism was absent. He took, by the end of the third year, relatively little relish in disappointing me over and over again, but he just couldn't or wouldn't stop. The layman might say that he had some very bad habits, and there certainly was something casual and habitual about it.

I began to feel that the longer I went on containing this, the longer it would last. I started to have phantasies like 'All this child really needs is a good spank!' I had certainly begun to feel a weariness and boredom with the repetitive quality, after many years of interpreting the intense motives, but, like Mrs S., I didn't feet certain that I should feel bored. I alternated between searching for as yet undiscovered motives for the immobility, when I'm certain I sounded somewhat hypocritical, and beginning to make interpretations like 'You take for granted I'll go on forever', etc. which did at times carry the kind of veiled threat I spoke of earlier. As I have pointed out, there's a fine line there. If some proper work has been done on *oneself*, the same interpretation can be made without too much emotion, yet not altogether empty of emotion either. At this stage of uncertainty and unawareness I think I sometimes let it pop out vengefully.

In January of this year, I noticed that although I often gave up speaking when Cyrus interrupted me with his 'blah-blahs' or his obscene curses, I had never ceased to watch his dramatic antics. He often enacted very vividly some drama, usually a battle between two powerful heroes. He is a lively, appealing child, and in many ways, a pleasure to watch. He was also, as I've said, narcissistic. On January 14th, I began to watch him less. I found, for example, that I could just as easily interpret while looking at the floor. By January 17th, he had become much more alert; by the 18th, he actually listened to one or two interpretations, and by the 20th, he was actually pausing in his play to hear me out. I am not suggesting there is any magic in itself in the question of where one puts one's gaze; although in Richard's case, e.g. I believe it was very important to look. But with Cyrus I think the change of direction of my gaze was accompanied by many other changes. For example, there was a change in the length of my interpretations – they got shorter – and in my tone of voice – I think I allowed it to sound a little weary, a tiny bit bored. Maybe there was also a little chill in it. *I did not design and could not design, and am not recommending designing such changes.* I believe they *followed from* the examination of my counter-transference impressions that the child no longer needed, nor even particularly wanted to behave the way he did.

I have mentioned the tiny little hopeful signs. In between, however, things continued pretty much as usual, with obscene swearing, wild, excited, hugely noisy, exhibitionistic play.

On Monday 24th January I had to cancel a session because I was ill.

On Tuesday I felt that although his behaviour was unchanged, his eyes were on me much of the time.

On Wednesday the exciting battle of the giants went on as usual and his attacks on my voice were particularly cruel. I spoke firmly about his cruelty and he then played that he was shooting his enemy's tyres. Suddenly he said, 'They're flat', and looked very worried. I said he was afraid that I was exhausted and drained, and that that was why I'd gotten ill. I also said he was afraid I would run out of energy and hope and give up with him altogether. He gave me a very direct vulnerable look, and then rallied cockily and pointed his two fingers at me, pointing to the area between my breasts, pretending that his fingers were a gun, and said, 'I've got a good aim!' I agreed. I said he had perfect aim, that he knew exactly where to produce depression in me. I should have said 'he feels he knows', but even then there would have been no doubt that I was saying it from the heart. It seemed to hit him; he gave me a very clear-eyed look.

The next session, Thursday, was quite moving. I felt that almost for the first time, this very manipulative, charming, dishonest little boy spoke to me in a straightforward manner. At the beginning of the session, he said bitterly, 'You never listen, you just look round the room'. (I think that was high praise.) Later he said 'This place is like a prison'. He was protesting passionately, and yet the usual shrill melodramatic quality was absent. I interpreted that he felt the prison was himself and that he felt lately I wouldn't let him escape. Then he said, 'I feel sick'. I said, gently, since I felt very sorry for him at that moment, 'Perhaps you feel sick of yourself'. He said, unconvincingly, 'No – you'. Then he added, 'Well, mostly you'. He was near to tears. I said, 'A bit you, though'. To my surprise, he agreed.

The next session was Friday. He came a couple of minutes early and waited quietly. Downstairs he said, 'See, I'm empty-handed'. He often brings his own toys, which I have interpreted as his fear of coming empty-handed. Then he said, brightly and falsely, 'I'm looking *so* forward to Saturday'. I said, 'Well, you're not empty-minded'. He then insisted that at least he was empty-handed, and I acknowledged that he had made a considerable effort to manage that.

Then he decided to build what he called a 'torture place'. He was being shot at, but he was only an actor, it wasn't real shooting. He seemed to be trying to dilute the feelings of persecution, and the fascination with masochistic violence, but it was quite a struggle. I said that he felt it was very cruel to have to come here empty-handed, especially on a Friday and it was terribly cruel of me to be so full of stuff I was trying to give him. Here I was interpreting the feelings of persecution and defensiveness that I think were there, but as I did so, it began to change. This child readily despises and exploits containment. He got noisier and noisier and his voice became more and more horribly intrusive, so I began to speak about *his* cruelty. He refused to let me speak. I then said with much conviction that I did not believe he *did* think I was cruel. He seemed to hear me but went on playing. He played Evel Knievil, the stunt man with the bullet-proof vest, dodging the bullets. I said he felt I was the one who needed a bullet-proof vest. He looked worried, but got louder.

Then he changed to playing Luke Skywalker, the hero of *Star Wars*. Then he sort of collapsed on the couch, nearly fell off and looked close to tears. He made an effort to produce a riddle, a guessing game. Most of his conversation in the past consisted of this type of beginning 'Can you guess what?' or 'Do you know what . . .?' But this time his heart wasn't in it. What he said instead was, 'What's the difference between . . . garbage and Cyrus? No – Star Wars and Cyrus?' I tried to speak about the first, and he tried to push me on to the second. I stuck to the first, and said that I thought he was afraid that if he stopped his cruelty and noisy games, he'd be too empty-handed. There'd be just garbage in him. He said with passion, 'There is!' I said, 'You *feel* there is!' He was close to tears and shouting. He is a child who can be very persecuted by guilt, and I felt sorry for him, but I think I reassured him too quickly. Such rare moments of honesty about what a con-man he is do need delicate handling, but could perhaps have been allowed to last a little longer.

Then he moved half off the couch, looking at me from an upside-down position, and said, 'My name is Cyrus Joseph Khaled'. Then he told me his father had many more names than that. Then he mused, 'That's the first time I've ever told anyone my middle name'. I said, 'Perhaps that's a part you don't know, not garbagy, but not a stunt man either'. I searched for a word, and he said, very seriously, 'Clean?' Then he altered that to 'Neat'. I was still searching: I said, 'Yes, but I think it's more than that – it's something valuable – something which shouldn't be thrown away'. He said, out of the blue, and quite matter-of-factly, 'Rachel's the only one I show that part to' (his sister). There was more about this, and then he got talking about whether or not he could make himself dream the dreams at night he wanted to. Gradually the old stage pro returned, he got smoother and smoother and he began to confabulate. I said, 'You're spinning me a line'. He agreed with a sheepish grin, and sank back down on the couch. He said, sighing, 'I can't wait for Saturday'. But he helped me clear up.

A paper by David Tuckett (1983) called 'Words and the psychoanalytic interaction' discusses a review by Bullowa of the research on interactional synchrony. The researchers do frame-by-frame analysis of films of two people having a conversation. Bullowa argues that the research shows that language is inseparable from its bodily, mental and social matrices. Tuckett concludes that listening involves a process of physical and bodily response to the speaker which is involuntary and presumably unconscious. I have tried to suggest in this paper that while receptive containment in the counter-transference is a fundamental aspect of our work, transformation and the effective communication of the interpretation are equally fundamental to the therapist's activity. I would add that I think Bion's (1962) notion of alpha function, the mental process which allows thoughts to be thought about, and which endows experience with meaning, is highly relevant to this problem. If the therapist's aim is to help the patient to think with feeling, then he must make interpretations which can be experienced and heard by the patient as meaningful. These are more likely to arise when the therapist is honest with himself about his counter-transference, than when he denies it.

# References

Alvarez, A. (1981) 'Some thoughts on counter-transference and projective identification'. Unpublished.

Bick, E. (1964) 'Notes on infant observation in psychoanalytic training', *International Journal of Psycho-Analysis*, 45: 558–566.

Bick, E. (1968) 'The experience of the skin in early object relations', *International Journal of Psycho-Analysis*, 49: 484–486.

Bion, W.R. (1962) *Learning from Experience*. London: Heinemann.

Bion, W.R. (1965) *Transformations*. London: Heinemann.

Freud, S. with Breuer, J. (1895) *Studies on hysteria*, SE 2.

Freud, S. (1905) *Fragment of a case of hysteria*, SE 7.

Freud, S. (1918) *From the history of an infantile neurosis*, SE 17.

Freud, S. (1923) *The ego and the id*, SE 19.

Grotstein, J.S. (1981a) *Splitting and Projective Identification*. New York: Aronson.

Grotstein, J.S. (1981b) 'Wilfred R. Bion: the man, the psychoanalyst, the mystic. A perspective on his life and work'. In *Do I Dare Disturb the Universe?* Beverly Hills, CA: Caesura Press.

Heimann, P. (1950) 'On counter-transference', *International Journal of Psycho-Analysis*, 31: 81–84.

Heimann, P. (1960) 'Counter-transference', *British Journal of Medical Psychology*, 33: 9–15.

Joseph, B. (1978) 'Different types of anxiety and their handling in the analytic situation', *International Journal of Psycho-Analysis*, 59: 223–228.

Kermode, F. (1979) *The Genesis of Secrecy. On the Interpretation of Narrative.* London: Harvard University Press.

Klein, M. (1946) 'Notes on some schizoid mechanisms', In *The Writings of Melanie Klein*, Vol. III. London: Hogarth (1975).

Klein, M. (1952) 'The origins of transference', In *The Writings of Melanie Klein*, Vol. III. London: Hogarth (1975).

Klein, M. (1955) 'The psycho-analytic play technique: its history and significance', In *The Writings of Melanie Klein*, Vol. III. London: Hogarth (1975).

Macfarlane, A. (1977) *The Psychology of Childbirth*. London: Fontana/Open Books.

Meltzer, D. (1975) *Explorations in Autism*. Strath Tay: Clunie Press.

Meltzer, D. (1981) *Lectures on Dreams*. Tavistock Clinic.

Money-Kyrle, R. (1977) 'On being a psychoanalyst'. In *The Collected Papers of Roger Money-Kyrle*. Strath Tay: Clunie Press (1978).

Rosenfeld, H. (1965) *Psychotic States. A Psychoanalytical Approach*. London: Hogarth.

Rosenfeld, H. (1969) 'Contribution to the psychopathology of psychotic states: the importance of projective identification in the ego structure and object relations of the psychotic patient'. In Doueet, P. and Laurin, C. (eds.) *Problems of Psychosis*. The Hague: Excerpta Medica.

Rosenfeld, H. (1981) 'On the psychopathology and treatment of psychotic patients'. In Grotstein, J.S. (ed.) *Do I Dare Disturb the Universe?* Beverly Hills, CA: Caesura Press.

Segal, H. (1957) 'Notes on symbol formation', *International Journal of Psycho-Analysis*, 38: 391–397.

Spillius, E.B. (1983) 'Developments from the work of Melanie Klein', *International Journal of Psycho-Analysis*, 64, part 3.

Tuckett, D. (1983) 'Words and the psychoanalytic interaction'. Unpublished.

Tustin, F. (1972) *Autism and Childhood Psychosis*. London: Hogarth.

Tustin, F. (1981) *Autistic States in Children*. London: Routledge & Kegan Paul.

## POSTSCRIPT

Shortly after the publication of the above paper in the *Journal of Child Psychotherapy*, a colleague brought a message from Dr Herbert Rosenfeld offering to talk to me about the paper. I was honoured and fascinated because, although I knew him socially and had studied his works on schizophrenia and narcissism, I had not ever thought to ask for teaching or supervision from him, as he was not a child analyst.

He began by saying that the paper was interesting, but did I realise it was completely unfinished! He felt that I hadn't discussed in any sort of thorough way the technical implications of the firm stance taken by me and also by Mrs S. with our difficult patients described in the paper.

He then went on to share his views on working with patients with a psychopathic element in their personality. (He describes some patients at the extreme end of this spectrum in his chapter on destructive narcissism (in Rosenfeld, 1987), but he says relatively little there about technique.) What he wanted to say about technique was that with such patients, Bion's dictum regarding the shedding of memory and desire was inappropriate. On the contrary, with this kind of patient, he thought the analyst needed to be very vigilant – always a step ahead – not retaliatory, but prepared. He added that such patients may have to learn to respect us long before they love us or feel gratitude. We might nowadays understand that they were addicted to, or perversely excited by, their destructiveness, rather than just using it defensively or desperately and vengefully. We might therefore also need to do a lot of work on the addictive or perverse element (Joseph, 1982). I think Rosenfeld was talking about firmness, definitely not condemnation, which is usually counter-productive with such patients.

This was hugely helpful to me clinically, but I think now that the theoretical implications regarding steps in development *within the paranoid-schizoid position*, i.e. long before the developments of the depressive position, are also extremely important. A reduction of grandiosity, a sobering down, or reduction in excitement about destructiveness are developments indeed, even if real guilt and reparation are a long way off.

I finally 'finished' the paper by writing a new one on the more severely psychopathic patients many years later (Alvarez, 1995; see also Alvarez, 1996).

*March 2003*

## Postscript references

Alvarez, A. (1995) 'Motiveless malignity: problems in the psychotherapy of psychopathic patients'. *Journal of Child Psychotherapy*, 21(2): 167–182.

Alvarez, A. (1996) 'Different uses of the counter-transference with neurotic, borderline and psychotic patients.' In Tsiantis, J., Sandler, A.-M., Anastasopoulos, D. and Martindale, B. (eds.) *Countertransference in Psychoanalytic Psychotherapy with Children and Adolescents*. EFPP Clinical Monograph Series. London: Karnac.

Joseph, B. (1982) 'Addiction to near death.' In Feldman, M. and Spillius, E. (eds.) *Psychic Equilibrium and Psychic Change*. London: Tavistock/Routledge (1989).

Rosenfeld, H. (1987) *Impasse and Interpretation*. London, Tavistock.

# Part 2

# Mainly clinical

# Introduction

Such is the range of clinical work undertaken by child psychotherapists, that the papers that follow can only represent a small fraction of that contribution. They do, however, illustrate some of the clinical and technical issues that have continued to preoccupy the profession. Here I can only highlight a few of these.

Child psychotherapy still remains a scarce resource and for this reason, if no other, the problem of conducting appropriate assessments is critical. Rustin's paper offers a valuable way in to this thorny area of determining whether individual therapy is indeed the 'treatment of choice'. Equally critical, though perhaps less often debated, is the matter of the frequency of sessions that might be necessary to ensure that the work is going to be clinically effective. This issue was discussed to some extent in an early paper by Harris (1971) on the role of once-weekly treatment, written at a time when training cases were usually seen five times per week (unfortunately space did not allow the inclusion of this paper). There are real risks for the profession in losing sight of this tradition of *intensive* analytic work and offering less than might be required. If this leads to an intervention that is unsuccessful, some may well conclude that psychoanalytic psychotherapy is therefore not a helpful form of treatment. As Menzies-Lyth has commented (personal communication) one would not think of prescribing half the effective dose of an antibiotic in order to enable two patients to be treated!

Whilst Rustin's emphasis on exploring what the child is able to make of the offer of a space for thinking and reflection remains central to the assessment process, much further work and refinement has since taken place, including consideration of the role of brief interventions and the particular issues raised by certain clinical populations. These are well described in the book on this topic that Rustin has since co-edited (Rustin and Quagliata, 2000).

The study of the impact of trauma has always been at the heart of psychoanalysis, from Freud's early 'Studies in hysteria' which considered the consequences of childhood abuse to his interest in the trauma of war in

'Beyond the pleasure principle'. That preoccupation is also apparent in these papers, two of which explicitly address the clinical and technical issues involved. Both raise very pertinent questions about the role of reconstruction and the re-experiencing of the original trauma within the transference relationship. In later work, child psychotherapists have continued to explore this area: Tustin (1994) saw the infant's *subjective* experience of trauma as a key factor in the development of psychogenic autism and Reid (1999) has also suggested that it can play a central role. There has also been a recent special number of the *Journal* devoted to the subject of trauma (*Journal of Child Psychotherapy*, 27(3) 2001). This continuing interest has been further stimulated by recent work in the neuroscience field that has added to our understanding of the way trauma impacts on the brain (see, for example, Perry *et al.*, 1995, and Schore, 2001) as well as by work from infant mental health clinicians (see, for example, Gaensbauer, 2002).

Trauma is, of course, inherent to the experience of deprived children. The latter now form a large part of the case load of child psychotherapists, but in the early days of the profession there was considerable doubt as to whether such children were suitable for this kind of treatment. Early papers by Boston (1967, 1972) gave encouragement, and the paper by Henry reprinted here is a now classic, and moving, account of how a child psychotherapist *can* make emotional contact with such very damaged and hardened children who have suffered multiple changes of placement. It is saddening to note, however, in this case, that the long-term devoted care provided by one foster family failed to make an impact on this boy's state of mind, though this does serve to highlight how often additional skilled therapy is required if such children are to be able to free themselves from the cycle whereby they continue to deprive themselves of the help that might be available to them. (A later paper by Hopkins (2000) illustrates how, in different circumstances, therapy can help children move on to successfully form new attachments in an adoptive placement.) Subsequent to Henry's paper, Boston and Szur (1983) edited a book describing the ways in which some therapists were developing this work, work that has remained a central preoccupation for many child psychotherapists. This is again reflected in a recent special number of the *Journal* devoted to fostering and adoption (*Journal of Child Psychotherapy*, 26(3) 2000).

Just as these deprived children have now become a regular part of the case load of child psychotherapists, so subsequent developments in clinical work have continued to extend the range of patients for whom this kind of treatment may be beneficial. This includes, particularly, autistic and borderline children (see Alvarez, 1992; Lanyado and Horne, 1999).

Implicit in all of these clinical accounts is the question of what is the aim of child psychotherapy? As Henry notes:

I can understand Martin's puzzlement and reservations when he seems to be asking me in so many ways: 'If it hurts, how can you call it getting better?'

Similarly, at one stage in Adam's treatment, Hopkins found it 'hard . . . to believe that it could be of any benefit for him to face such a stark reality.' It is, however, the belief in the value of facing up to reality (both internal and external) that in many ways distinguishes the psychoanalytic approach from others that might be more symptom based (for a fuller discussion see Barrows, 2001). This also returns us to the issue of frequency of treatment raised by Harris (1971) and the question of the different aims that might apply in once weekly work as compared to four or five times weekly analysis.

Even in the latter instance, as Harris warns us and as echoed in Hopkins's paper, our therapeutic zeal (and omnipotence) has to be tempered with due humility and realism about the degree of change that we can hope to facilitate. Nonetheless we must not underestimate the 'beneficial effect of a relationship with a person who tries to comprehend, to stand firm and function while remaining receptive to the most violent and discouraging projections' (Harris, 1971).

# Chapter 5

# The experience of puberty

*Shirley Hoxter*

Originally published in the *Journal of Child Psychotherapy* (1964) 1(2): 13–25.

## Introduction

The specific feature which differentiates the adolescent from people of other ages is the experience of puberty, and much of the adolescent's behaviour in the community may be seen as an external expression of the unconscious anxieties and conflicts aroused by pubertal sexual development. It also appears that some of the community's reactions to adolescents express the anxiety of the adult when faced with the fact that a new generation is attaining sexual maturity. An adolescent girl reflected a widespread attitude when saying 'I know what juvenile delinquency means, but I am not sure which word means "young person" and which word means "criminal"'. The constant stories of teenage violence and teenage sexuality and the reactions of outraged protest, force upon one the realisation that prominent sections of the adolescent population and of the adult population alike are engaged in the warlike activity of acting out their oedipal rivalry.

This is often conducted in conformity to stereotyped patterns of conflict which enable both parties to avoid experiencing guilt and personal responsibility for the intense feelings of hostility and envy arising from their mutual sexual rivalry. Sometimes the conflict occurs on a vast scale and most of the population is drawn into participating in the melodrama at least vicariously. Or it may initially be conducted as a one-man war. A boy telephoned me late one night saying 'I have urgent news to tell you. I am at war with the LCC.[1]' This was followed by tenacious and partially successful efforts to get myself and other members of the clinic staff to act in conjunction with him and to become involved in conflict with many County Council officials. It was only just possible to prevent him from extending his war to the police and to Interpol.

The physical maturation of the adolescent, with its greatly increased sexual drives, is simultaneously accompanied by a resurgence of the

1 London County Council [ed.]

imperious feelings and phantasies which previously characterised the object relations of early childhood. The adolescent is faced with the task of relinquishing his parents as his original sexual objects and turning to others outside the family. This leads to further difficulties when impulses stemming from the infantile aspects of his sexuality continue to dominate his behaviour, both with his peers and with adults. The adolescent has the physical capacity to put into action much which would appear mainly as phantasy in the young child. He can really attack, destroy, rob, murder or commit suicide and he can really have sexual experiences of a heterosexual, homosexual or perverse nature. The young child can be protected and controlled by his parents, but the parents of the adolescent are powerless to do either if he opposes them with full force. The adolescent may then resort to defences of a pathological nature or he may act out his phantasies in antisocial behaviour. His delinquency may provoke the representatives of authority into imposing the control which he half seeks. Sometimes he persists in his defiance until the authorities show punitive behaviour of sufficient harshness to act as a confirmation that the repressive tyrants of his phantasies have an external existence which justifies his hostile rebellion. For these reasons the adolescent's attempts to be independent and his attempts to withdraw his oedipal conflicts from the family frequently arouse great and justified concern in his parents. Their opposition to his behaviour brings the battle back into the home. Often the adolescent unconsciously, and sometimes consciously, feels that this opposition is entirely due to his parents' spiteful determination to frustrate him and to their resentment of his claims for independence and adult sexuality. He then fights his parents bitterly and does all he can to arouse their envy of his youthful sexuality and to exacerbate their anxieties concerning the menopause, old age and death.

This is the pressure of conflict which requires to be contained within the therapy situation and indeed within the therapist herself. For it is the therapist's task to use the transference relationship to help the adolescent to take back into himself the dangers and conflicts which he is projecting into the external world. The adolescent himself often experiences the impact of puberty as a situation of extreme internal danger. To seek relief from this he may live dangerously and through his violent or self-destructive behaviour project his own feelings of alarm into the therapist so that she is under strong pressure to take steps to protect or restrain him; yet to do so may be taken as a confirmation that the dangers are external ones or that the therapist also finds them intolerable as internal experiences. This situation of inner danger is not primarily due to anxieties relating to the development of sexual maturity but arises from a fear of being overwhelmed by the infantile aspects of sexuality. During the relative quiescence of the latency period there has usually been established an internal system of civilisation; a structure of defences whereby law and order and sublimations have been established to some extent. At puberty the internal system of control may be threatened with disruption by the re-emergence of the omnipotent, sadistic and envious aspects of the sexual drives and phantasies which accompanied the object relationships of the first few years of life. Severe anxiety is then experienced and frequently there is a resort to the modes of defence which pertained to the earliest years.

Particular difficulties arise from the adolescent's failure to differentiate between the mature and the infantile aspects of sexuality and from his equating rebellion against dependence with genuine independence. Adolescents who put their infantile phantasies into action frequently regard this regressive behaviour as genuine independence and maturity. The adults who attempt to restrain them tend to be regarded as sexual rivals who stand in their way. A similar lack of differentiation between the mature and the infantile aspects of sexuality frequently underlies the condition of those adolescents who express fears of growing up and of achieving sexual maturity and independence. They are often identified with the authoritarian aspects of their internal parental figures. They tend to remain in a mental state of protracted latency for, unconsciously, they fear that 'growing up' means regression to the completely uncontrolled expression of infantile sexuality.

## Case material

The nature of the anxieties and conflicts aroused by pubertal sexual development will now be examined more closely and related to some aspects of therapeutic techniques which appear to be particularly relevant to work with adolescents[2]. For this purpose I will use material from the treatment sessions of three adolescents. The material selected relates especially to the area of these patients' phantasies and feelings about their sexuality.

### First case. Bruce (aged 12½ to 13½)

The fear of being completely overwhelmed by an uprising of violently strong feelings and phantasies relating to the infantile aspects of sexuality was clearly shown by Bruce, who was physically well developed for his age. Before being able to verbalise his phantasies Bruce had gone through a long

---

2 The theoretical concepts underlying my work and the techniques which I follow are based upon the work of Freud and the contributions of Melanie Klein and her followers. The attendance of my adolescent patients has varied from one to five times weekly, the majority attending twice weekly. I do not vary my techniques according to the frequency of attendance although I do modify my level of aspiration for those who attend less frequently. The cases mentioned in this paper attended two or three times weekly.

period of violent hostility to me, attempting to force his own fears into me and to render me helpless and humiliated. He dreaded close contact with people of either sex and of any age. He frequently went about armed with a knife and tended either to flee or to get into fights when other boys approached him.

As he approached his thirteenth birthday Bruce expressed not only his pride about growing up but also his terror. He feared that he would change into a 'teenage werewolf'. His expectation was that puberty entailed a metamorphosis which would turn him into a savage and ruthless beast. He feared that the sexual beast in him would completely devour the human in him. The precarious state of latency which he had achieved had already been threatened during a period of intense masturbation in the course of which he had had many dreams. To give an example:

> Bruce dreamt that he was in an old-fashioned house. His grandmother was showing him round. He was looking at a beautiful antique tea-set when suddenly there was a blinding explosion. A nuclear bomb had fallen near London. He covered his eyes and shuddered. He grabbed his grandmother and asked with great urgency, 'What are the effects of a nuclear explosion?' Then he was in the setting of London streets, partially devastated by the bomb. His mother, pushing a pram, was looking for shelter. A man came by wearing a jacket like that of his father. He grabbed hold of him and asked, 'What are the effects of a nuclear explosion? How much of this radiation stuff do we have to sop up?' The man said, 'I don't know but look what is happening to the children'. Bruce saw that a small boy was growing into a very tall man as he walked down the road. The boy became huge and chased after Bruce and the man. They ran to a skyscraper and climbed up and up, but it was no good. For when they got to the top they found that the boy had grown as tall as the skyscraper. The man tried to escape, he jumped off the skyscraper and was killed.

This dream shows many aspects of the masturbatory experience and the phantasies accompanying it. Bruce's associations enabled his anxious, repeated question, 'What are the effects of a nuclear explosion?' to be understood to mean, 'What are the effects of explosive masturbation?' His question concerning the radiation which had to be 'sopped up' referred to a nocturnal emission, which he later said had occurred, and showed his anxiety concerning the effects of this. The dream answered his questions and showed that the effects of his masturbation, or rather of the phantasies accompanying this masturbation, were to endanger the life of his internal father and also the life of his internal mother, and to destroy her fertility, represented by the pram (Bruce was an only child). The boy who eventually grew as tall as a skyscraper symbolised Bruce's penis and his experience of an erection. The dream showed the dangerous omnipotence accompanying this experience which culminated in triumphant murderous rivalry with his father. In a wider sense this is what 'growing up' meant to Bruce. It is of importance to note that Bruce was represented by two figures, one of whom turned to father for help with his anxieties and was allied to father in the situation of danger, and who was also concerned that mother should find shelter. The other, the sexual Bruce, drove father to his death and also threatened the existence of the Bruce who had a good relationship with father.

A few weeks later Bruce had a dream in which he was identified with the sadistic and omnipotent part of himself which he called 'B.2' (Bruce 2). In the dream 'B.2' raided a bank and stole all the money. There were many women in the bank, whom he raped and killed, sawing their bodies into many pieces. Bruce was horrified by this dream and said that the worst of it was that 'B.2 enjoyed it all and got away with it'. Giving his own interpretation of the dream he said 'B.2 lies coiled up inside me, waiting to spring out at night, then he goes to the woman, like to you, to raid her. He wants to get his own back'. This very clearly expressed his feeling that his sadism resided in his penis and was released like a coiled-up spring – or beast – when he masturbated and experienced an erection. The dream emphasised the ruthless, greedy sadism of the re-emerging infantile sexuality. Many adolescents, less disturbed than Bruce, when talking directly or indirectly of their partially buried infantile sexuality, often equate it with a mad or criminal part of themselves, which must be kept locked up and which they fear their masturbation will release. Bruce said that this dream had been stimulated by a wireless programme on homosexuality. He said that he understood homosexuality to mean 'when men and women get mixed up. When women raid men like B.2 raided the women at the bank'. It emerged that his phantasy of the parental intercourse was of a situation in which each partner violently raided and attempted to steal parts of the other partner's body, resulting in a 'mix-up' of the sexes.

Later material arising from a time when Bruce collected pictures of semi-nude girls threw further light on this situation. His phantasies of making love to the girls in these pictures sometimes commenced tenderly, but usually led to his feeling that he violently invaded their bodies not only with his penis but with the whole of himself. He then felt himself to become the woman whose body he had entered and felt that he himself became the victim of an assault by a man. The pain and confusion of this vivid phantasy was such that he thought the only way to regain his masculine identity was, in his own words, 'to commit suicide to kill the woman in me'.

In the context of his adolescent interest in pin-up girls Bruce showed that his phantasies were not those of having an adult sexual relationship, but more closely resembled the infant's phantasies (as described by Klein) of a possessive invasion of parts of the mother's body with consequent confusion of identity and of body boundaries. These phantasies also showed that his apparent heterosexual interests were intricately interwoven with his homosexuality.

Bruce was a severely disturbed boy who was at times overwhelmed by anxieties of a psychotic nature. But similar phantasies (although appearing in a more disguised form) are revealed in the psychotherapy even of those who have had a relatively healthy latency period, as in the two further cases to be discussed.

### Second case. Sally (aged 13)

Internal situations which have been submerged and almost inaccessible during latency may erupt at puberty causing acute anxiety. This is sometimes reflected in an apparent change of character which resembles the metamorphosis dreaded by Bruce.

A situation of this nature occurred in the case of Sally as she approached the onset of menstruation. She was referred for treatment following a long series of vague illnesses and of undiagnosed abdominal pains, which were not relieved when she had her appendix removed. She had appeared to be a demure and compliant little girl, although rather depressed. At school she had been considered a sweet-natured, model pupil. In the term preceding the commencement of treatment she appeared to change into a truculent and defiant trouble-maker, constantly provoking her teachers by her impudence and unconcealed contempt.

Sally was the second daughter of rather elderly parents. She had slept in her parents' bedroom until she was nine. Her father, who ran a small garage, was reported to be moody, irritable and hypercritical. Her mother often protected Sally from the father's outbursts and Sally spoke adoringly of her, reserving for her teachers (and later her therapist) the onslaughts of her envious rivalry. Sally brought her sexual anxieties into the treatment situation straight away, by saying that she did not want evening appointments as she was afraid of being out alone after dark, in case she might be followed by a man. She gave a detailed story of an occasion when a man had spoken and exposed himself to her. She had run away and he had made no attempt to follow, but many later associations showed that she feared that every man wanted to rape her and that she might even be kidnapped from her bed. Additional material relating to her sexual fears arose in the first few weeks of treatment. In the fifth week there was a break for a holiday, during which Sally had her first menstrual period.

On returning from holiday she did not at first tell me of this event. She angrily criticised her teachers, tearing them to pieces with her scornful remarks and complaining that they made unjust accusations against her. She became angrily defensive when she found that I did not comply with her attempts to get me to side with her against the teachers. Later she was able to say that she was afraid that she might want to fight me and that I would be unable to cope with her or to defend myself. She thought she might want to scream and scream but if she did so the neighbours would think that she was murdering me or being murdered by me. She said that sometimes she would like to get a gun and shoot and that, as a child, she had pretended to be a cowboy and to shoot out of the window. She added excitedly that she was very bloodthirsty and often felt that she would like to rip off someone's clothes, and that it would be lovely to tear and rend everything. Sally was here showing a glimpse of her phantasy that the attacks, which she thought might take place between us, would resemble the sexual assaults which she so frequently feared from men. She also revealed a glimpse of the sadistic aspects of her own homosexuality. In the following session she told me of a dream which she had had during the holidays. The dream was interpreted in terms of the phantasies which she had about the internal structure of her body and genitals, after which she told me of her first menstrual period and discussed some of her mixed feelings about this. The phantasies and intense anxiety which she experienced concerning her menstruation appeared more clearly in the following session.

Sally came full of angry complaints about her father. He had gone into her room and found an un-emptied pot under her bed. He had scolded her about this, saying that the room stank and that she was dirty. Sally was furious; she admitted that she had forgotten to empty the pot, but defended herself with many excuses, stressing that it was quite untrue that the room stank, as she always sprayed it with scent. Anyway, she said, it was none of her father's business, he did not have to come into her room. She complained that her father was always poking and prying about in her room, running his finger over the furniture to see if it was dusted. She suspected that he also rummaged among the blouses in her wardrobe; she kept some special things there which he should never see. It was not right that he should come into her room, she was too old for that now. She would like to get a padlock for the door and lock him out. In case he managed to get in she would place a bowl of dirty water for him to step into. This account was built up and elaborated as she made repeated bids to get me to side with her against her father.

I said that, in part, she felt that she was a growing up young woman and should be allowed privacy and treated with respect. This went with her feelings of pride and pleasure at having begun her periods. But she also had quite different feelings about her periods and felt that it meant that she had something dirty and smelly inside her. She was afraid that if this part of her was found she would be regarded as a dirty and smelly child. I said that Sally felt me to be like father; she felt that I came poking and prying, not into her room, but into her mind, to find the things she felt ashamed about. Last time we had talked about some of her thoughts and feelings concerning the sexual parts of her body. It had felt to her as though I was really prying into her body and finding her menstruation, like father prying into her room and finding the pot under the bed. She was afraid that I would find that she had dirty things in her mind and her body and that I would angrily accuse her, saying that her sexuality was something disgusting and stinking. I recalled the secret things which she kept among her blouses, saying that I thought she also felt that there were some good things about her sexual development, perhaps particularly her breasts, but she did not want these to be found, it was safer to keep them secret.

Sally did not accept these interpretations but continued to try and argue me into agreeing that it was all father's fault and none of her own. She made many further complaints about her father's behaviour to her. One of these was a complaint that sometimes, in the early mornings, father came bursting into her room, shouting and waking her up, and giving her a shock. Then he left the door open, causing a draught which gave her earache.

Father was here accused of violent intrusion and of causing an abrupt awakening, shock and pain. Considered in relation to her previous material this accusation could be understood to express her unconscious belief that she had been raped by her father. This reflected Sally's unconscious phantasy that her period was caused by the injury of a sexual assault and expressed her feeling of shock at the sudden discovery of her internal sexuality. She had projected onto her father her guilt concerning the sadistic aspects of her own sexual curiosity, which must have been greatly stimulated when she slept in her parents' bedroom and wished to 'poke and pry' into the primal scene. The terror of awakening to observe this scene was also reflected in frequently recurring dreams, in which she had been unable to open her eyes or unable to scream or to run away. Her accusation of her father also showed a projection of her guilt concerning the sadistic aspects of her own homosexuality, in which she appeared to be identified with a cruel, prying penis, and which she had expressed in her wishes to shoot and tear off clothing. Her curiosity and her homosexual wishes had been stimulated by her feelings towards me, standing for the mother, in the transference, and it was now my privacy and my body into which she wished to poke and pry. Most aspects of this situation were interpreted to Sally, but without direct reference to her father or mother. The interpretations were made in the transference along the following lines. I said that Sally felt that my words woke her up with such a shock (like father's shouting) and made her aware of her sexuality. I related this to her way of experiencing her period and also to her previously expressed thoughts concerning sexual assaults, adding that she felt that I was doing this to her when she felt my words penetrating her mind, rousing her and making her aware of thoughts and feelings inside her, some of which she felt were shocking and painful.

Although she neither directly denied nor accepted these interpretations, she gradually became less hostile and resistant and modified her attitude.

She discussed the ways in which she resembled her parents, saying that she thought she was like her mother in appearance but more like her father in her character, being moody and grumpy. She did not at this point blame her father for her character but said it was a pity and she wished she could be nicer.

With the diminishing of her projections, Sally was able to become more in touch with the good aspects of her relationships and to recall happier times when she had enjoyed playing with her father. These modifications were sustained in the next session when Sally was friendly and co-operative and spoke of new friends and interests. By focusing her infantile sadism and her persecutory anxieties in the transference relationship, the more mature and realistic aspects of her personality became a little more free to be expressed in positive relationships outside the therapy situation.

*Aspects of technique*

Sally exerted tremendous pressure to try and get me involved in her conflicts and to side with her against her father and teachers. In the course of the session concerning her father's entry into her room, she gave many details which suggested that her father did, in fact, do much to disparage her femininity and to try and humiliate her. I also got the impression that he might have been deeply disturbed by her menstruation. In spite of this impression that Sally's complaints had a basis of truth, I avoided adopting an attitude which might have been taken to imply sympathetic support for her against her father. Such an attitude might more quickly have produced an appearance of co-operation, but would unconsciously have been felt as a placation or as an alliance with her infantile sadism which might have aroused anxiety. In the long run such an attitude would vitiate any possibility of using the therapy to achieve a better state of integration.

I aimed to make it clear to Sally that my interpretations related to her feelings concerning myself in the transference and not to any actual behaviour of her father. If, in such a situation, one's interpretations are related to the external parent, there is a strong risk that the therapy will increase rather than diminish the tendency to act out. There is also the likelihood that the sessions will become completely blocked by endless arguments concerning the external parents and how much they are 'to blame' for the patient's difficulties. These situations arise more frequently with adolescents than with younger children, and I consider that it is essential that the emphasis of the interpretations should be on relating the unconscious anxieties and conflicts to the internal situation and to the transference of this onto the therapist.

I considered that Sally would not be in a position to understand her father or his influence upon her with any objectivity until, through work in the transference, she had gained a greater capacity to recognise her projections and to discriminate between internal and external reality, and also until the reasons for her feelings of guilt about her sexuality had been far more fully understood. It is likely that it might take several years of work on these lines before reaching the stage when it would be useful to help her to understand and discriminate between which aspects of her internal, raping, father stemmed from her own projections and which aspects stemmed from her internalisation of her father's projections and, possibly, of his actual sexual approaches to her. Considerations such as these influence my 'timing' of interpretations. I find that a scrutiny of the transference manifestations gives the most valuable guide as to whether or not an interpretation of the unconscious material is ready to be made relevant and meaningful to the patient.

The technical aspects of obtaining and maintaining the patient's co-operation arise from a recognition of the essentially internal nature of his conflicts and the way in which the adolescent himself is divided into warring parts. One has to be careful not to allow the adolescent to mislead one into thinking that he is wholly identified either with the forces of rebellion or with the forces of repression and must give overt recognition to the acute anxiety which each part experiences when threatened by the other. With adolescents I have found it helpful to make it clear that an interpretation is directed to one particular part of the personality and that I recognise that the feelings and phantasies referred to are not shared by certain other parts and may even be strongly repudiated by other parts. For instance, Bruce's dream showed a part of himself that was allied to his parents as well as a part that was sadistic and hostile. He came to recognise that a part of him was characterised by arrogant omnipotence and sadism and called this 'Bruce 2', no longer having either to deny it or to feel that it completely obliterated the more realistic and more loving aspects of himself. With Sally, it was important to give explicit recognition to the part of herself which was proud of her sexual development and to her wish to be treated with respect.

Clarifications of this kind help the adolescent to accept interpretations concerning his infantile feelings and anxieties, including his dependency, without feeling that he is being treated as a child or that his dignity, adult achievements and independence are being challenged or ridiculed. I have found that this method helps me to maintain the cooperation of at least a fragment of the adolescent's personality while, at the same time, keeping the heat of the battle focused within the transference.

Adolescents who deny their sexuality and their infantile phantasies and impulses feel less threatened if one repeatedly makes clear the distinctions between infantile and adult sexuality. It is necessary to make it clear that one does not share their fear that a complete regression would result from the acceptance of their sexuality or from the acceptance of their dependency and immature features.

### Third case. James (aged 15)

James showed many of the features of an adolescent in a state of protracted latency. At an early stage of treatment he expressed the fear that every step he took towards growing up meant pushing his parents a step nearer to their graves, and he wished he could make 'time stand still'. However, he remained child-like only in patches and more often seemed to feel burdened with responsibility. He projected his destructive and rebellious impulses onto others and behaved like a repressive parent in harshly condemning them for irresponsible behaviour.

For a long time he denied both his own and his therapist's sexuality and showed anxious resistance to interpretations with sexual content. He had a number of sublimations but complained that he could not enjoy anything and showed real enthusiasm only for his hobby of stamp-collecting. This interest was later found to be invested with all the significance and satisfactions of his infantile sexuality. He had few friends of his own age and preferred the company of a man who fostered his interest in stamp-collecting. This relationship had an unconscious homosexual significance for him.

I will give details of a session which occurred when James had been receiving treatment for two years. At this stage he had worked through a long and painful ending of his 'love-affair' with stamp collecting and the man friend and was turning more to other interests and to people nearer his age. The session illustrates the ways in which a patient can use the method of consistently making explicit the differentiations between the mature and infantile aspects of sexuality and between the conflicting parts into which he himself is divided.

He commenced the session by saying that he had had a shock. He had seen a girl on a bus and to his horror experienced 'a terribly strong feeling' that he wanted to 'grab hold of her and to rush in and have intercourse'. He now realised that he had often had similar feelings but said 'usually the conscience part of me just pushes it aside or shuts it up'. He felt it was terribly dangerous, as he might feel like doing this to any girl, regardless of whether he liked her or not. He could not say why it would be terrible, it was not really anything to do with his age or his parents' reaction, it would be just as bad if he had behaved like this at 21. It was not really that he thought that intercourse was a bad thing. Sometimes he thought to himself 'If I want to why shouldn't I? Who is there to stop me and what's wrong with it anyway?' Yet, he concluded, he knew that it would be wrong and felt that his conscience was all against it.

I pointed out that he had not been thinking of the girl as a person but just as a body which he wanted to use and suggested that this might be one of the things that he felt was so terribly wrong. I referred to an area concerning which there had been much previous material and work and which I will try to summarise very briefly. This related to a part of himself which we came to call 'the parasite baby'. The 'parasite baby' part of him wished to use me, standing for the mother's breast, as his host. This entailed embedding himself in me and living on me in a way which was ruthlessly possessive and also endlessly dependent (for, as a parasite, he would never grow up to be able to sustain himself). As a host I existed only to serve the needs of the parasite baby and had no other function in life, in fact I had no life, no relationships, thoughts or feelings of my own, all that I had existed only to feed the parasite baby. In this session there was no need to go over this familiar material in any detail. I pointed out that his feelings towards this girl were the same as the feelings of the parasite baby part of him towards my breast. He wanted to grab hold of the girl's body, to use it as though it existed only to serve him and to force her to be host to his penis. I said that he felt that his body had now grown up and that he could really have sexual intercourse but he was afraid that his sexuality would be used entirely by the baby part which was felt to be so impatient, greedy and demanding, instead of being used by the more grown-up part of himself which really cared about people and did not want to use them just as bodies but wanted to love and be loved as we had often seen.

He followed this interpretation closely and discussed it for some time. Later he said that recently he had had many daydreams concerning rockets. It made him feel very excited to think of them, he sort of gloried in thinking of their power and strength. For the sake of peace he thought that Britain should get rid of them all, yet he hated the idea of disarmament. He interpreted this spontaneously for himself saying that the rockets stood for his sexuality, that his 'conscience father' said that he should give it all up but the baby part of himself felt that he 'would miss it terribly'. I queried whether it was just the baby part which did not want to give up sexuality and pointed out that he felt his 'conscience father' to be saying that his penis was only an instrument of aggression and therefore should be done away with. With mounting excitement he said that his thoughts were about starting a war of aggression. It gave him a thrill to think of his rockets rushing through the air to land in another country, causing terrific havoc and destruction and smashing the other country's forces at base. I said that this showed why he thought it would be so bad and dangerous for him to have intercourse. When he masturbated he gloried in the power of his penis and felt that it would rush like a rocket into my body, smash me up and cause tremendous damage. He also felt that inside me he would find the penis of my husband, the father, represented by the forces of the country which he invaded, and he wanted to attack and smash this penis. These were the reasons for his feeling that the father conscience demanded that he should disarm, give up his penis and his sexuality altogether.

He warmly agreed with this interpretation and said that he could now really see why he had had to turn right away from people and take up stamp-collecting. It was, he added, as though his father had said, 'It is not safe for you to go with people. If you have got to do this, do it with the kings and queens and countries on the stamps!' He added that he had told himself that if Britain disarmed all the other countries would see that she was harmless and that then surely no country would be so bad as to attack a little unarmed one. I stressed the placatory way in which he castrated himself and wished to appear as a passive sexless little child or as a woman. He had told himself that if he had no penis no father would fear him as a rival and then, surely, no father would be so cruel as to attack him.

He discussed this for a little and then was silent. I spoke of the way in which his sexuality had continued secretly and omnipotently while he presented this safely sexless exterior. He said he had not really been listening to me, but his next association showed that this secret intercourse had in fact been taking place. He said that he had been thinking that on the way home there might be a long queue for train tickets. In this case he would go right ahead through the barrier and pay at the other end. He had thought that the ticket collector at the other end might not believe that he had come only a short distance, he might suspect him of having travelled further. He would then say, 'If you don't believe me you can telephone Mrs Hoxter and ask her'. I said that the ticket collector stood for my husband. He was thinking that my husband might not believe that he had just come for therapy and had just talked about sex, he might suspect that he had gone much further, that he had been too impatient to wait to grow up like other people but had pushed through the barrier and had sexual intercourse with me. He would then say to my husband, 'Ask Mrs Hoxter and she will tell you that I didn't go any further than talk'. He gave a mock groan and said, 'Yes, it must be that I really do feel that talking about sex is as bad as having sex'. I said that one part of him made no distinction between talking about sex and having sex, and I added that while he had been talking, putting his sexual thoughts and feelings into words to go into my mind, he had felt that he was really putting sexual parts of his body, his penis, into me. He replied, 'That is why I used never to be able to talk about sex, or even to think about it'.

This session confirmed many previous indications that James's denial of his own sexuality and his hidden tendency to passive homosexuality were largely determined by his flight from the sadistic aspects of his hetero-sexuality and the fear of rivalry with his father. It is likely that, if he had not been in therapy, his impulses towards the girl would have been repressed and followed by renewed placation and flight to a homosexual position. In reality he had a good relationship with his non-authoritarian father. The domineering, harsh super-ego with which he often identified when criticising other people derived its power and cruelty from the omnipotence and sadism of his own infantile sexuality.

*Identity*

Much previous work had been done on the placatory nature of James's co-operation in therapy. He tended to idealise me and then flatteringly to model himself on this image and to serve me with what he felt I demanded. (This had been a pronounced feature of his relationship to the man who encouraged his stamp-collecting.) Traces of this may be detected in the session presented. It was frequently necessary to analyse the way in which he was seductively open to influence from me, and to avoid being enticed into fascinating intellectual discussions.

The adolescent attempts to develop a new identity for himself, which is neither that of his previous childhood nor a mere imitation of his parents. When the foundations of his previous identifications are shaken he may experience profound feelings of confusion and loss. He plunges into new relationships but tends to do so with the projective force and idealisation of infancy. He is likely to find a hero figure (or rebel hero), to incorporate this figure and to use it, both consciously and unconsciously, as his model. He may use his therapist in this way. But such idealisation can only lead to further confusion about what is his 'real' self and is often followed by a resentful smashing or expulsion of the hero figure. For the hero is felt to have become another parent, imposing himself as a model to be worshipped and flattered by slavish imitation in a manner which crushes all true independence.

Adolescents who have been able to achieve identifications with their parents based, not upon placation or rivalry, but upon love and genuine appreciation of the parents' creative capacities, experience less acute conflicts at puberty. During latency such adolescents have often achieved considerable capacity for sublimation and reparation. This greatly supports them when facing the frustrations and stresses of puberty. The loving aspects of their infantile sexuality can be allied to their increased adult powers and used to give fuller expression to their creativity, to their urge for adventure, discovery and knowledge and to their protective and reparative drives. Their adolescent rebellion can also be sublimated, and they constructively challenge the assumptions and values of adults. These are the adolescents who make it possible for progress and reform to take place from one generation to another.

## Conclusion

The material which has been presented relates to three crucial experiences of pubertal sexuality; in Bruce's case a masturbatory experience; in Sally's case the onset of menstruation; and in James's case a strong urge to intercourse. The emergence of the biological aspects of adult sexuality was accompanied by the simultaneous resurgence of the feelings, drives and relationships of infantile sexuality. The internal parental images which had been built up by introjections during infancy again came vividly to life and were accompanied by the same strong feelings and by the same anxieties and defences as those which originally occurred in childhood. The material showed a close interplay of heterosexual and homosexual impulses and the influence of pre-genital sexuality upon coexistent genital experiences. It was also shown that the impulses to forceful and possessive invasion of their objects led to them becoming 'mixed up' and identified with parts of other people, causing damage to the integrity of their personal identities. Phantasies of violent and cruel sexuality dominated each experience causing a situation of acute shock and danger.

These points of resemblance may apply as general characteristics of the experience of puberty, although in each case, as in those presented, the experience will be greatly influenced by the psychopathology and personality of the individual.

## References

Freud, S. (1905) 'Three essays on the theory of sexuality', SE 7: 143–245.

Klein, M. (1932a) 'The technique of analysis in puberty'. In *The Psychoanalysis of Children*. London: Hogarth.

Klein, M. (1932b) 'Early stages of the oedipus conflict and of super-ego formation'. In *The Psychoanalysis of Children*. London: Hogarth.

Klein, M. (1933) 'The early development of the conscience in the child'. In *Contributions to Psychoanalysis 1921–1945*. London: Hogarth (1948).

Klein, M. (1946) 'Notes on some schizoid mechanisms'. In Riviere, J. (ed.) *Developments in Psychoanalysis*. London: Hogarth (1952).

Klein, M. (1955) 'On identification', pp. 309–345. In Klein, M., Heimann, P. and Money-Kyrle, R. (eds.) *New Directions in Psychoanalysis*. London: Tavistock.

# Chapter 6

# Doubly deprived[1]

*Gianna Henry*

Originally published in the *Journal of Child Psychotherapy* (1974) 3(4): 15–28.

I intend to present some aspects of my work with a patient whom I have been treating for just over two years, initially on a once-weekly basis and twice a week since June 1973. Martin was referred to the clinic for very considerable learning difficulties (he was nearly fourteen when he started treatment and his reading age was six), for aggressive behaviour and stealing. He had made a suicidal attempt two years prior to referral when he tried to jump from a second-floor window.

## History

Martin is the illegitimate child of West Indian parents. His mother died when he was seven years old, but she had had no contact with Martin after he had been placed in residential care; he was at the time two months old. His father had disappeared at the beginning of the mother's pregnancy. Martin had three placements up to the age of two, when he was fostered by an English couple with a child of their own, a boy four years older than Martin. He was with the foster parents for ten years until fostering broke down. Martin was at the time 12 years old. It seems that the foster parents found Martin increasingly unmanageable because of his stealing and very defiant behaviour. They had reached the point where they felt that they were 'unable to accept him or have any trust in him'.

There is no indication of the impact that the attempted suicide one year before the breakdown of fostering, might have had on the foster parents and how it might possibly have contributed to their feeling at a loss. They reported that the difficulties with Martin had very considerably increased from the time when he was informed of his natural mother's death. He was then seven years old.

---

1 This paper was presented at the Study Weekend of the Association of Child Psychotherapists in March 1974.

When Martin left the foster home, he returned to a children's home and apparently there were no outward signs of his being distressed about the move. There are many indications in the case history of the foster parents' deep feeling of failure in their relationship with Martin, and they saw his coldness and detachment as confirmation that they had never meant a great deal to him. The first contact after the move to the children's home was a phone call which had to be cut short because the foster mother was crying so much she could not talk. Both foster parents had visited Martin at the home. Their son refused to come because he said 'Martin had hurt his mother too much'. They left after meeting Martin feeling that 'nothing had happened. He appeared to have happily settled himself down'. They said they would prefer to discontinue contact with Martin and have in fact completely lost touch with him since then.

I have described the breaking down of fostering in some detail as it is relevant to the main issue of this paper; namely this patient's 'double deprivation'. Firstly the one inflicted upon him by external circumstances of which he had no control whatsoever, secondly the deprivation derived from internal sources: from his crippling defences and from the quality of his internal objects which provided him with so little support as to make him an orphan inwardly as well as outwardly.

## Identification with an idealised internal object

When Martin started treatment he had spent just over a year at the children's home and he was attending a large secondary modern school. He was subsequently moved to a school for maladjusted children, which proved a much more suitable setting for such a very disturbed child.

The most alarmed and alarming reports came at first from the school where Martin had become dangerously aggressive to other children. In spite of daily careful inspection he had developed a talent for smuggling knives into the school and suddenly flicking them open, terrorising other children. On one occasion, which had been followed by suspension, he had pointed a knife at a child's throat and the child had very nearly fainted with fear. Martin did not seem to show any reaction to punishments or reproaches. While provoking very violent emotions in others, he himself appeared to be, most of the time, devoid of feelings. As he was to tell me some months later, 'a teacher at the old school said that I am the only person he has come across who has no feelings'.

When I first met Martin, I also perceived an alarming quality of numbness about him, as if, although his suicidal attempt had not succeeded, he was really only going through the motions of being alive, through the motions of coming for treatment, very regularly and punctually (in fact he was invariably early), but without being in the least in touch with his motivations for coming. The environment was indeed highly motivated and, at that time, carrying the weight of all the feelings Martin was not perceiving himself. His numbness was in fact, partly at least, a consequence of his enormous skill in splitting off and disposing of feelings or parts of himself into other people, unfortunately in a very scattered way, for instance in the terrorising of children at school.

There was only one thing in life which Martin seemed to invest with enormous importance and this was his appearance. I had heard before he started treatment that he often took more than one hour getting ready before going out, and the care he put into the most minute details showed at first sight, even when he was in a school uniform. When I saw him during a school holiday, I had a better opportunity of catching glimpses of his personal taste. He seemed to pay an enormous amount of attention to the choice of colours; the matching or contrasting of pink and pale green, of various shades of red and orange; he often wore bracelets; chains with a pendant; for a brief period he started wearing one earring. He had many rings on each hand; some of them looked fairly harmless, but at times he arrived at his sessions with a full set of knuckle rings. This made a particularly striking contrast when he was wearing pale and rather feminine colours. He has a very handsome face, but at first it was very mask-like and had little change of expression. His hair was short, carefully divided in the middle with a very straight parting, and slightly puffed on the sides. As I have often seen him use a comb in his sessions, I realised that this puffing involved a very elaborate procedure; a sort of backcombing, made very difficult by his frizzy hair.

I mentioned earlier the very disconcerting, unreachable quality I perceived in Martin at the beginning of treatment. There was *always* a feeling of his not being all there, which made it very difficult to establish contact with him. But I gradually came to realise that there was often a very specific mood attached to the lack of contact. While not listening, or treating whatever I said as if he only perceived a remote sound, he appeared to be totally absorbed in a detail of his appearance; at times it might be something very minor, like removing tiny specks of dust or fluff from his jacket; at times his movements became very feminine, almost in a caricatured way. For instance, using his sunglasses as a mirror, he could spend lengthy periods smoothing his eyebrows with his fingertips; or he could become totally absorbed in the care of his nails. Once he actually came to his session with nail-varnish on the nails of both hands. He treated, on those occasions, my attempts to reach him with an interpretation as if I were a sort of annoying child, or a noise in the background. I should not disturb him while he was busy with something, so much more important than anything I could possibly say. Indeed the identification with an idealised internal object was at this time very important to him, being, precarious as it was, the only thing which held him together. One particular session provided a vivid example of the type of projective identification I was confronted with, a form of entering inside an object in a sort of hand-to-glove-puppet relationship, which is very similar to examples given by Melanie Klein (1955) in her paper 'On identification'.

Martin was wearing an anorak with a fur-trimmed hood, I was to learn later that its name (it could not be more appropriate in the context) is a 'parka'. He pulled the hood right over his head, then he took a comb out of his pocket and he started combing the long-haired fur around his hood as if he were curling it – with long sensuous, very feminine strokes. He really behaved as if he perceived himself 'parked' inside someone else's skin. The impact of his behaviour was heightened by the fact that he was wearing on this occasion, as on many others, menacing rings on his right-hand fingers, but seemed completely oblivious of them.

In this session, and in the ones I have previously described, there were some verbal responses to my attempts to reach him, in the nature of 'Yes, what is it you wanted to say?', 'I have got no time for your rubbish', 'Tough, you have got to suffer', 'You are talking to a brick wall'. His tone of voice, on those occasions, was cold, contemptuous and very hard. Indeed it was like talking to a brick wall and after some trials and errors, I realised that this was the most important quality of Martin's communication. That he had to put me in the position of the child who tries to make contact with somebody who has no time to listen, a hard and vain mother who says 'Tough, you have got to suffer', while she is curling her hair and treats with scorn and contempt the weakling who is trying to get some of her attention. I am referring to Martin's internal object – but this appeared to be, from subsequent material, the phantasy that he had formed about the reason why his mother had left him just after his birth. She was too vain and self-centred and hard to care for a small baby.

The purpose of Martin's unreachable attitude was now, as it had probably been many times in the past, the one of splitting and projecting into somebody else both the feelings that he could not tolerate and a part of himself, the needy child he had to disown, while he identified himself with the unavailable object which at this time he idealised, felt completely at one with, and thus in control of it.

When I said to Martin that I thought he behaved with me as if I were a nuisance child, trying to talk to a mother who is only interested with the reflection of her face in the mirror and can't be bothered to listen, a very hard mother, like a brick wall, he answered: 'There is only one way to find out whether you are a brick wall or not. You hit your head against a brick wall, if it hurts, you are not'. The implication of this statement is very enlightening in terms of the development of Martin's defences. He appeared to be saying that the only way not to get hurt if you have got this sort of an object is to identify with it, become a brick wall yourself and leave the hurt to someone else. The use of this type of defence brought about the numbness I referred to above, both through identification with an insensitive internal object, and through the impoverishing splitting of feelings and parts of the self into other people. After all, the foster mother, not Martin, was crying on the phone, while he behaved as if nothing had happened, but the foster parents had subsequently made themselves unavailable to further contact. This chain reaction had probably occurred many times in Martin's life.

The pressure that Martin could put on an external object to give up trying, to give up any hope that he could be reached was very strong. I think that the very forceful impact he had on people in this respect, must have deprived him many times of positive experiences. He had developed a talent, not only for hardening himself, but for hardening people around him and making them deaf to the real nature of his need. Any further deprivation and experience of an external hard object was reintrojected and cemented the hardness of his internal object.

## The Pakistani

It is understandable that Martin should have such dread of getting in touch with feelings of dependency, when he had inside himself a very insensitive object; he had so often contributed to hardening his external objects and was not as yet sure that it would not happen with me, although the sentence I quoted earlier on, implied at least a hope that I might bear the impact of his behaviour and not become a brick wall.

Martin's profound contempt and hatred for a split off, needy part of himself has been a recurrent theme in treatment; it was initially to be known to us as 'The Pakistani'.

Although Martin is coloured himself, his prejudice against Pakistanis was fierce and sanctimonious and he had often chosen Pakistani children as the target of his attacks in school. He used to say about them 'They can't fend for themselves, or they wouldn't have come over here for help, would they?' 'They are inferior, they are savages, not like us British'. This inferior and needy savage had not only to be despised, but crushed and obliterated: 'Oh, I love Pakistanis,' Martin said once, 'you hit them and they come for more and more and more until you kill them', and he caressed menacingly, the knuckle rings which covered all fingers on his right hand. This is probably very similar to what he felt would happen to the weakling, the fool who kept hitting his head against an insensitive hard mother; he would not survive it for long. Subsequent material has brought much more into the open Martin's anxieties about death, but he was certainly projecting the fear of death into the children he used to terrorise in school with knives. This type of acting out had fluctuated, but it completely ceased at the beginning of the second year of treatment, when signs of integration of this split-off part began to emerge. Martin told me one day: 'I'm not after all the Pakistanis in the world, I'm not man-hunting, I am just after one bloke'. He started scribbling, then, on the side of his box, he wrote his name, his address, and his telephone number.

## Grievances

As gradually, very tentatively, Martin began to realise that the Pakistani he had been bashing, despising, depriving of the help he needed was within himself and caught the first glimpses of insight into this area of need, of wanting help, wishing for me to retrieve him when he lost touch (the address and the telephone number), he began to reproach me increasingly for hardness, coldness, negligence, in failing to provide what he needed. He could idealise the aloof, detached, narcissistic quality of his object only as long as he kept the needy child completely split off. While he used this defence, he *was* the insensitive mother, he completely identified with her. The feelings that she evoked had to be felt by the despised trampled Pakistanis, not by him. As he began to perceive *his* feelings of need, he also got in touch with *his* grievances. His appearance mirrored very strikingly his change of attitude and the shift in his identifications. He would at times come to the clinic wearing trousers too short for him, a torn jumper, holes in his socks. In the session previous to a holiday break, he was wearing a very thick 'second skin' (Bick, 1968): a shirt, two jumpers, a cardigan and his anorak and it was not a very cold day. As soon as he sat down, he touched the radiator as if shivering and said: 'Call this central heating? Cold water running through a mass of metal.' When I linked this reproach for coldness and his holding himself together with many protective layers to the forth-coming holiday break, Martin moved to an eroticised and much safer area of grievances. He said I was such a cold person, because I came from a cold country (he was convinced I was Polish) and all we have in Poland is snow and ice, while he comes from Africa where they have beautiful tropical fishes and sunshine. While saying that, his attitude became very seductive, as if he wished to imply that he had all the warmth, the passion, the glamour of Africa, as opposed to me: a metallic object with cold water in my veins. (The mass of metal with cold water running through it.)

On occasions the grievances had a marked defensive quality to them, and Martin appeared to go to great lengths to put himself in a position where he could reproach me of neglect.

From the very first days of treatment, he had come very early to the clinic. At least half an hour, often an hour earlier than his appointment. I have always seen him at ten o'clock and, at times, he was waiting outside when the clinic was opened at nine o'clock. We knew from the house-parents that he always left home after breakfast at eight o'clock and that he often walked all the way to the clinic (about four miles) in order to save his fare money. The reasons for coming early have been different at different times in treatment; the behaviour has remained the same, but its meaning has changed many times over those two years. At the time when grievances began to emerge, coming early appeared to serve a very specific purpose. No matter how punctual I was, from Martin's point of view I had kept him waiting a long time; I was not available when he arrived. It is true that I *had* kept him waiting since the previous session and the sessions were very spaced out.

Martin looked very sullen, as he left the waiting room. He often took a comic along and he looked through it for the first two or three minutes or looked outside the window, very much out of touch with me, then suddenly turned towards the clock which had obviously moved from ten o'clock and remarked for instance: 'Late again', or shrugged his shoulders as if to say: 'You are hopeless'. On one occasion he said, referring to the previous session: 'You were half a minute late last time'.

I think that the main defensive purpose served by the grievances, was that Martin felt much more comfortable in a known situation, confronted with an object which he did not value, someone who could be no good and no use to him, somebody not to be trusted. This was a dimension where he moved with great ease, and a very familiar one. He had not really trusted anybody in his life. He was not prepared to take chances. His defences, for instance the projective identification with the internal insensitive mother, had an enormous advantage over a relationship with any live object. It could be conjured up at any moment, it was always available and Martin felt in full control, while he could not fall back all the time on my help. In fact he could only, at first, for 50 minutes out of all the hours of the week and I wondered about a reference to the seven days of the week, when he told me once that he had 'seven layers of skin that covered the soft spot'. Not just a 'crust of the weekend' but a crust of the week. I decided that, as soon as I had a vacancy, I would offer him a second session. (I only wish it had been possible to increase the number of sessions to five times weekly.) Martin reacted to the offer, saying that he would only come if he could choose the day and time. Why couldn't I see him on Saturday mornings? Why couldn't the clinic stay open at weekends? Anyhow he did not need to come twice a week, in fact he did not even need to come once. His spasmodic need to be in control was very clearly spelled out: 'If I were not in control I would not be here', 'If I am not in control, all you have got is the choice of death: hanging, electric chair, drowning, decapitation'.

I thought at first that it would be better to allow him to work through his anxieties and wait for the time when he would be able to say that he wished to accept the session, but I came to realise that, were he able to say so openly that he needed more help, he would not be so ill and in need of it. In fact, to my surprise, he seemed very relieved when eventually I arranged for him to have a second session without waiting for his blessing. He always appeared to experience relief when there was an acknowledgement in the outside world of how little he could as yet look after himself and his needs.

Although I feel that it was worthwhile to disrupt the rhythm of treatment in order to increase the sessions, I realised that this change in the known pattern had temporarily shaken Martin's feeling of safety in the therapeutic 'setting' (I am using the word setting in the context described by Meltzer (1967) in *The Psychoanalytic Process*). I also think that the increased number of sessions was at first experienced as a rather cruel tantalising game. If I could give him a little more, then why so little? Then Martin brought to one of his sessions the advertisement of a restaurant open 'most hours of day and night', providing me with a model of how things should be. He told me one day, looking at the 'emergency numbers' on the telephone dial and talking about emergencies: 'But I am not an emergency, am I? Or I would come every day'. He referred to the time of the session as 'miserable 50 minutes'. He told me after I had referred to myself as 'mother' in a transference interpretation, that 'there are no mothers in a place like this' (he referred to the clinic and, I expect, just as much to a children's home). 'Only people doing their job and getting paid for it. There might be some mothers, but that means they have got children at home'. This reproach about being no more than yet another part-time person in his life has been a very recurrent one. It always appeared to imply that if I put him in touch with a feeling of need, if I was responsible for his knowing that he had a soft spot *inside* himself and not lodged in any odd Pakistani, I could only help him by offering the actual mothering he had been deprived of, or deprived himself of and a very idealised, always available mothering. I should not expose him to the pain of knowing what he had missed without providing it, in the present, if not in the past. Whenever I fell short of those expectations and I was bound to *all the time*, I was felt to be playing a cruel tantalising game.

## Physical and mental violence

I came to understand only later that Martin's repeated accusations of my wanting to make him cry were, at least partly, serving the purpose of turning me into the executioner and himself into the victim who was only fighting in self-defence and was, thus, immune to guilt.

Towards the end of the first year of treatment, while reproaching me for cruelty, Martin threatened me in a number of sessions with physical violence. A key session in this respect was one very close to our first Christmas break. He had spoken and complained about the rain on his way to the clinic, he had referred to the doll's house (an open-plan one) in the corner and said: 'That house is no good: it would let the rain in'. He had put his face out of the window, it was still raining, and wiped his face as he came back in. When I said that he seemed to be talking about getting his face wet with tears, that he felt, like the doll's house, I did not provide enough protection against the rain-tears, Martin caressed his knuckle rings with a smile as if getting ready to punch me and said, 'You can get your face wet with rain, with tears, with blood, and yours is going to be wet with blood before mine is wet with tears'.

It might be relevant that the risk of physical violence being acted out or, better, 'acted in' treatment (Meltzer, 1967) coincided with the end of aggressive behaviour elsewhere. The problem came to be gathered more in the transference. Although physical violence did not actually ever occur, I think that Martin needed to bring about a situation where I would take very seriously the possibility that it could occur and bear the feelings that this aroused. I found both of Mary Boston's papers (1967, 1972) on her work with a patient from a children's home very helpful in highlighting problems which may be recurrent in the treatment of institutionalised children. In her 1972 paper, Mary Boston refers to the patient's phantasy, greatly reinforced by reality, that his hostile impulses might be responsible for the parents' disappearance and points out: 'Understanding the hostility and phantasies may not be sufficient. The new object, the therapist, has to prove that he can contain the violence and reduce its omnipotence by withstanding it and surviving as the original object in the patient's phantasy did not' (Boston, 1972).

I feel that this issue is very relevant in Martin's case, because subsequent material showed that his anxieties about the extent of his omnipotence were very strong and that it is well possible that his disturbance became exacerbated when he heard of his mother's death because it was experienced by him as a further confirmation in reality of the power of his murderous phantasies. He had told me that I would only have the choice of death if I escaped his control. His mother did and she died. Other very overwhelming feelings had also been aroused by her death, as it shattered all hopes that she would ever come back and it was experienced by Martin as the ultimate proof of her narcissistic, selfish, withdrawal. 'She is having a lovely holiday, pushing up the daisies', he said bitterly, very close to one of my holiday breaks.

At the time when Martin was threatening me with his knuckle rings or, suddenly, flicked a knife open and stabbed his box ('We'll have to get a new box', 'We'll have to get a new Mrs Henry'), he spoke about his mother having died of foot-and-mouth disease and produced many other gruesome sadistic phantasies. They were very divorced from his feelings and had very marked anal masturbatory quality to them. He called them his 'walks in the graveyard' and they provided an image of the large portion of his internal world which resembled a graveyard.

There was not in those instances a glimpse of guilt feelings as *I* was supposed to feel all the guilt for wanting to make him cry, as his mother had wanted to make him cry. I was confronted with the grievances of a lifetime; he behaved as if he were either phantasising attacks or threatening physical violence in self-defence.

Once the threat of physical violence receded, the impact of the violence did not diminish, it remained as mental violence, but it became to a certain extent easier to work, because it is very difficult to gather one's thoughts and interpret when a knife can appear out of nowhere. (The surprise element was a very central one.)

Martin let me know that this type of danger was over in a way which is very typical of how he shows me he has gained a piece of insight, giving it back to me in a sort of patronising way. I was talking quite unaware of moving my hands, while doing so. Martin touched one of my hands with a finger, gently pressing it towards the table and said: 'We can just talk, you don't need to use your hands'. By projection I had become the acting-out patient.

On this occasion I also think that eroticisation of the relationship (touching my hand, the seductive behaviour, the quality of innuendo in Martin's words) had been used as a defence; in this case against tender feelings.

Martin found any feelings of warmth, closeness, tenderness so painful that he had to dispose of them very quickly. Either he eroticised them and turned them into excitement or he had to 'execute' them. 'My hurt is not my business. I execute it,' he said once while cutting in two halves, with a sharp movement a piece of string he was holding in his hands. I think that this sign language provides a very good example of the 'attacks on linking' described by Bion (1959) which have been a core of mental violence in Martin and, possibly, one of the greatest sources of his deprivation.

In his paper 'Attacks on linking' Bion (1959) says: 'I employ the term link because I wish to discuss the patient's relationship with a function, rather than with the object that subserves a function; my concern is not only with the breast or penis or verbal thought, but with their function of providing a link between two objects'. Elsewhere, in the same paper, Bion compares this approach to physiology as different from anatomy.

If, using the model proposed by Bion, I attempt to summarise the most frequent 'attacks on linking' that occurred in Martin's treatment, I shall refer firstly to his emptying of meaning and thus of feeling, a piece of insight he had just acquired: attacks on links within his mind. He used this method as the quickest remedy against any painful feelings as he much preferred to be in a muddle than to be in pain. He could achieve this purpose by taking a word out of context and 'executing it'. To quote an example, after he had emerged from one of his delusional identifications with the vain mother and, for a moment, seemed really to feel and to understand how little sustenance this narcissistic object could provide for him, there was an abrupt change of mood, he picked out of context the word 'character' I had just used in connection with the vain mother and said: 'Character, Character? Oh yes, I like carrots'. It was as quick and sudden as the flicking open of knives, in no time the meaning and the feeling were executed, the part of Martin that knew where it hurts and why it hurts was executed, and the consequence was a loss of contact between his mind and my mind.

This loss of contact is the second type of attacks on linking to which I wish to refer. Martin was very much in need of a container (Bion, 1962) for the feelings he could not bear himself and of the experience that they could be survived, understood and processed for him by an external object. Bion suggests that a very extensive use in treatment of this type of projective identification, a stepping stone in development, probably implies that patients have been cheated out of the use of this mechanism in infancy. It is very likely that this might be so for children cared for in institutions. But the reaction to being given what has been needed for so long, is often accompanied by very painful feelings. As Bion (1959) points out: 'the patient feels he is being allowed an opportunity of which he had hitherto been cheated: the poignancy of the deprivation is thereby rendered the more acute and so are the feelings of resentment at the deprivation'. I think that the rapid 'execution' of feelings of being understood, of being in touch and the consequent loss of contact with me were defences against this painful experience.

A third type of attacks, intimately connected with the first two, was aimed at disrupting links within my mind. Martin very openly expressed his intolerance of my being anything more than a passive container for his projections. 'You are just a great big dustbin stuffed with rubbish: Dustbins don't talk'. 'If you find out something about me, just keep it to yourself, will you?' The development he fought against was the moment when I did not comply with the purely receptive role and tried to understand the meaning of what was happening. There the disruption often started. On some occasions my sentences were interrupted after the first two or three words, especially if I had started a sentence with the words: 'I think that . . .'. 'You think everything, don't you?' 'You are a brain-box'. He did not as yet know the content of my sentence; he was fighting the thinking, not the thoughts. If I stopped talking, as a silence was undoubtedly preferable to a battle of wits, he would say: 'Come on – proceed – what is it you were trying to say? Can't you remember?' Indeed this behaviour was also a meaningful communication as Martin was once more telling me about a very destructive part of himself, another version of the 'Paki-basher' that was paralysing *his* capacity to think and showing me how it happened. The whole painful issue of the impaired use of his mind, of his incapacity to retain knowledge ('Can't you remember?'), to link and to learn was being put across.

I often interpreted this behaviour as a communication, but there was something very crucial in those disruptions which was meant as an attack. Its nature appeared to me very similar to the quality of attacks described by Bion (1959) as follows: 'The couple engaged in a creative act are felt to have an enviable emotional experience. He (the patient) being identified . . . with the excluded party, has a painful emotional experience. On many occasions the patient had a hatred of emotions and, therefore, by a short extension of life itself. This hatred contributed to the murderous attacks on that which links the pair, on the pair itself and on the object generated by the pair', and elsewhere: 'Envy and hatred of a capacity for understanding, was leading him to take in a good understanding object, in order to destroy and eject it, a procedure which had often lead to persecution by the destroyed and ejected object'.

In my opinion, Martin expressed something which can be understood on those lines when he said 'I want to overwork that little man that runs around your head, putting together all the data'. Back in school, he was going to find out about computers. (His learning difficulties had, by this time, the second half of the second year, considerably lessened.) He thought the best way to blow up the valves, was to overload a computer; I should give a holiday to my little man. 'Why didn't I throw him out of the window and let him have a bit of fresh air?' The attack on linking is here spelled out as a wish to get rid of my 'little man', to disrupt the combined object, to break the link, which in this case appears to be represented by the father's penis inside the mother, and thus make any creative process impossible. A very primitive type of jealousy and envy, as well as intolerance of psychic pain were bringing about Martin's repeated attempts at deadening the life of his object and, whether the image is a computer jammed with unprocessed data or a mute metallic dustbin overloaded with projections, the result of those attacks left Martin with a very lifeless, cold and frightening object inside. The task of resuscitation is huge and only just beginning.

It has been important for Martin to reach some understanding of the connections between his attacks in the transference and the deadly nature of his internal object. His impairment in learning in spite of the evidence he gave in his destructiveness of having a good mind, was certainly connected with the fragmentation of his internal world and he had been confronted daily throughout his life with this deprivation, fortunately a reversible one.

It is certainly relevant that he had himself experienced so many broken links during the first two years of his life when he must so often have lost people he had made some contact with, in the turnover of staff within the same institution and in the three changes of placements.

## Wish to be retrieved

During this last year, especially in the second half, there have been many indications that Martin is relying on my work to re-establish the links when they are broken, so that he will not be allowed to get lost in his muddle or otherwise drift away. Although he let me know that he has gained some insight in this area in his manic, patronising way, and with a very overdetermined communication, he has caught a glimpse of it. 'I have read the Bible', he told me very recently – 'and it says there: He who muddles shall perish in the eternal flames and he who speaks the truth shall live forever'. He also told me that 'you can put a piece of rope to all sort of good uses, for instance you need it to tie a boat to the shore, so that it doesn't drift away, or you can tie the rope to a buoy'. He laughed as soon as he became aware of the double meaning of the word and said 'I know what you are going to say'. He showed me in the same session, using the string for pulling the curtains, a very safe knot used by mountain climbers which he tied round both his legs. He said it was safe because it had a double loop. Some acknowledgement perhaps that it is safer to be held by both parents. He said that even if he threw himself out of the window he wouldn't fall, he would just hang by his legs. The reference to his attempted suicide is striking, but, as Martin has never mentioned it, I have not referred to it in my interpretations. There has been plenty of material in the sessions that put us in touch with his suicidal impulses and, at this stage, with his fear of them. Martin has often asked me why don't I just 'let him rot in peace', 'six feet underground is a peaceful place', 'the brain only stops working when you are dead'. 'Dead people lose life, but they gain death'. He also said: 'If I were to kill myself I know the quickest way of doing it. You jump out of a window, head first'.

Very often his 'attacks on linking' during a session, his throwing his mind and feelings out of the window and the deadening of his object, had a suicidal quality of brutal anaesthesia. I could talk about the suicide, while it was happening. I do not think that Martin could dare me to let him drift away into madness or actual death without having developed some trust in an object that would not let it happen. During the past months there have been indications that he can at times experience a greater feeling of trust towards me and that he is capable, although in a rather intermittent way, of a more dependent relationship. It is possible that this development might have been accelerated by events external to treatment which have made him feel very much at risk.

Martin was supposed to leave the present home when he was 16 and he had often said in past years that he wished to join the army. A great deal of material about the meaning the army had for him had been brought to his sessions. It stood at first for a 'licence to kill', later more clearly for a 'licence to get killed', 'a passport to death' as Martin called it. Although he felt himself much less motivated to joining the army, which would have obviously meant the end of treatment, nobody in his environment doubted that this would be the best solution. Martin no longer gave cause for concern either at school or at the home, and had made good progress from the external point of view; if he could pass the exams and join the Regulars, all were in agreement that he should. Martin brought the problem quite openly to his session when he asked me, 'so what's going to happen when I am 16?' He also brought to the clinic, at this time, a picture of one of the homes where he had stayed as a small child. On another occasion he brought a leaflet from the local authority council and related services and he browsed through it. He pointed at 'Territorial and Army Volunteer Reserve' and said 'we don't want that, do we?'. He looked at length at the page listing child care and child guidance.

I knew that Martin would not have been able to say openly, as yet, to anybody that he still needed a great deal of child care and child guidance. I was surprised in fact that he had gone as far as implying it. I felt a strong pressure towards making direct steps in order to relieve his worry about the future, but it seemed more useful for me to deal in treatment with the strong anxieties that this situation aroused in him. It was very fortunate that I could rely on a great deal of support from the psychiatrist at the clinic in putting across to the houseparents, the school and representatives of social services, how undesirable it would have been for Martin to stop treatment at this stage and join the army. One of the problems was where should he go instead, and luckily a suitable placement could be found. It was suggested by the school that he could stay on for six months after school-leaving age because he had developed a great interest in photography and he could have some professional training in it.

I think that it was important for Martin to know that other people at the clinic were concerned with the factual arrangements in his life. If he were to feel that I was organising his future, I think he might have experienced this change in the known pattern as very confusing and tantalising. His reaction to the offer of the second session had given me food for thought in this respect. The crucial problem, if a change of technique is introduced at a given stage during treatment is the need to set the limit again at some point and to choose at which point to do so. It would have been very difficult to set a limit which made sense to Martin as to how far I could go and what I could actually do for him, if I overstepped in the least my role. If I was taking care of his future placements, he might well have wondered why I did not offer him a home myself. Because of the extent of his deprivation and his craving for a 'full-time mother' he will never have in external reality, I think that I can better help him by setting very clear limits to what he can expect. If any change is possible, then he can start hoping again that I might, at some stage, make up for *all* he has missed, while I can only help him lessen the extent of the deprivation which derives from internal sources.

It is difficult to know at this stage how far he can be helped in this direction. I think that there is an indication that he must have had some positive experiences in his early days because he would have been, otherwise, more impervious to treatment. When he first came it was difficult to get in touch with his wish to stay alive, but I think it is significant that he had not become psychotic, although he used a profusion of psychotic defences, that he *had* stayed alive and Spitz's work (Spitz, 1945) tells us about babies in similar circumstances who did not and he had in fact cried for help by producing alarming symptoms, while other institutionalised children go through life dead or hollow inside without anybody noticing it. At the time when Martin, having gathered his disturbance into treatment, offered a well-adjusted image to the environment and was considered to be fit for the Army I realised what risks institutionalised children run when they offer the appearance of being intact. How much more convenient it is for everybody.

I think it is a hopeful sign that in the instance I have just mentioned Martin appeared to be able to stand on the side of his real need and to ask for more 'child care and child guidance'. It seems to me an indication that he was in touch with an object within himself who can treat his needs with respect and ask for them to be taken seriously: a role which he had completely left to me in the past. In fact Martin impoverished, depleted and deprived himself, through the use of splitting and projection both of the good and bad parts of his self and object. The progressive reintegration which is taking place affords some hope that Martin's deprivation can be gradually lessened.

It cannot be denied though that Martin has also been *deprived* of something by his treatment. The previous changes of placement have probably been relatively painless. He let himself be moved like a suitcase, a fairly empty one, and left the tears to someone else. But he is not finding it so easy at present. When the prospective foster parents came to take him to their house for a weekend, they found him very cosily tucked up in bed with the blanket up to his nose, engrossed in reading a book. He said that he would prefer for the break to be definite, go to their house and stay there, he did not want to come and go. He was asked whether he would accept to go to them if he could bring something that mattered with him. As he was so engrossed in reading, would he like to bring that book; Martin answered he would only go if he could take all 'his family' with him. Fortunately it will be possible to arrange for him to have regular contacts with the present house parents in the future, and he says he wishes to see them once a week, but it is undeniable that this move is yet another loss in his life and he has shed now some of the protective layers that made him quite immune to any feelings of loss. Early in treatment he had told me very proudly: 'I never miss anybody – people miss me'. I can understand Martin's puzzlement and reservations when he seems to be asking me in so many ways: 'If it hurts, how can you call it getting better?'

## References

Bick, E. (1968) 'The experience of the skin in early object relations', *International Journal of Psycho-Analysis*, 49.
Bion, W.R. (1959) 'Attacks on linking', *International Journal of Psycho-Analysis*, 40.

Bion, W.R. (1962) *Learning from Experience*. London: Heinemann.

Boston, M. (1967) 'Some effects of external circumstances on the inner experience of two child patients', *Journal of Child Psychotherapy*, 2 (1).

Boston, M. (1972) 'Psychotherapy with a boy from a children's home', *Journal of Child Psychotherapy*, 3(2).

Klein, M. (1955) 'On identification'. In Klein, M., Heimann, P. and Money-Kyrle, R. (eds.) *New Directions in Psychoanalysis*. London: Tavistock.

Meltzer, D. (1967) *The Psychoanalytic Process*. London: Heinemann.

Spitz, R.A. (1945) 'Hospitalism. An inquiry into the genesis of psychiatric conditions in early childhood'. In *The Psychoanalytic Study of the Child*. Vol. 1. New York: International University Press.

# Chapter 7

# Adolescent re-enactment, trauma and reconstruction[1]

*Margret Tonnesmann*

Originally published in the *Journal of Child Psychotherapy* (1980) 6: 23–44.

Ernest Jones, in his classical paper 'Some problems of adolescence' (1922) speaks of the great changes that occur at the completion of adolescence and states, 'At puberty a regression takes place in the direction of infancy, . . . and the person lives over again, though on another plane, the development he passed through in the first five years of his life'. Jones reasons that this is the key to many of the problems of adolescence '. . . it signifies that the individual *recapitulates and expands* in the second decennium of life the development he passed through during the first five years of life . . .' Moreover, Jones stresses that there is regression of '. . . other mental aspects than the purely sexual ones'. This paper was written before Freud introduced his structural theory in 'The ego and the id' (1923). But I think we can nevertheless postulate that Jones already alluded to the regression of ego-functioning when he talked about those 'other mental aspects'.

Adolescence has been for long the 'step-child' of psycho-analysis, as Anna Freud pointed out in 1958. Certainly, the names of such outstanding pioneers as Aichhorn, Bernfeld and Hoffer come to mind. But only over the last 20 years or so have psycho-analysts investigated the adolescent process more extensively, and its significance for the theory and practice of psycho-analysis has become more evident.

## The normative crisis of adolescence

Adolescence is a developmental phase, a process which has a definite beginning with the onset of biological puberty and the re-organisation of the sexual instinct, and ends when the maturational processes have consolidated into what we call adulthood. Adolescence, the age between, is a *normative crisis situation*. It requires the relinquishment of the attachment to primary object(s) and incestuous figures and the modification of reliance

1 Written in honour of Paula Heimann for her 75th birthday.

upon parental ego-support and the parentally influenced ego-ideal and super-ego. It is a process of adaptation to adulthood in respect of hetero-sexual object-finding, self-object representation, ego synthesis, ego-ideal formation and super-ego restructuring (Buxbaum, 1958; Blos, 1962; Erikson, 1956; Spiegel, 1951, 1958).

Many authors have more recently compared the adolescent crisis with the work of mourning. They have emphasised one of the outstanding features of adolescent mourning; regression in the service of progression and adaptation, in the service of the ego. There is also a regression in ego-functioning. Primitive modes of defence and sometimes a breakthrough of primary process can be observed before greater synthesis of ego-functioning proceeds. Moreover there is regression in the adolescent's object-relating, sometimes to the level of primary identification, before libidinal detachment from the infantile love objects is achieved (Blos, 1963, 1967; Erikson, 1956; Geleerd, 1961, 1964; Jacobson, 1961; Kris, 1952; Lampl-de Groot, 1960; Root, 1957).

Erikson (1956) mentions another characteristic of primary process func-tioning in adolescents, namely the lack of a sense of time, and he postulates that adolescence could be seen as an institutional *moratorium* which should be granted by the environment so that growth of a stable psycho-social ego-identity can be secured.

## Adolescent mourning and reality testing

Freud (1917) defines mourning as a thought preoccupation with the deceased, leading time and again to the painful, grief-stricken realisation that the love object is lost. The adolescent does not mourn present-day love objects, he is concerned with the loss of his infantile objects, i.e., he is preoccupied with the loss of the internalised objects of his infancy and childhood. It is a mourning process, therefore, which does not result in a grief reaction on the testing of actual reality. Instead, the adolescent uses reality as a substitute to turn to, which often results in poor reality testing (Blos, 1963). His outside world may then become a stage with co-actors on which his childhood and infancy can be relived and memories which were either never conscious (primary repression) or which stem from later traumatic events (rendering the ego helpless relative to the maturational state of its stimulus barriers) can be re-enacted and so belatedly mastered (Blos, 1967; Ritvo, 1972).

## Adolescent mourning and re-enactment

In the symposium on 'Acting Out' at the 25th International Congress of Psycho-Analysis, Anna Freud (1968) drew attention to the present-day confusion about the concept of acting out. This arises because the original meaning of the term does not fit with current theoretical advances: the development of ego-psychology; the widening of instinct theory; the shift of interest and exploration from the phallic-oedipal phase to pre-oedipal events, mother–infant interaction and the rudiments of personality development. Freud (1914) had introduced the term 'acting out' to refer to a specific manifestation of resistance, when the patient repeats forgotten past events in the transference instead of remembering them. As Anna Freud pointed out, in the context of the widening scope of psycho-analytic treatment the concept of acting out has undergone a change from denoting resistance against recovering the past to denoting experiential attempts at re-enactment or enactment in the clinical situation. Between the original use of the concept as formulated by Freud in 1914 and its present application, came the introduction of the structural theory (Freud, 1923). With this advance a change occurred in the comprehension of transference manifestations from their being seen as the repetition of past events to their being understood as a new edition of repressed instinctual urges and wishes. As a result acting out became for a while a slightly derogative term denoting the instant discharge of impulses by a weak ego not capable of enduring unpleasure and tensions. The compulsion to repeat psychic traumata in the service of ultimate mastery, however, has been seen as a special case, lying beyond the realm of the pleasure principle (Freud, 1920).

The 'acted mourning' of the adolescent is more in the nature of a regressive re-enactment than an 'acting out'. Like all mourning work this acted mourning has an adaptive function, that of freeing libido. It is moreover a progressive process: it leads to the formation of an ego-identity (Erikson, 1956), a temporal continuous self (Blos, 1962), a continuity of ego-feelings (Federn, 1932, 1934). This is achieved through the synthetic functioning of the ego (Nunberg, 1931), one of the predominant ego-functions of later adolescence (Blos, 1963). Out of the adolescent's state of chaotic timelessness evolves a synthesis of past, present and future adulthood. The adolescent achieves what Blos (1963) has called 'a self rooted in personal history'. *En route* to this, however, the adolescent *repeats* in action all those early traumata[2], deprivations and sometimes privations which were disruptive to the continuity of development (Blos, 1963), when the immature ego's stimulus barriers were flooded and the ego defended itself

---

2 Anna Freud (1964/67) states that '. . . the concept of trauma should be profitably restricted to those stages in human life when structuralisation has taken place and ego mediation is the normal order of the day. While the infant is an undifferentiated being, he experiences distress, not trauma in the strict sense of the word. But this distress of the infant is probably identical with the older being's helplessness before recovery from trauma. What the two have in common is the absence of a functioning ego'. In this paper 'trauma' refers to the ego distress of the infant as well as the older child's ego state of severe helplessness in response to traumatic events.

by dissociating such experiences, which led to alterations, splits and rifts in the ego (Freud, 1927, 1939, 1940a, 1940c).

Such dissociated traumata are not available to be memorised. The adolescent therefore actively re-enacts them by seeking out and staging experiences which under fortunate circumstances might allow for belated mastery of passively suffered intrusions or neglect.

## Vicissitudes of failure of adolescent mourning: arrest or foreclosure

Freud stressed the repetitive quality of the working-through process of mourning, i.e., of libidinal detachment from the lost object. The adolescent's mourning bears witness to this in the continuous turmoil of regression and progression/adaptation in the enacted repetition of his infancy and childhood. Early needs not met by the original environment are creatively restaged in experiences which often have a self-healing function. Ego functioning may temporarily regress to preceding developmental levels and it seems no wonder that we find rapidly changing neurotic and psychotic symptomatology which does not structure itself into a definite illness, so that society at large often speaks of 'weird adolescent behaviour'. The creation of his 'self-with-a-sense-of-personal history' (Blos, 1963) is very private to the adolescent who needs time and space to facilitate the unfolding of his personal drama. If this moratorium is not granted, either because the intrapsychic ego resources of the individual are not sufficiently developed to achieve this organisational psychic activity of 're-enacting', or because his environmental circumstances prevent it, then, I believe, we often find a typical pathological outcome either in adolescent arrest or in a foreclosure with premature pseudo-adaptation to adulthood.

In a large psycho-analytic study of adult patients who suffered parental loss during their childhood and adolescence, Altschul (1968), Fleming and Altschul (1963) and Pollock (1961) found that denial of the meaningfulness of the loss led to the restriction of further ego development and to ego-arrest. I would like to suggest that *adolescent arrest* can also be understood as a denial of early trauma. Periodically, hyper-cathexis of these dissociated traumata brings about the compulsion to repeat (re-enact) them without resulting in their active mastery, and the counter-force of denial is re-established. Hence, the integration and synthesis of the self and self-object representations of infancy and childhood, which is understood in this paper as an essential part of the developmental process of adolescent growth, remains impaired.

*Foreclosure of adolescence*, however, is seen here as the organisation of a rigid defence structure. It is compatible with a compulsive reactive adjustment to the demands of adulthood. But the actualisation of the self in creative pursuits and spontaneous experimentation, so essential to the maturational process of adaptation, cannot take place. Moreover, the encounters of the self with the other are equally limited to reactive patterns of relationships.

If adolescence is arrested or frozen in a foreclosure, dissociated early traumata may not be recovered or early lacunae may not be filled, and so the self will be impoverished and liable to experiences of futility and lack of enjoyment in adult pursuits. This in turn may lead to a structured illness in adulthood; it may be experienced by the adult as a void for which help is sought; it may give rise to repeated attempts at regressive acting in adulthood (with concomitant clashes with an environment that expects adult behaviour) or it may give rise to typical behaviour patterns or breakdowns when the next *normative crisis*, the 'mid-life crisis', approaches.

Some analysts therefore recommend various special techniques in treating adolescent patients, to cater for their particular needs (Blos, 1967; Eissler, 1958; Geleerd, 1957; Ritvo, 1972; Root, 1957; Sklansky, 1972). Others warn against a too liberal recommendation of psycho-analytic treatment and regard it as preferable 'to help the helpers' (A. Freud, 1958; Miller, 1969; Winnicott, 1968). Even if the reasoning of these authors is based on criteria different from those postulated here, they may well be aware of the danger that too active an interpretative approach can lead to a prematurely achieved adulthood.

During the early days of my analytic career I analysed a 15-year-old girl, Norah, seeing her five times a week. She was an in-patient in a neurosis-unit and came from a disturbed family who could not cope with their outgoing, unruly and rebellious daughter and sister. She was referred from a medical ward where it was found that, prior to admission, she had taken small amounts of rat-poisoning regularly over a couple of weeks. The diagnosis of early schizophrenia was in the air, but her behaviour turned out to be a typical adolescent enactment of the fact, denied by her family, that mother had tried to abort her. During her stay in hospital she acted out continuously, was weird and wild in a way that the other, mainly adult patients, the nursing staff and ward doctors all found hardly bearable at times. My interpretative work was very active and focused on analysing defences and transferences, not different from the analysis of any adult suffering from a neurosis. Clinically, Norah improved considerably within two years, and treatment was terminated for reasons outside my or Norah's control.

A year or so later, Norah met me by chance and – having read somewhere that patients should pay for their psychotherapy – she said to me 'I feel I have paid a heavy price for my treatment. Not with money, but I am always with older people nowadays. I assume I have matured during my treatment somehow – but like a plant that might grow too quickly in a hot-house.'

I believe that Norah's comments are true. In the light of my later experiences I consider that her analysis may have led to a foreclosure of adolescence resulting in pseudo-adaptation to adulthood.

## The repetition of adolescence during psycho-analytic treatment

A. Freud (1958), speaking of the poverty of psycho-analytic investigations into adolescence, adduced as one of the reasons the fact that adolescence is not reproduced in a transference neurosis: adolescence can be freely remembered during treatment and is not covered by amnesia as is the infantile neurosis. Geleerd (1961) postulated that elements of the transference neurosis as such, in particular its characteristic acting in our adult patients, repeat the adolescent phase. Other authors (Hurn, 1970; Lampl-de Groot, 1960) suggest that adolescent behaviour as a transference manifestation is repeated mainly during the end-phase of psycho-analysis.

I, myself, would like to put forward the idea that characteristic forms of adolescent re-enactment appear at any stage during the analysis of those adult patients who, during their adolescence, were not able to integrate dissociated experiences of early traumata, privation or deprivation.

## Adolescent re-enactment as a phase-specific mode of communicating early traumata, deprivation and privation

Blos (1966) defines adolescent acting out as a *phase-specific characteristic* (my italics) similar to the child's play and the adult's use of direct verbal communication. Thus he delimits it from acting out in impulsive disorders and reasons that it is an organised psychic action which can serve three different aims: it can be a manifestation of the unconscious motivation of the youngster's parents; it can be a tension-regulator protecting against conflict anxiety, or it can protect the psychic organism against anxiety due to structural disintegration. It is, then, '. . . the establishment of that particular experiential congruence by which present reality provides a link to a traumatic past' (Blos, 1963).

It is this latter adolescent acting out for which I would prefer the term 'adolescent re-enacting'. The actualisation of the self in the analysis of patients who suffer from arrested maturation, from so-called narcissistic disorders or from atypical depressions may be achieved through the provision of an analytic setting which allows for 'adolescent re-enactment'. The patient is thus enabled to recreate experientially those dissociated traumata and deficiencies of his early life which led to rifts and lacunae in his ego-organisation and which have escaped successful recovery and integration during adolescence. Such patients present with disorders the origin of which we place in early childhood, within the area of overwhelming and traumatic somato-psychic or ego-self experiences, the area of 'basic fault' (Balint, 1968) of substructures due to passively suffered intrusions (Heimann, 1966); of 'cumulative trauma' (Khan, 1963a, 1974); of 'false self organizations' (Winnicott, 1960a). In such patients adolescence is inevitably arrested or foreclosed so that the creation of a self-with-a-sense-of-personal-history, a temporal continuous ego (Blos, 1962), is not achieved. It may be argued that those who, despite privation, deprivation or early traumata, do not experience a lasting impoverishment of the self have had the good fortune to achieve sufficient self-healing through the provision of sufficient time and space during their adolescent moratorium.

Freud (1939), although pessimistic about the probability of self-cure through the repetition of trauma, did not dismiss the possibility altogether. He wrote that a neurotic illness which could break out at puberty or a little later '. . . may also be looked upon as an attempt at cure – as an effort once more to reconcile with the rest those portions of the ego that have been split off by the influence of the trauma and to unite them into a powerful whole *vis-à-vis* the external world. An attempt of this kind seldom succeeds, however, unless the work of analysis comes to its help, and even then not always'.

In my experience, characteristic forms of adolescent re-enactment of traumatic loss and/or separation during early childhood occurred in the analyses of several of my patients whose ages varied from late adolescence to the forties. I can select only a few to illustrate my thesis.

## Fugue states during the analytic hour: the recovery of the lost original object

Norman, an unusually gifted 25-year-old man, was English by birth. All his relations of the parental generation spoke English. However, since his grandparents had emigrated from a German-speaking minority community, he had heard adult members of the family speak German at an early age and he later learnt the German language formally at school. He was a premenopausal child. His father was of advanced age at his birth, and his mother for a longish period after confinement suffered from depression. Various aunts and his grandmother, who lived in the home, took care of him. His grandmother died when he was barely one year old and during his childhood he suffered the loss of other early attachment figures.

Clinically, Norman suffered from a narcissistic character disorder but he also suffered from an arrested adolescence as he had not succeeded in integrating the infantile trauma of multiple mothering. He presented a history of various attempts to re-enact the multiple mothering during his early adolescence. He had become obsessed for a while with an ancient culture. (When he related this to me in great detail during the analysis, I became confused for a while and found it difficult to memorise the symbolic qualities and emotional meaning of the various gods and goddesses as they repeatedly emerged during the sessions. In a reversal of roles, I had to experience the confusion Norman suffered as an infant when he was exposed to repeated changes in his caring environment.) During his school days, he had a marked tendency to shift his interests from one subject to another as he also turned from one teacher to the next, always breaking off before he could reach the standard of proficiency expected of him.

During his analysis, Norman occasionally spoke German but it did not come easily to him and he had a definite English accent. At the beginning of a session, in the third year of his analysis, he was silent. Then, completely absorbed and unselfconscious, he started to sing Goethe's 'Harzreise im Winter', in the original German text, set to part of Brahms's 'Alto Rhapsody'.

Ah, who can heal the pain of one who finds poison in balsam? He has drunk the hate of mankind from the cup of love! First scorned, now scorning, he secretly wastes his own merit in useless searching for himself. If there is in your Psalter, Father of Love, a melody that can reach his ear, revive his heart! Turn your unclouded light down on the thousand fountains beside the thirsting soul in the wasteland.

(Mann, tr. 1962)

Norman had recited bits of this poem occasionally before – but somewhat hesitantly and with his usual English accent. Several lines had served us well during different stages of the analysis: Norman's father had used his son (aged 9) as a guinea-pig for pharmacological experiments. Norman, in identification with his father, cruelly attacked and ruthlessly used people inside and outside the analytic situation before we could recover the little boy's admiration and love for his powerful father. Equally, Norman suffered from early life onwards from various food allergies. Good food (and equally interpretations experienced as feeding him) often became poisonous. It was in this context that Norman worked out his rage with the multiple mothering figures constantly demanding new adjustments of the infant and so interfering with his developing sense of continuity-of-being.

When he sang the poem fluently with a definite German accent, I recognised the one typical of the German enclave from which his grandparents had come. I responded by listening with contentment. The patient suddenly became aware of my presence and, visibly embarrassed, started to talk about music. I did not take up his embarrassment, as I felt it dynamically more important to verbalise his short mildly dissociated state while it was still emotionally available to him. So I interrupted him and said that while I had been listening to his singing I wondered whether he might have been in touch with a sensual memory of his grandmother who, he knew, had sung German nursery rhymes to him. He had never been sure whether he had a hazy memory of this, or whether it was his own fantasy attached to a piece of hearsay history. (However, he had one clear memory of her sitting in a chair trying to catch him as he was playfully toddling by, and he had been excited and frightened of being caught – he had a markedly precocious development throughout his childhood.) He responded to my suggestion by telling me about his need to be alone to listen to music. At such times he could get into so dazed a state that he found it difficult to come back to reality. He recited in German the last line from a Schubert song '. . . and carried me away into a better world'. But this time he spoke it with his usual English accent.

In the following session Norman brought a dream. He had fallen asleep at his desk. In the dream he found himself standing on a coloured etching of an ancient map. He stood on a concave-shaped shore gazing over a river to a convex-shaped landscape marked on the map as hilly. Suddenly he felt that the gap between the shores was narrowing but he was too frightened to move to the other side, fearing that he might be unable to return. The breast-symbol was obvious in the convex shape, and the patient remarked that the landscape marked as hilly must represent a body shape. It seemed to be a confirmatory dream as it repeated in a visual image his forlorn singing in the mild fugue stage in the service of recovering dissociated early memories. During the previous session, he had already talked about his difficulties in returning to 'reality'. His memory was that he had been frightened of being caught when playing with granny and I reminded him that, on waking up from the twilight state in the session, he had immediately switched to intellectual verbalisations (i.e., secondary process), as if anxious that he might be caught by me and regress to primary, symbiotic relatedness. He had, therefore, quickly re-established his inner ego-boundaries against the recovery of the early sensory feeling-stage which he – like Goethe's Wanderer – was in search of.

It was about a year later that Norman came to a session after he had accomplished a difficult task. I could observe his becoming quiet, slightly sleepy and silent which, I felt, had a contented quality. Suddenly, he started to sing again with the same ease and the same German accent as on the earlier occasion. But now, he sang 'Sheep may safely graze when a good shepherd guards them', from the Bach Cantata. I reminded him again of his only secure memory of grandmother, namely, when she was trying to catch the little toddler 'sheep'. This time, however, he was relaxed and felt happy when he became aware of my presence. There was no anxiety and, as expressed in the Cantata, he moved with far more freedom in his intra-psychic space, a regression truly in the service of the ego.

Heimann (1956) when talking about the patient's recovery of his lost original object says: '. . . it is truly an experience with his original objects, they are alive to him and present, they are felt as an essential part of himself and his present life even though they are dead . . . His ego is an integrated whole and functions optimally. There is some happiness within the sadness and remorse . . . The analyst remains a listener, a bystander . . .'. This description refers to those original objects which the patient can recall in memory. Norman had lost his grandmother, one of his original objects, before he was in command of language. Hence, her recall in memory was of a different order, and he re-enacted a very early, pre-traumatic relationship twice during his analysis. The first time my presence meant an interference, and he was embarrassed when becoming aware of me. The second time he had included me and felt me to be there. 'Acting out', Greenacre said in 1950, is a form of remembering and '. . . consists in a distortion in the relation of action to speech and verbalised thought, arising most often from severe disturbance of the second year. . . . Even when the action involved in acting out includes speech, the latter is usually secondary to the action which is the more important function'. Norman's singing and his correct accent was of an imitative character and could be seen as *the* instrumental motor action of his meaningful experiences, an observation in accordance with Greenacre (1950) who mentions the changed quality of tone when speech is used as a vehicle for acting-out.

Thus during his analysis, Norman could finally master the traumatic experience of multiple mothering during his infancy which he had tried but failed to do in various ways during his adolescence.


### Recovery of pre-traumatic mood: hope and the child's conceptualisation of time and space

Mr S., an artistically gifted patient in his forties, got up suddenly from the couch, moved to the other side of the room, stood still and said: 'Now I understand, it is as if the present has been the couch, and here is the future'. He then returned to the couch, lay down again and described a feeling of elation. He had finally understood that a grey present does not mean greyness forever. It was a very moving moment for both of us, and it signified the emergence of hope after a long period of depression. This patient had an early prolonged separation from his mother, and we could re-construct his sense of timeless greyness as the hopeless despair of the child's mourning reaction (Bowlby, 1960, 1963). Mr S. expressed his memory by an action before we could use language for its reconstruction. Within the paradox which belongs to the child's creation of his world, he had used space in his acting to experience time and the concept of future to recover a pre-traumatic past, a past of his when hope was still taken for granted.

## Recovery of separation traumata in confusional states

Mr A. was in his forties and aware that he was approaching the mid-life crisis when he came to me for his second analysis. The first one had taken place during his twenties, and he felt that he had been helped greatly in his career, where he had indeed reached a top managerial position. However, he was still unmarried, felt increasingly lonely and suffered at times from an overwhelming sense of futility. Lately, on several occasions, he had found himself getting into a panic which left him in a mild confusional state for a few hours. Each time he had been curiously aware of his own confusion and thus had been able to withdraw from the social scene so that nobody knew about these episodes.

Mr A. had suffered a severe separation trauma. He and his older sister were taken away from their mother and fostered out to different homes when they were 8 and 9 years old. Neither the children nor their mother had been able to cope with this sudden, traumatic separation, and mother had suffered ever after from agitated, depressive episodes. Mr A.'s analysis began stormily! There was a good deal of adolescent provocation in his behaviour which I came to understand as his acting his mother's part. I was made to feel what the patient felt when nothing he tried to lift mother's depression had any effect on her or re-established contact with her. The sessions were filled with memories of a 'bad' mother from the time of adolescence, interspersed with earlier memories. He maintained that he could remember being neglected as an infant by his mother, and accused her of depriving him emotionally.

However, such memories or impressions were not confirmed by any 'somatic memory' (Heimann, 1962) appearing in dream images, somatic discomfort or illness. I was reminded of Freud's early use of the concept of 'screen memories' as describing something that occurred earlier than chronologically situated (cf., Strachey, 1962). Concurrently another feature developed. Whenever we had a good session, Mr A. would immediately erase it with complete amnesia. Once he even said 'I am frightened to leave, because I know that by the time I get back to my car, I will have forgotten it all, and I don't know *how* to overcome this awful amnesia'. This led me to suggest that he might have had a good relationship to his early mother, which he had kept so secret that it became a secret even to himself and was lost like the good sessions. He confirmed this by telling me that he could not talk about his feelings for his mother in his foster home as the staff made hurtful, disparaging remarks about her. This marked a change in the analysis, and a period of vehement 're-enacting' of his childhood memories followed. For a while, I was only just able to avoid hospitalising the patient. He started to have 'mild confusional states' several times during the course of a day, when he suddenly felt unable to perceive and test reality, but was at the same time aware of his misinterpreting what others did and said. He started to phone me in states of confusion, but I could usually give him instant relief by reconstructing a part of the past traumatic events which he seemed to be re-enacting. Like an adolescent, he used his environment to stage a dissociated traumatic incident from the past, any small and in itself insignificant occurrence acting as a trigger (Greenacre, 1967). The patient himself called such states, very aptly, 'my mini-psychoses'. When he returned to his actual reality, he often left ashamed of having phoned me and judged himself as weak in a self-accusatory depressive fashion. Testing my availability on the phone was in the service of another adolescent re-enactment. Mr A. experientially mastered actively his once passively suffered separation from his mother. She had never been available to her children more than a few hours of the day.

Slowly, the patient integrated these dissociated traumatic experiences. An example might illustrate this: he suddenly took to phoning me very early in the morning, and what he related over the phone seemed to me associations to dreams he could not remember. He felt despairing, there was no hope, he had lost all trust in me! I would suggest to him that he must have dreamt about his good early mother and was re-experiencing all his grief about having lost her. During a session, he reported that he felt better after such phone calls. Indeed these sessions were filled with happy memories about which he talked in a self-absorbed way, often surprised that he could recover them. The early morning phone calls went on for a few days, until one morning when the patient appeared to me to be whining in a very aggressive way. This was no longer 'acted mourning': it was acting out with the aim of discharging aggression. I responded by showing him how he was now taking revenge on his mother, who had woken him up early in the morning when he came home occasionally at weekends from the foster home, complaining and whining about him and his father. There was a moment's silence over the phone, and then he said that he did not want to behave like his mother. Later that day in his session, he conveyed his anxieties that his early phone calls might have damaged my health. He reported that he had worked extremely hard during the day hoping to please me. (We knew from certain memories that the only pleasure his mother showed her pubertal son was when he brought good school reports.) The difference between his reacting with shame to telephone calls which related to mourning his lost good mother and reacting with guilt when concerned with mastering a passive–aggressive striving by turning it into an active one, was most marked. Another differentiating feature was that calls which were linked with past ego-distress and trauma were short and the patient felt embarrassed rather than triumphant. When, however, conflictual material was related to me, there was a bid to involve me in a collusion with gratificatory games based on instinctual strivings of an infantile sado-masochistic nature.

'Needs should be met, wishes should be frustrated', Winnicott once said (personal communication). 'Adolescent re-enactment' of dissociated traumata and pre-oedipal material has to be accepted as the paradox it is, namely, regression in the service of the ego, progression and adaptation. 'Adolescent acting out' aiming at the discharge of instinctual tensions has to be dealt with differently. The diverse aims of the phone calls exemplify this point. 'Adolescent re-enacting' refers to regressive states of the ego; 'adolescent acting out' refers to defensive instinctual regression.

## Re-enactment in psychoanalysis with adolescent patients

Blos (1963) has stressed how difficult it is to differentiate between the various forms of adolescent acting out. My experiences fully confirm this view. The moments of sudden swings from the re-enactment of traumata and pre-verbal experiences to the acting out of conflictual oedipal memories covered by infantile amnesia, or even direct discharge of instinctual tension states, require the analyst's continuous attendance to his own counter-transference reactions (Heimann, 1950, 1960; Little, 1951, 1960; Searles, 1961; Winnicott, 1960a). Counter-transference reactions stem on the one hand from the patient's verbal and non-verbal communication and on the other hand from the analyst's inner psychic responses. Parents are guided by their intuitions when relating to their children, responding to their needs or distracting their infantile sexual wishes. In a similar way analysts' counter-transference reactions differ when they meet a state of need or of impulse-determined acting out in their patients. We may here remember Freud's rule of 'abstinence' (Freud, 1915). I would suggest that this was based specifically on his awareness of patients' acting out of instinctual impulses. It is well documented in the recollections of some of Freud's patients (e.g., the Wolf-Man (Gardiner, 1972) or Doolittle (1971)) that he also responded freely to his patients' needs!

All the adult patients whom I have discussed had been exposed to early traumata of loss or separation. They all presented as suffering from various conditions like depression, anxiety states or narcissistic disorders. They fulfilled their social roles satisfactorily and were highly respected and liked by their friends. To put it differently: during their adolescence they had achieved a sufficient degree of healthy mourning to build up a relatively stable 'ego-identity' and a relatively firm adult self-representation. It was mainly in the area of 'self-experience' and in the development of healthy narcissism (Heimann, 1962) that there was serious impairment, because the traumatic experiences were dissociated and not recovered during the patient's adolescent moratorium. For various reasons all these patients had an *atypical* adolescence, and over the years I have learnt to take into account the history of the patient's adolescence, as well as of his early childhood, when trying to obtain some idea of the quality of his environmental provision. Adolescent re-enactment as a mode of communicating early trauma is on the whole a self-limiting event in the analysis of adult patients. Only *dissociated* past experiences are re-enacted, and once they are understood the patient returns to the adult mode of verbal communication. Such re-enactment is sometimes presented as a twilight or somnambulistic state; occasionally, I have found an extensive use of defensive disavowal of reality and poor reality testing or a state of de-realisation. Yet, most patients maintained simultaneously that therapeutic split of the ego involved in the 'working alliance'.

In adolescent patients, however, 'acting' is the predominant means of communication and we have to offer ourselves more often than not to be 'acted out' on as Werner (1966) put it. What might be experienced by the adult patient as a fugue state is presented by the adolescent in a vehement totality of impaired ego-functioning. This may appear as florid manic states, schizophrenic-like psychotic episodes with delusions, hallucinations and inappropriateness of affect or sometimes compulsive perverse activity (see Spotnitz, 1961).

## Failed re-enactment of infantile trauma or psychotic episodes?

Charles, age 23, had suffered several psychotic episodes for which he was hospitalised, from the time he left school at the age of 18. On some occasions admission was precipitated by an impulsive suicidal attempt. He maintained that each time he had felt unable any longer to bear the pain of perceiving his body as ugly, incomplete or in pieces. All these episodes followed the abrupt emotional detachment and physical departure of his twin sister at the age of 18. He responded with feelings of great loneliness and deep narcissistic hurt.

During his last admission, he was compulsively preoccupied with his forehead. He explained that he had been cutting his hair, when the scissors suddenly slipped producing an uneven line. Trying to remedy this he cut off more and more, in increasing panic, until his forehead was bare and visible. This led to feelings of estrangement from his own body image, and he was compelled to look into a mirror several times a day. The hospital staff felt that he had shown definite signs of ego-fragmentation.

At an early stage of his analysis, which started shortly after his discharge from hospital, it became clear that the hair-cutting incident was a typical adolescent re-enactment of a hospitalisation trauma. At the age of two he had an eye operation and the curly hair over his forehead had been cut off. Cutting his hair himself was an unconscious attempt to master actively what he had suffered passively. It is worth noting that this endeavour emphatically involved the functioning of his eyes: he looked into the mirror. However, his attempt failed and only recreated the early traumatic experience resulting in panic and confusion. Reconstruction of the trauma during the analysis relieved the patient, and, for the first time, he felt that some explanation for his confusional states were available to him. He claimed that he had some awareness during such states, but felt unable to overcome them. The in-patient psychiatrist had understood and interpreted the hair cutting as manifestations of typical adolescent masturbatory equivalents. This had angered Charles greatly, and he felt misunderstood and belittled – another manifestation of his adolescent state.

I realised that during his last admission his ego might have simply been functioning in accordance with the developmental age at which the trauma (the eye operation) had occurred; that there was no ego-fragmentation became clear to me when Charles became confused again (see Greenacre, 1967). This happened shortly after our reconstructing some of the events of his early childhood hospitalisation. One day Charles did not turn up for his session during the early evening. It was about midnight when he rang me, talking in a strange, high-pitched voice, confused and obviously panic-stricken. I could feel that he was out of contact with me, and in an attempt to reach him I shouted into the phone that I expected him to come to a session immediately. My rationale was that his voice made me suspect that he was regressed again and therefore a strict parental-like demand at that moment might meet the actual ego state of the patient. He came by taxi, presenting as perplexed and confused and showing an unusual clumsiness which I knew had been a prominent feature during his childhood. I could only slowly understand from his confused talk that he had been picked up by a man but suddenly felt panicky. Using my observation that the patient had regressed to very childlike ego-functioning – it could be said he appeared as if imitating a little boy – I asked him whether this man might have been an old friend from a past experience in the eye-hospital. He was puzzled at first, but I asked again, and he then told me that there had been a patient in the ward who read stories to him. Charles often went into his bed. As he remembered this he gradually became his adolescent self again. His voice changed back to normal, and his tense body posture slowly relaxed. Later, the parents confirmed to the patient the correctness of his memory. The unanswered question, however, was what had triggered off this fugue state. Charles could remember only that the bus had taken an unusual route, then there was a blank. But this, I felt, was more in the nature of an externalisation of his own ego-functioning. The description of his fugue state in the image of the bus embarking on an unusual route indicated some dim awareness of his intra-psychic state. Charles left this midnight session embarrassed, but composed and without any further trace of confusion.

From further reconstructive work it emerged that the child experienced the eye operation as a gross, forceful interference with his body as a whole, as well as a castration. His body image became impaired and this reinforced identification with his twin sister. Childhood memories showed clearly his gender uncertainty but he never linked this in any way with the dissociated hospitalisation experience, which he tried to master in adolescent re-enacting as described above. On both these occasions, when cutting his hair as well as when he phoned me in the fugue state, his attempt failed and, instead, a repetition of the original scene resulted, as Deutsch (1963) and Greenacre (1963) have described. On these occasions he used me as a mirror who reflected his body image back to him by reconstructing his experiences of the disturbing appearance in the hospital ward mirrors. I would like to postulate here that this mirror function of mine was part of the original scene. There the doctor-patient on the ward, with whom Charles shared the bed at times, had reflected the male body back to the blindfolded boy.

In his analysis, Charles became able to separate his self-image from that of his sister and mourn the loss of their close relationship during childhood. Identification with his own gender could then proceed, and his self became rooted in his personal history. As I now reconsider my question in the title of this section, I would answer: episodes which look psychotic are often a re-enactment of early traumata; they can be understood and analysed and thus lead to experiences of growth and integration of the self.

Greenacre (1967) refers to Freud's assumption that those traumata which have broken through the stimulus barrier of the ego tend to disrupt and disorganise normal perceptions and the formation of normal memory traces. Hence, trauma may leave its own pattern manifested in the compulsion to repeat. This phenomenon, Greenacre says, seems similar to imprinting. Contrary to Freud who considered the compulsion to repeat as an essentially regressive force, she has postulated that it could also be seen as the organism's attempt to establish a better harmony in its internal milieu. It is then supported by forces from the forward thrust of deep but continuous maturational factors. Moreover, she has supposed that traumatised patients seem to be especially prone to suffer sudden confusional states at critical periods, at the threshold of or just at entering a new phase of life. Reality testing can sometimes be so impaired that such patients require hospit-alisation. But they recover as abruptly as they had fallen ill. She further says that '. . . sometimes, it even seemed that the attack had brought a degree of renewal, permitting a return to a higher integrative level'.

## Re-enactment of infantile trauma through delinquent behaviour

Eileen, aged 17, was brought by her father. He expressed great concern about his daughter's strange behaviour over the last year and he described her as suffering from a 'double personality'. She had become delinquent, lying and stealing, as if without any conscience. But when confronted she could become 'her old self again', full of remorse, only to resort demonstratively to completely unconcerned behaviour a few minutes later. When I asked the father about any early separation experiences or significant losses he answered in the negative. Later, however, Eileen's mother phoned me in great distress. It was true that early separation had occurred. When Eileen was four years old, she had been in a nursing home for a tonsillectomy, and the specialist had advised the parents against visiting her. When collecting the child nine days later, the mother noticed a marked change. For years afterwards Eileen became very clinging and made a great fuss when left in the nanny's care, even just for one evening. Eileen's mother knew at the time that it would be wrong not to visit Eileen, but she had followed the specialist's advice.

Eileen was somewhat reluctant to make the longish journey for her sessions, but soon settled and regressed to symbiotic relatedness. She often talked in a curious private language which I returned in such a way that her communications became meaningful to her while her own verbalisation was often far removed from what she meant to convey. Every time this happened, it gave her great relief. The significant adolescent re-enacting involved in this mode of speech became clear when she told me of her mother's behaviour! Mother had tried to teach her children words very early in order to discourage them from wanting to walk, being afraid that too early weight bearing might be harmful to the bone structure of the children's legs.

Fairly early on during her analysis, Eileen re-enacted outside the sessions, in several mild, short fugue states, what she had experienced in the nursing home. She had hardly any memory of it, but we could reconstruct that she had felt exposed to the physical force of the nurses, whom she fought before she surrendered. Confirmatory dreams often helped the reconstruction. Sometimes Eileen responded with visual images to my interpretations. Slowly her bed, her room, the face of a very angry nurse emerged. Concomitantly her delinquent behaviour could be analysed. It became clear that it served in part as an active re-enactment of passively suffered intrusions during her hospitalisation.

Gradually her delinquent behaviour lessened, and she became more aware of the beginnings of such fugue states, which she called 'not feeling well'. One day she reported that she did not feel well over the weekend and went several times to the mirror to make sure she was still herself. She then became quiet, and I observed that the expression on her face changed. Suddenly she sat up as if wanting to get off the couch, and said that, when her parents came to collect her from the nursing home, a young nurse sitting on the window-sill said: 'Look who is coming there!' She rushed out of bed to the wardrobe-mirror to see whether she still looked the same and tried to touch her own mirror image. For the first time there was happiness in her voice, when she said, 'Now I know why it has always been such a comfort to me to look into the mirror'.

This session led to a change in Eileen. She gave up her most unsuitable, delinquent boyfriend, at whose place she had been found time and again on the occasions when she absconded from home. Much to her mother's annoyance she had always taken with her an object which she knew to be dear to her mother. This could be seen as another bit of acted communication of her complaints: that in the nursing home she was not allowed her transitional object, or a loved and familiar toy, but only a clean, new teddy. Her 'strange behaviour' (as the parents called it) stopped, but sporadically, she was prone to 'feeling unwell' in acute stress situations.

Why did Eileen react so strongly to the relatively short hospitalisation? Another episode from her very early history might shed some light on this: when Eileen was six weeks old, she was hospitalised for an operation for pyloric stenosis. Dreams and other analytic material suggested that this early illness interfered with her developing sensual body awareness and its introjection (Greenacre, 1953a, b, 1958, 1967). It left somatic memories (Heimann, 1962) of violent intrusion and of equally violent expulsion in reaction to the flooding of stimuli. Eileen had a bad start in life. But mother and she tried to compensate for this by prolonged symbiotic relatedness within the private space of their baby-talk. This was interrupted by Eileen's renewed hospitalisation, at the age of four, when she repeated her experiences of passively suffered violent intrusions. The development of ego-functioning was delayed. Eileen had not yet achieved proper object representation. Since an object representation of mother was not available to her during her nine days long separation, her self image and her body-ego image changed. Thus, she had to re-discover herself in the mirror before she was reunited with her parents. On her return home, she showed signs of post-separation clinging (Bowlby, 1963) and regressed to symbiotic relatedness again. This discontinuity of her development became apparent during her adolescence. She re-enacted it and became delinquent and compliant. But she was also a youngster of 17 regressed to symbiotic relatedness.

The first phase of the analysis could therefore be seen as an active mastery of her beginning, resulting this time in a better 'fit' or understanding of the clue-cue system that 'pyloric babies' can be expected to have. Eileen used the analytic relationship with me to re-enact her early childhood experiences. Because she was of the adolescent age group, I limited my interventions for some time to reconstruction. After she had recalled (in mild fugue states) the dissociated trauma of the nursing-home experiences, in particular the recovery of her identity when her parents came to collect her, a more coherent self slowly evolved. I then became also the object of her oedipal strivings in the transference which were more often than not acted out in adolescent fashion. Somatic memories or imprints of the pyloric stenosis and the first operation re-emerged when she suffered an acute somatic illness towards the end of the analysis. As Eileen had developed by then a sensitive self-awareness, she was able to understand these as an integral part of her somato-psychic existence.

## Adolescent re-enactment: the analyst as need-fulfilling part-object and supplementary ego

Both Charles and Eileen suffered early somatic traumata when separated from their mother; these interfered with the continuity of the development of the body image. Hence, they characteristically used the *analyst as a mirror* which, by verbalising their acted repetition in search of an active mastery of the trauma, had to give back to them a body image of wholeness which had suffered somatic injuries. Prior to treatment they both sought in vain help from the real mirror. Fenichel (1945) in his classical paper on 'neurotic acting out' mentions the oral libidinal striving in all acting out, namely that objects are used as need-fulfilling part-objects. During the earlier phases of the analysis of adolescents, when the re-enactment of early and earliest childhood experiences is prominent in their psychic functioning, we should provide for a setting in which they can use us to 'act out on'. (This is equally true of those adult patients who regress to the adolescent mode of acted communication when early traumata are about to be recovered.) Only after sufficient adolescent 'acted' mourning of childhood experiences, of regressive and progressive shifts in psychic functioning, has been 'lived through' (instead of 'worked through' as in adult analysis) can the underlying mode of oral-libidinal strivings be interpreted in the transference without interfering with this developmental process of maturation.

'Adolescent re-enacting', however, as has been shown for acting out in general, is 'a source for the gaining of material' (Fenichel, 1945), 'a communication' (Limentani, 1965), 'a chief ally in certain disorders' (Khan, 1964), a 'memorising' (Greenacre, 1950) during analytic treatment. It provides direct access to the patient's childhood and allows for its experiential recovery and mastery helped by the analyst's reconstructions. The analyst thus becomes the patient's supplementary ego (Heimann, 1956) and enables the patient to structuralise and synthesise those early traumatic experiences or deficiencies which had been dissociated at the time. Depending on the developmental level of psychic functioning at which the dissociated traumatic events take place, various configurations of psychic pathology ensue. (See Balint, 1968; Greenacre, 1953a, b; Freud, 1927; Heimann, 1962, 1966; James, 1960, 1962; Khan, 1974; Little, 1951; Milner, 1969; Searles, 1965; Winnicott, 1958, 1965, 1971.)

The dissociation of infantile trauma, intrusion, loss, deprivation or privation leads to discontinuity of development and concurrent lacunae in the ego. This may be the reason why adolescent re-enactment is so often experienced in special states of consciousness such as twilight, fugue, hypnagogic or somnambulic states or, if experienced habitually, in de-realisation states. Freud (1914) and Greenacre (1950) mentioned such phenomena, when discussing problems of acting out. Sometimes patients maintain that they are simultaneously aware of actual reality, and Freud (1927) described patients who presented two simultaneous areas of cognitive functioning, where overwhelming traumatic anxiety during childhood (loss of the father) had led to a rift or split in the ego.

## Discussion

I have tried to show how the developmental phase of adolescence with its predominant mode of acted communication is repeated during the analyses of those adult patients who present with deficiencies in the actualisation of their selves. Such conditions can manifest themselves in disturbances of the self's relationship to the other as well as in difficulties of the self in pursuing creative goals. It is my thesis that these patients in fact suffer from various degrees of foreclosure or arrest of adolescence. In clinical terminology, however, their diagnoses range from anxiety states, atypical depression, narcissistic disorders and borderline states to schizo-affective disorders.

Moreover, I have drawn attention to our adolescent patients' strong preference for acted rather than spoken communications, and I have indicated some implications for the diagnosis and treatment of this age group.

Over the last 20 years or so, analysts have studied more systematically the ego psychological processes of adolescence. Thus, the concept of the adolescent's 'acted mourning' of his meaningful childhood experiences has evolved. It has been defined as a regressive process that is in the service of consolidation of the adaptive and synthetic functions of the ego, the formation of an ego-identity, the integration of the self and self-awareness. Freud stated in 1905 that the most painful task of adolescence is the detachment from the parental authority. The ego-psychological approach to adolescence adds another dimension to this.

The adolescent not only acts out his oedipal conflicts, he also re-enacts his pre-oedipal and sometimes non-verbal and somatic infancy. He has therefore a second chance actively to master and integrate the privations, deprivations, traumatic distress, intrusions and neglect which he had been passively exposed to and suffered during his early life. Traumata of later childhood, in so far as they rendered the immature ego instantly helpless by the flooding of stimuli rather than causing an intra-psychic conflictual response, are re-enacted in a similar way. If, however, the damage has been too extensive so that sufficient intra-psychic organisational ego resources are not available, or if the environmental provisions are not good enough, this second chance is bound to fail.

According to my experience, the experiential re-enactment of the deficiencies, traumata or neglect of infancy and childhood becomes possible for the adult patient through regression to the adolescent's mode of acted communication during psycho-analytic treatment. 'Acted mourning' may then occur, fostering further regression in which the patient re-enacts the original infantile scene with the analyst. If during the course of the analysis the analyst allows time for this configuration to unfold, perhaps one could even say, if he provides for an *analytic moratorium*, the patient may be given another chance to experientially recover and so finally master and integrate those areas of his earliest history which were not available to him prior to treatment.

In this paper, I have chosen clinical material from five patients who had suffered traumata of loss, separation or somatic intrusion during their childhood. Each had dissociated the traumatic event at the time, which had resulted in splits and lacunae in the ego. Hence, they could recover the traumatic scene only through special states of consciousness.

I have tried to describe how I responded to the experiential quality of the patient's re-enactment, and how I was guided by my counter-transference reactions. In my opinion this finally allowed the patient to integrate and so actively master his trauma. Moreover, the working alliance between patient and analyst was on the whole maintained. But this was naturally dependent on the level of ego-functioning to which the patient temporarily regressed during the experiential re-enactment of the original scene. Furthermore, I have tried to illustrate how reconstruction of those traumatic events which the experiential re-enactment signified led sometimes to further re-enactment of even earlier incidents in typical adolescent creative pursuits.

I believe, however, that it is not only dissociated traumata of loss and separation that are experientially re-enacted during the analysis. Balint's concept of the 'area of basic fault' (1968), Heimann's 'passively suffered intrusions' (1966), Khan's 'cumulative trauma' (1963a) or Winnicott's 'false self' (1954) all delineate failure during infancy which lies outside the realm of infantile conflict. The relevant clinical material from adult patients with which they and many other authors have illuminated these and similar concepts (see Greenacre, 1953b; James, 1960, 1962; Little, 1951; Milner, 1969; Searles, 1965; and others) could also be interpreted as adolescent experiential re-enactment of the patient's infancy.

During such phases of re-enactment the patient relates to the analyst as a need-fulfilling part-object. Critics may say that the analyst's failure to interpret this as a transference manifestation (which it is!) is a collusion with the patient's acting out manoeuvres. I have tried to indicate how the analyst's counter-transference can be a reliable guide in differentiating between the patient's engagement in experiential re-enactment and the patient's acting out of transference wishes or instinctual tension states. If the analyst responds to re-enactment by interpreting it as a manifestation of transference resistance, he may repeat the failure of the environmental provisions during the patient's adolescent phase, and so foreclosure of adolescence with pseudo-adaptation to adulthood and impoverishment of the self may persist. If on the other hand the analyst responds to re-enactment as the patient's supplementary ego he will allow enough time for the experiential recovery of the infantile trauma to unfold, before he reconstructs the original scene. In this way he will help the patient to integrate the original experience into the self and to achieve the development of healthy narcissism. In our clinical practice, however, the analysis of the self and the analysis of transference neurosis take place side by side. The analyst interprets the patient's transference wishes whenever he judges this as the dynamically most appropriate intervention. He then aims at the recovery of infantile conflicts and interprets the defences against their recall in memory.

The development of ego psychology has widened the scope for the psycho-analytic treatment of disorders other than transference neuroses. I have tried to show that ego-psychological investigations into the developmental phase of adolescence have enlarged our understanding of analytic processes which occur in the analysis of patients suffering from disorders of the self. One might even postulate that regressive adolescent acted mourning, the experiential re-enactment of infancy, serves a function similar to that of screen memories in the discovery of repressed memories.

'Analysis has shown how the child lives on, almost unchanged, in the sick man as well as in the dreamer and the artist' (Freud, 1925). The analysis of the transference neurosis and the analysis of the self both aim at freeing the child from being locked in the patient's sickness. Psycho-analysis of the infantile neurosis, making the unconscious conscious, frees the child in man from the persisting oedipal struggles which lead to inhibitions and symptoms. Psycho-analysis of the self frees the infant in man from crippling deficiencies and the vicissitudes of neglect and so enables the self to become aware of its most personal history. The self can then actualise itself in its public encounters with the other and in the privacy of its creative pursuits.

# References

Altschul, S. (1968) 'Denial and ego arrest', *Journal of the American Psychoanalytic Association*, 16.

Balint, M. (1937) 'Early developmental states of the ego. Primary object love'. In *Primary Love and Psycho-Analytic Technique*. London: Tavistock (1965).

Balint, M. (1968) *The Basic Fault*. London: Tavistock.

Blos, P. (1962) *On Adolescence: A Psycho-Analytic Interpretation*. Glencoe, IL: The Free Press of Glencoe.

Blos, P. (1963) 'The concepts of acting-out in relation to the adolescent processes'. In Rexford, E.N. (ed.) *A Developmental Approach to Acting-Out*. Monographs of the Journal of the American Academy of Child Psychiatry, I. New York: International University Press (1966).

Blos, P. (1967) 'The second individuation process of adolescence', *Psychoanalytic Study of the Child*, 22.

Bowlby, J. (1960) 'Grief and mourning in infancy and early childhood', *Psychoanalytic Study of the Child*, 15.

Bowlby, J. (1963) 'Pathological mourning and childhood mourning', *Journal of the American Psychoanalytical Association*, 11.

Bowlby, J. (1973) *Separation Anxiety and Anger*. London: Hogarth.

Buxbaum, E. (1958) Ed. of 'Psychology of adolescence'. Panel Report. *Journal of the American Psychoanalytical Association*, 6.

Deutsch, H. (1963) 'Acting out in the transference'. In Rexford, E.N. (ed.) *A Developmental Approach to Problems of Acting Out*. Monographs of the Journal of the American Academy of Child Psychiatry, 1. New York: International University Press (1966).

Doolittle, H. (1971) *HD – Tribute to Freud*. South Hinksey, Oxford: Carcanet Press.

Eissler, K.R. (1958) 'Notes on problems of technique in the psychoanalytic treatment of adolescents: With some remarks on perversions'. *Psychoanalytic Study of the Child*, 13.

Erikson, E.H. (1956) 'The problem of ego identity', *Journal of the American Psychoanalytical Association*, 4.

Federn, P. (1932) 'Mental hygiene in the ego and schizophrenia'. In *Ego and the Psychosis*. New York: Basic Books (1952).

Federn, P. (1934) 'The awakening of the ego in dreams'. In *Ego and the Psychosis*. New York: Basic Books (1952).

Fenichel, O. (1945) 'Neurotic acting out'. In *The Collected Papers of Otto Fenichel*, Vol. II. New York: Norton Press (1954).

Fleming, J. and Altschul, S. (1963) 'Activation of mourning and growth in psychoanalysis', *International Journal of Psycho-Analysis*, 44.

Freud, A. (1952) 'Notes on a connection between the states of negativism and of emotional surrender', *International Journal of Psycho-Analysis*, 33.

Freud, A. (1958) 'Adolescence'. In *Research at the Hampstead Child-Therapy Clinic and Other Papers*. London: Hogarth (1970).

Freud, A. (1964/67) 'Comments on psychic trauma'. *Research at the Hampstead Child-Therapy Clinic and Other Papers*. London: Hogarth (1970).

Freud, A. (1968) 'Acting out', *International Journal of Psycho-Analysis*, 49.

Freud, S. (1905) 'Three essays on the theory of sexuality', SE 7.

Freud, S. (1914) 'Remembering, repeating and working through', SE 12.

Freud, S. (1915) 'Observations on transference love', SE 12.

Freud, S. (1917 [1915]) 'Mourning and melancholia', SE 14.

Freud, S. (1920) 'Beyond the pleasure principle', SE 18.

Freud, S. (1923) 'The ego and the id', SE 19.

Freud, S. (1925) 'Preface to Aichhorn's *Wayward Youth*', SE 19.

Freud, S. (1927) 'Fetishism', SE 21.

Freud, S. (1939 [1937–39]) 'Moses and monotheism', SE 23.

Freud, S. (1940a) 'An outline of psycho-analysis', SE 23.

Freud, S. (1940c) 'Splitting of the ego in the process of defence', SE 23.

Gardiner, M. (1972) *The Wolf-Man and Sigmund Freud*. London: Hogarth.

Geleerd, E.R. (1957) 'Some aspects of psychoanalytic technique in adolescence', *Psychoanalytic Study of the Child*, 12.

Geleerd, E.R. (1961) 'Some aspects of ego vicissitudes in adolescence', *Journal of the American Psychoanalytical Association*, 9.

Geleerd, E.R. (1964) 'Adolescence and adaptive regression', *Bulletin of the Menninger Clinic*, 28.

Greenacre, P. (1950) 'General problems of acting out', *Psychoanalytic Quarterly*, 14.

Greenacre, P. (1953a) 'Certain relationships between fetishism and faulty development of the body-image', *Psychoanalytic Study of the Child*, 8.

Greenacre, P. (1953b) *Trauma, Growth and Personality*. London: Hogarth.

Greenacre, P. (1957) 'The childhood of the artist. Libidinal phase development and giftedness', *Psychoanalytic Study of the Child*, 12.

Greenacre, P. (1958) 'Early physical determinants in the development of the sense of identity', *Journal of the American Psychoanalytic Association*, 6.

Greenacre, P. (1963) 'Problems of acting out in the transference relationship'. In *Emotional Growth*, Vol. II. New York: International University Press (1971).

Greenacre, P. (1967) 'The influence of infantile trauma on genetic patterns'. In *Emotional Growth*, Vol. I. New York: International University Press (1971).

Greenacre, P. (1968) 'The psychoanalytic process, transference and acting out', *International Journal of Psycho-Analysis*, 49.

Greenacre, P. (1969) 'Discussion of Dr. Galenson's paper on "The nature of thought in childhood play"'. In *Emotional Growth*, Vol. I. New York: International University Press (1971).

Heimann, P. (1950) 'On counter-transference', *International Journal of Psycho-Analysis*, 31.

Heimann, P. (1956) 'Dynamics of transference interpretations', *International Journal of Psycho-Analysis*, 37.

Heimann, P. (1960) 'Counter-transference', *British Journal of Medical Psychology*, 33.

Heimann, P. (1962) 'Notes on the anal stage', *International Journal of Psycho-Analysis*, 43.

Heimann, P. (1966) 'Comments on Dr. Kernberg's paper', *International Journal of Psycho-Analysis*, 47.

Hurn, H.T. (1970) 'Adolescent transference: A problem of the terminal phase of analysis', *Journal of the American Psychoanalytical Association*, 18.

Jacobson, E. (1961) 'Adolescent moods and the remodelling of psychic structures in adolescence', *The Psychoanalytic Study of the Child*, 16.

James, H.M. (1960) 'Premature ego-development', *International Journal of Psycho-Analysis*, 41.

James, H.M. (1962) 'Infantile narcissistic trauma', *International Journal of Psycho-Analysis*, 43.

Jones, E. (1922) 'Some problems of adolescence'. In *Papers on Psychoanalysis*. London: Baillière, Tindall and Cox (1948).

Khan, M.M.R. (1963a) 'The concept of cumulative trauma', *Psychoanalytic Study of the Child*, 13.

Khan, M.M.R. (1963b) 'Silence as communication', *Bulletin of the Menninger Clinic*, 27.

Khan, M.M.R. (1964) 'Ego distortion, cumulative trauma and the role of reconstruction in the analytic situation', *International Journal of Psycho-Analysis*, 45.

Khan, M.M.R. (1974) *The Analysis of the Self*. London: Hogarth.

Kris, E. (1952) *Psychoanalytic Explorations in Art*. New York: International University Press.

Lampl-de Groot, J. (1960) 'On adolescence', *Psychoanalytic Study of the Child*, 15.

Limentani, A. (1965) 'A re-evaluation of acting out in relation to working through', *Scientific Bulletin of the Psycho-Analytical Society*, 1.

Little, M. (1951) 'Counter-transference and the patient's response to it', *International Journal of Psycho-Analysis*, 32.

Little, M. (1960) 'Counter-transference', *British Journal of Medical Psychology*, 33.

Mann, W. (1962) (tr.) Rhapsody Opus 53. London: EMI.

Miller, D. (1969) *The Age Between*. London: Cornmarket/Hutchinson.

Milner, M. (1969) *The Hands of the Living God*. London: Hogarth.

Nunberg, H. (1931) 'The synthetic function of the ego', *International Journal of Psycho-Analysis*, 12.

Pollock, G.H. (1961) 'Mourning and adaptation', *International Journal of Psycho-Analysis*, 42.

Ritvo, S. (1972) 'Late adolescence, developmental and clinical considerations', *Psychoanalytic Study of the Child*, 26.

Root, N.N. (1957) 'A neurosis in adolescence', *Psychoanalytic Study of the Child*, 12.

Searles, H.F. (1961) 'Phases of patient and therapist interaction in the psychotherapy of chronic schizophrenia', *British Journal of Medical Psychology*, 34.

Searles, H.F. (1965) *Collected Papers on Schizophrenia and Related Subjects*. London: Hogarth.

Sklansky, M.A. (1972) Ed. of 'Indications and contraindications for the psychoanalysis of the adolescent'. Panel Report. *Journal of the American Psychoanalytical Association*, 20.

Spiegel, L.A. (1951) 'A review of contributions to the psychoanalytic theory of adolescence: Individual aspects', *Psychoanalytic Study of the Child*, 6.

Spiegel, L.A. (1958) 'Comments on the psychoanalytic psychology of adolescence', *Psychoanalytic Study of the Child*, 13.

Spotnitz, H. (1961) 'Adolescence and schizophrenia: Problems of differentiation'. In Lorand, S. and Schneer, H.I. (eds.) *Adolescents: Psychoanalytic Approach to Problems and Therapy*. New York: Paul B. Hoeber.

Strachey, J. (1962) 'Editor's Note'. In Freud, S. (1899) 'Screen memories', SE 3.

Werner, H. (1966) 'Discussion' to Peter Blos 'The concept of acting out in relation to the adolescent process'. In Rexford, E.N. (ed.) *A Developmental Approach to Acting Out*. Monographs of the Journal of the American Academy of Child Psychiatry, 1. New York: International University Press.

Winnicott, D.W. (1954) 'Metapsychological and clinical aspects of regression within the psycho-analytic set-up', *International Journal of Psycho-Analysis*, 36 (1955).

Winnicott, D.W. (1956) 'Clinical varieties of transference', *International Journal of Psycho-Analysis*, 37.

Winnicott, D.W. (1958) *Collected Papers*. London: Tavistock.

Winnicott, D.W. (1960a) 'Counter-transference', *British Journal of Medical Psychology*, 33.

Winnicott, D.W. (1960b) 'Ego distortion in terms of true and false self'. In *The Maturational Process and the Facilitating Environment*. London: Hogarth (1965).

Winnicott, D.W. (1965) *The Maturational Processes and the Facilitating Environment*. London: Hogarth.

Winnicott, D.W. (1968) 'Contemporary concepts of adolescent development and the implication for higher education'. In *Playing and Reality*. London: Tavistock (1971).

Winnicott, D.W. (1969) 'The use of an object and relating through identifications', *International Journal of Psycho-Analysis*, 50.

Winnicott, D.W. (1971) *Playing and Reality*. London: Tavistock.

## Chapter 8

# Finding a way to the child[1]

*Margaret Rustin*

Originally published in the *Journal of Child Psychotherapy* (1982) 8(2): 145–150.

I am going to describe some assessment work with the only child, a six-year-old boy, of a divorced mother.

They had been referred to the clinic by their GP who was asking for psychotherapy for mother, which had previously been recommended at another clinic, and indicating that the child's state of mind and health gave considerable cause for concern.

Mrs S. had consulted her GP about her persistent headaches and leg pains, and about Alex's hair, which was falling out. Hospital investigations suggested that all their symptoms were fundamentally psychosomatic and not organic. Some months later, mother again expressed worry about Alex, who was speaking of 'wanting to die', saying that he would use a knife, and also sleep-walking. His mother felt he was disturbed by his frequent visits to his father – agreed access was three times weekly.

When this case was first considered, we thought it likely that both mother and son might need individual therapy. The degree of somatisation was worrying, but mother's persistent search for help was also striking. We felt concerned to provide a framework in our initial contact which could help her to distinguish between her personal needs and those of Alex – we had to devise an approach which took account both of her own difficulty and of her parental worry and active concern about Alex.

We decided to offer her an exploratory consultation with a social worker to sort out whether she wanted assessment for Alex, whether a treatment might be feasible practically, and to clarify the legal situation *vis-à-vis* care and control of the boy. A consultation took place in which it was explained to her that a therapist could be available for her subsequent to an assessment of Alex, and that a decision would be taken jointly with her about what help would be appropriate for him. Our initial work was therefore

---

1 Paper originally presented to the Inter-Clinic Conference in London, October 1982, as part of a series of papers describing the work of the Tavistock Clinic, on the theme of 'Concepts of Change'.

designed to try to clarify whether there was available a parental framework of responsible concern which would provide a reliable setting for work with the child. Mrs S. accepted this approach and kept to the appointments arranged, which involved a longish gap between exploration with her and assessment of Alex because of the summer holiday period.

I offered Mrs S. two assessment sessions for Alex to be followed by a meeting between myself and her to discuss the implications of what I had observed. When I went to the waiting room to meet them, I met a very grubby-looking, somewhat plump little boy, who gave a tight and miserable impression. Mother seemed warm and supportive towards him and he came with me without demur. In my room he went straight for the materials I had put out for him – drawing things, plasticine, small figures, animals and cars, scissors etc. – and without a glance at me or the room he began to play with them. I was not sure if he listened to my explanation about my role, the two meetings we would have and so on. He took out a car and made it drive head-on into the plastic bucket which held all the toys several times, giving me a feeling of brutal impact. He then took out plasticine and seemed to consider making something, but rejected it in favour of the doll figures. An intricate non-stop game began, in which events succeeded each other at lightning speed. The original set-up was of two families, one composed of mother and a boy doll, the other of grandmother (called mother), big boy (actually the father doll) and various smaller children (called babies) and miscellaneous other adults. The smaller and larger boys were fighting throughout, with murderous intent and great viciousness.

Most of my enquiries were ignored, but Alex did tell me that the anger of the smaller boy was because he was jealous of the babies in the other family – he had no babies in his house. The murderous attacks vividly enacted, led to continuous involvement of the police, the bigger 'boy' being taken off to prison, but never actually arriving and being held there, the smaller one when he was hurt being taken off by ambulance to hospital – he did not arrive either because the scene was changing too fast for any sequence to be completed. Alex half turned to me to explain: 'He can't go to prison because he's under 21', and when the ambulance arrived he added: 'They're taking him to hospital even though he's bad!' This was said in an expressionless tone of voice. I tried to interest him in the idea that this clinic where his mum had brought him to see me might be a worrying place because he might not be sure whether it was a place for helping people who were hurt or ill or for punishing people who were bad. Alex shook his head, and said no, he didn't think so.

In the game, the membership of the family groups changed continuously, and the moral status of the combatants was volatile. Themes which reappeared were the smaller boy's protection of his mother and the intense rivalry between the two boys, which was often shown by one climbing up on top of the head and shoulders of the other, claiming superior strength and pressing, as if to push the victim down into the ground. The nature of the physical struggle was tremendously cruel, with particular attacks on each other's eyes, mouth and genitals, and full of magical acrobatic feats.

I devoted my energies to trying to follow what was happening, and this Alex seemed to want me to get clear – when I would recap a sequence to express my understanding of it, he would correct me carefully if I had misunderstood him, and in his rather clumsy speech would pause momentarily to keep me on the track. I tried to make contact with him by talking about the violence and cruelty and the rage of the doll-figures, and about the confusion everyone seemed to be struggling with – who was in which family, who was good and who was bad, who was friend and who was enemy – but the game went on relentlessly and Alex showed no interest.

I found myself reviewing my own situation in the interview: I was witness to an interminable horror-story. Death was no end, since the protagonists were continually dying but immediately leaping to their feet and carrying on. I was struggling with an immensely confusing sequence of events in which no fixed point could be established – all relationships were changing constantly. The barrage of torture, pain, hatred and fear was increasing and no framework of meaning which could make sense of why any of this was happening could be grasped. A numb state of shock and a tense doom-laden expectation of more to come predominated.

I began to talk to Alex about how frightened and despairing all of these characters must feel and as I tried to put this idea into words, I felt a slight change in his emotional state. I could observe a lessening of his muscular tension, which had, up to this point, been holding him taut and motionless except for his hand movements, and he turned in his chair a little in my direction. The relentless pace of events in the game slowed down a bit. Feeling that I had established a small area of understanding between us, I asked about things he was afraid of. He turned around and looked at me, and halting the game told me about being frightened when Mummy goes out. He feels she will be kidnapped. At night he is afraid of burglars – they want to kill him and his Mummy with a knife. They are under his bed. I asked if these were bad dreams he had and he agreed, but the borderline between the nightmare and the wide-awake phantasy of danger seemed minimal. While Alex was telling me this, he seemed to be feeling some anxiety for the first time – he took hold of the plasticine and twisted it around in his hands, not making anything, but having something to hold on to – but my main impression was of a child who had almost gone blank with fear. His face was expressionless, but as if too much had passed and nothing could any longer be transformed into communicable form. The dry facts about terror were all that was left. I felt it was important for me to go on talking to him, and to speak quietly and slowly, and to try to create a frame for the experiences of this session, so I talked about the clinic as a place where children could talk about fears and worries, his need for me to understand about how frightened he was, and explained that we would arrange with Mummy in the waiting room at the end of the session for him to come and see me again next week, when he and I could talk some more about this and think about what would help him. He nodded intently. I talked to him about his mind being completely full of the things he had been showing me, leaving no room for anything else, and at this point his face seemed to show a glimmer of sadness and I experienced him as extremely vulnerable. After he had packed the toys away, I found myself to my surprise asking if he would like to wash his hands – he was dreadfully grubby, and seemed to enjoy his perfunctory rinse and wipe, and I was left pondering the very concrete impact that his appeal for care had made on me.

When we returned upstairs to the waiting room he wanted to turn his back on me very quickly and get back to school. When his mother brought him for the second interview a week later, I noticed there was a man accompanying them; Alex made no reference to him although he is mother's co-habitee of some months' standing.

The session began in a very similar vein. The cruelty escalated, with overt torture seeming now to be the aim of each of the two boys – not just to be the winner but to inflict extremes of pain and humiliation on the other. The desperation of each contender to be on top was also intensified, and the acrobatic feats attempted were of Superman proportions, and Alex spoke of both Superman and Spiderman when describing what was going on. The mother figure was now less protected from the violence, and got more and more involved on one side and the other.

A new theme emerged – Alex built a prison of plasticine where the three main figures were placed and detained by being dug deep into the plasticine – half buried, in fact – and he spoke of the huge weights on their feet and hands which were to prevent them escaping. When they did so, they were returned and the weights increased. This seemed a very vivid enactment of his experience of being deeply stuck in all these preoccupations and in despair about being able to free himself. The repetitious and doomed attempts to get free seemed an eloquent plea for an intervention which would allow some new element in, and betoken the possibility of change. For although the pell-mell activity continued, creating an illusion of speedy change and excitement, the overall impression grew of a quite deathly and timeless stasis, which would absorb whole lifetimes and beyond.

I began to talk again and said to Alex that I thought he needed to come to the clinic to see someone who would help him to think about all these frightening ideas that he felt stuck with. I explained that I would discuss this with Mummy, that I thought she wanted him to have this kind of help, and that I hoped we could then arrange for him to come regularly. I explained again that he would not be seeing me, but that I would find someone who could work with him here.

All this took some time to convey, and as he took it in, he stopped his game and took out a black pen and began to draw. He drew a picture of White Land, which he connected with space and the moon. This seemed to be a good place that he was going to travel to, but very speedily the paper began to fill with all kinds of elaborate weaponry to deal with the attackers who were expected. He talked quite easily to me about all this. I was interested both by the content of this picture, but even more so by the change in mode of communication – it seemed to me that when I had managed to create for him an idea of a clinic that was here to deal with his sort of worries, and that he experienced as real in so far as he felt me to be in touch with him, a fresh hope had kindled that there might be some good place that he could reach in his imagination. One might liken this to a baby waking up in a miserable persecuted frame of mind but nonetheless able to respond to the care offered by mother and to recognise her as something he was seeking. In Alex's situation, the care he requires seems particularly to be connected with being able to deal with a great deal of dirt felt as immensely powerful and blocking him off from anything more alive. He reminded me of the sort of baby who cannot possibly settle to feed or look around him until his dirty nappy has been dealt with. At the end of the second session, I was interested to note that he went to the basin in my room to wash, indicating his memory of the sequence of the earlier session, but initiating it himself.

In this case, the external frame for treatment of the child was in fact a solid one – despite grave personal difficulties for which mother is seeking help, she is able to be thoughtfully aware of her son's problems and is prepared to engage in treatment despite quite long journeys and father's opposition. She has some support in this from her boyfriend whom she brought with her to meet me and discuss Alex.

In the child's internal world, there is little evidence of a thinking frame which can help him to encompass his very complicated and confusing experiences. It has all been far too great a strain on an immature mind; in his real experiences his father invites him into a perverse collusion against mother, and his mother by her confused identification with his distress has been unable to provide any adult boundaries to protect him appropriately. However, in the assessment interviews, there is evidence that Alex could make use of a containing framework when I found a way to convey such a conception to him. I think this becomes a meaningful experience for him because I survived a degree of immersion in his nightmare world but emerged able to talk to him, so that he knew that I understood where he was.

Now I want to consider the experience I had with Alex in terms of my approach to the assessment of children for psychotherapy. The setting I offered was designed to make it possible for him to communicate with me about his inner world. This particular child's most urgent statement to me was not to be found in the content of his play and conversation but in the demonstration that the interviews provided of the monolithic character of his preoccupations. He was unable to respond to any ordinary enquiries about himself, what he liked, school, friends and so on. The world in which he might be said to be living if one looked at it from outside was in fact being crucially shaped by the powerful phantasies of his internal world which occupied his entire mental space. The impoverishment of his capacity to make contact with reality was the result of an as-yet uncontained phantasy life. One detail of the play in the second session relates to this particularly – in the plasticine prison, huge lumps of plasticine were fashioned into weights on the prisoners' heads which also covered their eyes, so that they existed in a world of darkness which could not be penetrated, and they had no functional perceptual apparatus for seeing.

Talking with his mother amplified this picture – she described how he was viewed at school as being in a world of his own, how unable he was to learn despite his teachers' conviction of his intelligence; also the nature of his play with other children – they had to play his games, which were always to do with death, and mother could describe how he successfully bullied his companions into the roles he designed for them. He was always the goody in these games, often with superhuman capacities, identified with one of the super-heroes as he had shown me, since only characters like them had a chance against the forces of omnipotent destruction of which he was so fearful.

The assessment I made was intended both to inform me of this child's situation in terms of emotional development and capacity for experience and to give me some indication as to whether change might be facilitated by a clinical intervention. For this reason, the technique I use in assessing children has elements of the attitude I would adopt in an on-going treatment setting, for I want to explore what use the child seems able to make of me and an unstructured interview. Whilst not interpreting any personal transference that I observe, I would want to test out the child's openness to linking comments, drawing together different aspects of what he shows me. I also find it important to keep a close eye on the emotional impact the child makes on me, and to think about the implications of this counter-transference evidence in coming to conclusions about treatability. In other words, I am using the assessment process to review the possibility of change in a patient being facilitated by a therapeutic setting and relationship. So the concepts of change which inform psychoanalytic psychotherapy also permeate my initial contact with a child although there are many important differences too.

The sessions with Alex demonstrated a very rudimentary capacity in him to form a relationship. Most of the time, I felt myself not experienced as another person in the room with him at all. Nor did he seem to feel he was in my room nor that the toys put out for him had been arranged by me.

However, what took place did indicate to me that at a much more primitive level he was aware of a need to be listened to and kept in mind, and he was able to elicit in me a sense of how to manage the situation for him in a way which would give him an idea that I could know about what filled his thoughts and nonetheless, by my attitude, by the way I talked to him, give him an experience of my mind as able to contain my experience with him within a larger framework. He felt the super-heroes were his only hope but he seemed able to perceive that a grown-up ally might be some use.

## POSTSCRIPT

This paper was originally framed by a parallel one 'Finding a way to the parents' and this perhaps explains its particular emphasis on the individual sessions with the child, with somewhat less attention to history and context than we might expect.

It is also interesting to note the absence of explicit theorisation and the assumption that a carefully described clinical case adequately demonstrates the mode of thinking employed by child psychotherapists. In later writing about assessment, one would find reference to theoretical models, since the earlier structures of child guidance work have been replaced by much more complex multi-disciplinary teams and multi-modal forms of assessment. Clarifying the importance of detailed observation, of the use of the counter-transference, of the stability of the setting, and of team consultation would be attempted, and the theoretical base in the understanding of unconscious phantasy and internal object relationships would be explicated. The diverse forms of patient/therapist communication in a clinical interview would be described and evaluated.

Readers are referred to Lanyado and Horne (1999) and Rustin and Quagliata (2000) for an up-to-date look at assessment. Nonetheless, the continuity in clinical thinking and practice is evident in this paper and the immediacy of the child's play holds one's attention. The vitality of case presentation as a primary mode of scientific discourse remains impressive.

*April 2003*

## Postscript references

Lanyado, M. and Horne, A. (1999) *The Handbook of Child Psychotherapy*. London: Routledge.

Rustin, M. and Quagliata, E. (2000) *Assessment in Child Psychotherapy*. London: Duckworth.

# Chapter 9

# Solving the mystery of monsters: Steps towards the recovery from trauma[1]

*Juliet Hopkins*

Originally published in the *Journal of Child Psychotherapy* (1986) 12(1): 61–71.

Freud wrote in 1909 that 'a thing which has not been understood inevitably reappears; like an unlaid ghost it cannot rest until the mystery has been solved and the spell broken.'

This paper is concerned with solving the mystery and breaking the spell which binds children who have become the victims of trauma. It illustrates how psychotherapy can free children from the worst effects of trauma by enabling them to accept both the reality of the traumatic event and of the feelings which it aroused. In this way both these elements of the traumatic experience can be integrated and a start made in the process of recovery. I give examples from the psychotherapy of two children and consider the stages by which recovery from trauma takes place, and discuss the role of the child psychotherapist in facilitating it.

In defining trauma I follow Freud's statement of 1926: 'The essence of a traumatic situation is an experience of helplessness on the part of the ego in the face of accumulation of excitation, whether of external or internal origin.' This definition links the specific external event with internal psychic conditions and indicates the shattering, devastating and generally overwhelming effect of a trauma. Spontaneous recovery from such an event is possible, though commonly subsequent development is altered and takes a pathological course, as it did in the case of the two children whose clinical material I want to present. These children had both been subjected to recurrent traumas from their earliest years. They both had serious learning difficulties, and they were both preoccupied with monsters to the exclusion of all other interests. But I have selected them mainly because of the different response to trauma which each represents: one child retained detailed knowledge of the traumas but had no awareness that these events had been the cause of any suffering; the other child had retained no conscious knowledge of the traumas but remained overwhelmed by the distressing emotions which these events had aroused.

---

1 This paper was presented at the ACP Study Weekend in March 1986.

## (1) Psychotherapy with Adam

Adam was referred to our clinic at the age of eight years because he could not read in spite of good intelligence (Hopkins, 1977). He had an encyclopaedic knowledge of dinosaurs and monsters, but otherwise was uninterested in learning. He was unhappy and bullied at school. At home he spent his time playing with models of dinosaurs and drawing endless pictures of imaginary monsters. His parents, who were concerned and caring people, complained of his apathy and felt there was 'a certain meanness' about his emotions.

Adam had been born with a hereditary blood disease which made him pale, weak and anaemic and which required transfusions every few months. His parents were told he might not survive. As an infant he found weekly blood tests and regular transfusions extremely distressing, and his mother always stayed with him in hospital. However, when he was just four years old, he responded to reassuring explanations about his treatment by becoming completely confident, and he no longer appeared to need his mother in hospital. From this time onward he rejected physical cuddling and became very independent and self-reliant. His parents proudly reported that he had been very brave about a major abdominal operation at the age of seven years. When I met Adam at the age of eight years he described hospital as his favourite place. He knew all about his unusual illness and its treatment and was devoted to the doctors who had saved his life.

In the first of his once-weekly psychotherapy sessions, Adam told me about his eager co-operation in medical research and his 'best Christmas ever', spent in hospital. At the same time he was modelling a dinosaur which fell into a caveman's trap, and was eaten alive slowly, starting at the tail. He said that luckily the dinosaur didn't feel much because it was very insensitive. I acknowledged Adam's eager wish to co-operate with me too, but I thought his play revealed fears that I would deceive and attack him, just as he must have felt the kind doctors had done with their horrible treatment. I also compared the dinosaur's insensitivity to the way Adam appeared to have become insensitive to the distress which he could have been expected to feel about a chronic illness and its treatment.

Adam was interested in my ideas and showed me in drawings what his imaginary monsters were like. Each one aimed to deceive its prey. For example, if you protected yourself from its dangerous mouth it would be its tail which hid a lethal sting. Some monsters had snouts like drills which penetrated underground and tapped veins of gold which they stole. I thought that these monsters transparently disguised Adam's fears of treacherous attack and his dread of doctor's needles which penetrated his veins and stole his precious blood. Adam had apparently become a perfect patient at the cost of losing conscious awareness of his feelings about his treatment. His dread of doctors had been displaced on to monsters.

In the course of Adam's therapy with me which lasted nearly two years, he gradually re-experienced his anxiety, anger and distress about his illness and its treatment. This occurred first in the transference when Adam broke into violent rebellion against his psychotherapy, claiming that it was very unfair and unkind that he should have been picked on to have this sort of treatment, and begging instead for more physical treatment at the hospital.

It was in the second year of Adam's therapy that he gradually became painfully aware that cruel fate had picked on him to suffer a chronic illness and to endure endless physical treatment for it. He became intensely persecuted about it and also very depressed. His realisation of the trauma was so distressing for him it was hard for me to believe that it could be of any benefit for him to face such a stark reality. I felt as though I myself had been responsible for traumatising him. Gradually he changed from feeling crushed by the realisation to lamenting his fate and to becoming angry about it. In his play he openly identified with savage monsters seeking revenge. He was very frightened of expressing his anger openly to me or at home, but little by little he took courage to do so with his parents, and finally exploded into violent tantrums which he hadn't had since he was very small.

When Adam rediscovered his anger he also rediscovered his early love for his parents which he hadn't expressed since he was four years old. He became cuddly and affectionate, lost his preoccupation with monsters, developed other interests, and began to learn well in school. His emotional 'meanness' had gone, and he had become able, to a limited extent, to think about his illness and its implications as a chronic misfortune and handicap in his life. For example, he groaned at the prospect of always being seen to be different from other children because he couldn't play games, and he resented the need to explain his condition, in contrast to the way in which he used to be proud to be special.

## (2) Psychotherapy with Sylvia

Sylvia was referred to our clinic at the age of six years because she was hyperactive, unmanageable and unable to learn, in spite of receiving special education at a school for maladjusted children. She had been previously assessed as borderline psychotic (Hopkins, 1984). Sylvia, like Adam, was obsessed with monsters. She constantly talked of them and dramatised attacks both on them and by them. Much of the detail of her monster play derived from the TV series *Dr Who*.

Sylvia's history was related by her widowed mother, a defensive young Italian woman who supplied only the barest details and made no mention of the traumas which she later confessed. She said that Sylvia had screamed endlessly as a baby and had thrown violent tantrums as a toddler. She was so backward when she started nursery school that she was thought to be mentally retarded. Her father had died in a car crash shortly before her fourth birthday and her behaviour had become increasingly unmanageable after this event.

In therapy, Sylvia quickly became extremely messy and aggressive, attacking me constantly in the role of a monster and enacting fantasies in which she herself was attacked by a variety of monsters too. She called the furniture 'Daleks' and seemed convinced that chairs moved across the room to strike her, causing her to duck and cower in terror. As treatment progressed Sylvia increasingly demanded that I should act the part of terrifying monsters who pursued her with roars and threatened to eat her up. 'Be a Dalek', 'Be a carpet monster' or 'Be a light-switch monster', she said. By making me enact the monsters I thought she was trying to localise and control her terror of being attacked. But this stratagem was never wholly successful for she often screamed out in terror that a chair, a light or an unseen monster was attacking her; at such moments she seemed to be hallucinated.

I first interpreted one of her dramas as an attempt to communicate the past when she told me, 'Be a cross dream!' She made herself a bed and hid under the blanket. 'Roar!' she shouted. When I did, she asked, 'Are you a real mummy? Are you a daddy too?' 'Yes' I said. 'Speak Italian then!' said Sylvia. 'I'm Never-Mind-Boy in bed. I'm not Sylvia. Sylvia was too frightened.' I said she was trying to remember what it was like when she was little and her mummy and daddy had terrible rows in Italian and she had been too frightened to bear it. Sylvia was moved by my reconstruction and wanted me to tell her more about what had happened in the past. At this stage of her treatment, during part of each session she would repeatedly enact a drama in a particularly urgent manner. I understood this as a request for me to reconstruct past events, which were at first more rows between her fighting parents. Sylvia now claimed to remember their fights. 'Dad beat my mummy up,' she said with conviction.

Soon Sylvia voiced more memories of her own. One session when she asked me, 'Be a fierce daddy monster and frighten me very much,' I said I thought she was trying to remember how she had been frightened of her own fierce daddy. Sylvia suddenly looked at me with great amazement and said, 'My dad broke up our house! It was another house. He threw all the furniture.' She was perplexed about where this event had happened, and I told her I knew she had lived with her dad in a different house which her family left just before he died.

Sylvia's vivid recollection of her father throwing furniture helped me to understand her terrors of flying Dalek furniture and her own need to fling the furniture herself. She quickly responded to interpretation about her wish to throw furniture in order to terrify me, so that I would know how she had felt when her father did it. As a result, she lost her terror of being attacked by furniture and also stopped throwing it.

In her role of Never-Mind-Boy Sylvia then began to think increasingly about the past. Just as her recollection of her father throwing furniture had laid the Dalek monsters to rest, so her recollection that her father had died in a car accident, collecting a carpet, led to the disappearance of her need to make me attack her dressed as a 'carpet monster'. Sylvia's attacks on the lights in my room and her terror of the 'light-switch monster' seemed related to her intense fear of the dark and her almost equal fear of turning on the light to reveal her monster parents fighting together. Discussion of these fears stopped Sylvia's attacks on the lights, and the light-switch monster also disappeared. She no longer seemed to be hallucinated.

In 1937 Freud reached the conclusion that there is 'not only method in madness but also a fragment of historical truth.' He wrote: 'Perhaps it may be a general characteristic of hallucinations, to which sufficient attention has not hitherto been paid, that in them something that has been experienced in infancy and then forgotten returns.'

After I had reconstructed some of the forgotten events which had kept returning to Sylvia in the disguise of monsters, she began to bring happier memories about her father. She liked to sit on top of my cupboard because it was 'just like riding on my daddy's back.' She told me with delight how she could now remember going to the park with her daddy and paddling with him in the pool. Sylvia was then in touch with her love for her friendly father as well as with her hatred and fear of her fierce and angry father. Following this she grew openly depressed and cried recurrently as she genuinely mourned the dad she had loved as well as feared and hated. Before this she had dealt with his death by disavowal.

It was a whole year after Sylvia had shared her memories of her father's violence with me, that her mother at last confirmed these memories by confessing that her husband had thrown furniture in his rages and had broken the arms off the chairs. She also confessed that he had beaten Sylvia frequently and had thrown her across the room. When Sylvia was a screaming baby he had kicked both mother and daughter out of the house, or else he would have killed Sylvia. His violence outside the home had led him into serious trouble with the police.

The effect on Sylvia of recalling her traumatic experiences with her father was dramatic. She became much more manageable and was able to talk about what angered her. She was no longer possessed by preoccupation with monsters but began to develop other play themes, to draw pictures and to talk about them. At school she became sufficiently in touch with reality to learn, and after completing two years of twice-weekly psychotherapy she was able to transfer to a school for normal children.

## The meaning of monsters

The course of each of these children's psychotherapy illustrates Freud's idea (1920) that compulsive repetition in children's play is a means of mastering anxieties associated with trauma. It also illustrates a possible meaning of monsters.

For both Adam and Sylvia, monsters appeared to represent a compromise between their terrors of real aggressive assaults and terrors related to their own aggressive impulses. This is likely to be the case whenever a repetitive preoccupation with monsters is concerned. In practice it means that details of monsters can often give us clues to the people or events which have aroused the terror and rage which the monsters represent.

## Stages in the recovery from trauma

Adam and Sylvia were both freed from their repetitive pre-occupation with monsters by recognising the traumas which the monsters had disguised. The analytic work had provided the understanding which solved the mystery, laid the ghosts and broke the spell. But revealing the monster's disguise was only a step in the children's recognition of the underlying traumas. Such recognition involves both a cognitive and an emotional awareness, it proceeds slowly and it is hard to say at what stage, if ever, it is complete.

Adam was interested, during his very first session, in my idea that his monsters might be doctors; he soon brought more material to amplify this view which he easily came to accept. However, it was not until the second year of his therapy, after he had re-lived the persecutory aspect of his medical treatment with me in the transference, that he could get in touch with his feelings about the suffering which he had undergone. He had of course known about the fact of his illness and his need for medical treatment as long as he could remember, but it now came as a terrible shock to him to realise that cruel fate had discriminated against him and had not simply made him uniquely special as he had supposed.

The shocking realisation that a congenital illness or a handicap is a catastrophe is an occurrence in the lives of many handicapped children. For example, Anna Freud (1967) has described how traumatic the discovery of blindness can be to a congenitally blind child. For Adam, the shock of acknowledging his handicap was followed by a retreat to bed for more than two weeks with flu, but it was after his recovery from this apparent set-back that he gained the freedom to express both his love and his anger and started to learn in school.

Sylvia's first acknowledgement of the reality of the traumas which she had endured was achieved through my reconstructions of the violence in her past. Reconstruction effectively gave her permission, in a safe setting, to recall and share what she already knew but was not supposed to know. The analytic literature (e.g. Bowlby, 1985; Khan, 1972; Rosen, 1955; Tonnesmann, 1980) suggests that the therapist's ability to construct external events is of particular importance when the patient has taken psychotic flight from reality, or when important adults in the patient's life have put a tabu on knowing. In both these conditions, which applied to Sylvia, the therapist risks colluding with the patient's defences if he treats the traumatic events only as fantasies. He may also risk repeating the behaviour of the original traumatogenic adult, for, as Balint (1969) points out, it is common for an adult who has traumatised a child to behave afterwards as though nothing had happened.

For both children, the intellectual and emotional acknowledgement of trauma achieved during therapy resulted in the significant improvements in their development already reported. However, in many respects the improvements were very limited. When therapy ended, Adam remained a passive, subdued boy, no longer bullied at school, but still without friends. Sylvia was still a borderline psychotic child, preoccupied with violence. A further limitation to their improvement was shown by both children's continuing propensity to repeat their traumas, a tendency which has been considered to be diagnostic of a traumatised child.

Adam's need to repeat his traumas was demonstrated by his voluntary submission to experimental medical procedures. Although he became very resentful of his illness and recognised his fear of doctors, he remained devoted to the medical team at the hospital where he was treated. He willingly continued to volunteer as a guinea pig in medical research and to submit himself to further painful investigations. The manner in which he described his collaboration suggested that he took a masochistic pleasure in his submission to experiments. It seemed likely that masochism might remain a significant feature in his pathology, as it has been found to be in some victims of medical and surgical assault in early childhood (Glenn, 1984). However, there were also other motives in Adam's participation as guinea-pig. His willing co-operation allowed him a sense of mastery and control over the inevitable, he was proud of his courage, won the admiration of doctors and nurses and aimed to help to discover a cure for his disease.

Sylvia's continuing propensity to repeat her traumas was manifest in her persistent provocation of violence. She did this recurrently in her treatment with me where her assaults taxed my patience to the limits and made it extremely hard to resist retaliation. She also provoked her mother repeatedly at home. Her mother confessed that she was driven to being brutal to her, and no doubt this meant that she was colluding in recreating Sylvia's early traumatic experiences. However, at school Sylvia gave up her provocative behaviour. She stopped attacking her teacher and the other children and ceased to be constantly involved in fights.

Neither Adam nor Sylvia was successfully freed from the aftermath of trauma. In order to recover more fully than they were able to do, children need to accept not only the reality of the traumatic events and the feelings which they engendered, but to become able to grieve about the damage done to them and to express appropriate anger about this. Adam was able to do this to some extent as far as his congenital illness was concerned, but not with regard to his medical treatment. Sylvia's initial acknowledgement of her trauma was followed by a phase of active mourning, but this was due to her new capacity to recognise the death of her father and to weep for him. She never reached the point of recognising what harm her father had done to her and she never became able to grieve for her misfortune in having had a father who had battered her and a mother who had failed to protect her. By the time that treatment ended she had reached the point of recognising that she felt psychologically damaged and in danger of becoming mad, but she blamed me for it. '*You* broke me. *You* tore me apart,' she said, and she took revenge on me by threatening suicide and by making renewed assaults.

At this stage of psychotherapy, Sylvia had moved beyond the initial feelings of terror and rage evoked by the trauma to an emotional recognition of the damage which had been done to her. In the transference, she attributed the cause of the damage to me, because I had put her in touch with it. Much further work would have been needed to enable her to recognise where the blame belonged, to grieve for her terrible misfortune, to achieve some detachment from it and to relinquish the past sufficiently to prevent the need to re-enact it in the present. The initial intellectual and emotional recognition of trauma is only the beginning of a very long and painful process of working through. Only if this process is successful can a patient finally experience grief and anger for what has happened, and then detachment and relinquishment.

Both Adam's and Sylvia's psychotherapy had ended prematurely, after about two years, at their parents' insistence. More treatment would probably have helped them further, but it remains debatable whether recovery from severe infantile traumas, like Adam's and Sylvia's, can ever be complete. Greenacre (1953) maintains that no truly traumatic event is ever wholly assimilated and that increased vulnerability inevitably remains, predisposing the individual to break down at some later date if faced with some repetition or near repetition of the original injury. In the case of an on-going trauma, like Adam's illness and its treatment, from which there is no escape, the question of a complete recovery cannot exist. After the traumatic impact of the initial realisation of the chronic catastrophe, there can be a period of assimilation and recovery, as Adam demonstrated, but he was bound to have to experience further traumatic crises as he faced the implications of his handicap for each new developmental stage. Although the social implications of his chronic illness were likely to become increasingly distressing, his medical treatment should have lost the monstrous qualities which it had for him as a very young child.

## The role of parents

Parents frequently contribute to the original trauma and always influence the course of their child's recovery.

In a review of psychoanalytic literature of trauma, Balint (1969) concluded that not one of the childhood traumas reported had occurred according to the model of a railway accident. On the contrary, 'there existed a close and intimate relationship between the child and the adult who inflicted the trauma upon him', so violating the child's love and trust.

Even when parents are not the direct psychological cause of a trauma, as Adam's parents were not, probably they never escape blame in the child's mind. At the most basic level they have failed to protect the child from harm and have violated his trust in their omnipotence. Often, and probably always in the case of very young children, the trauma becomes attributed to the parents in the child's fantasies. For example, Adam went through a long period in therapy in which the monster doctors had clearly become monster parents who cruelly attacked him or else abandoned him while they fought each other. Another example is provided in Anny Katan's account (1973) of the analysis of six women who had been raped in childhood. All but one of these women in fantasy attributed the rapes to their innocent fathers.

Whereas children may *feel* their parents to have been responsible for the occurrence of traumas, there is no doubt that parents *are* at least partly responsible for determining the outcome of their children's reactions to these overwhelming events. Several authors have pointed out that many children do recover from truly traumatic experiences, given adequate environmental support. However, Adam's parents had inadvertently encouraged the repression of his distress about his hospitalisation and treatment by their appeals to him to be calm and reasonable. Sylvia's mother had encouraged her flight from reality by her refusal to mention Sylvia's father or to acknowledge his violence. Regular casework at the clinic helped Adam's parents to feel less guilty about his hereditary illness and so to be more tolerant of his distress about it as this emerged during therapy. Similar help for Sylvia's mother freed her to lift the tabu on speaking to Sylvia about her father and his violence. Changes in their parents' attitudes were beneficial to both children, although the crucial changes in the children's own attitudes were independently achieved by them in their psychotherapy. It was their own understanding of the meaning of monsters which solved the mystery and broke the spell of repetition.

## The therapist's role in helping children to understand external reality

The remainder of this paper focuses on the technical issue of the therapist's role in enabling children to recognise traumatic or adverse aspects of external reality, when these adverse aspects are contributed by their parents. I am not thinking only of the blatantly traumatic effects of physical or sexual abuse, but also of the less dramatic but damaging influences of, for example, parental mental illness or of rejection and scapegoating of the child. Evidently the first step in giving a child a minimum of protection or of autonomy from these adverse influences is for him to recognise what is happening to him.

Children have strong inclinations not to notice their parents' deficiencies. Their loyalty to the parents they love and their wishes for perfect parents are both very strong, and so is their susceptibility to pressure from their parents to be seen in a favourable light. In addition, young children have not achieved the experience or objectivity necessary to know that relationships could be different, let alone to be able to see their parents as people with their own problems. All this means that it is significantly harder for children than for adolescents to become aware of parental pathology or neglect, and the younger the child the harder the task.

The central aim of the work of child psychotherapists has always been to analyse the transference so that children are enabled to discriminate between their own projections, their introjection of their parents' projections and their parents' actual contributions. Melanie Klein clearly illustrated how effective this can be, particularly when, as can be the case, children's internal parents are more sadistic and severe than their actual parents are. Adam provides an obvious example of a child who became able to express and enjoy affection with his parents, only after therapy had helped him to discriminate between his cruel internal monster parents and his real parents who had always done their best to help him. It can prove harder to help children to give up idealised versions of their internal parents in order to recognise monstrous behaviour in their actual parents.

I have found in my clinical experience that therapy may often get stuck at the point where a child clings to his internal, subjective, egocentric view of an external problem and steadily resists a more objective appraisal. This impasse can occur because the child prefers to feel responsible for, even guilty about, an external situation which he can control within the ambit of his omnipotence, rather than to admit his helplessness in the face of an intolerable reality. Looking back, I now wonder whether I have sometimes colluded with a child in turning a blind eye to painful aspects of external reality, while hoping that the issues could be sufficiently disentangled within the transference to enable the child to make the necessary changes in perception himself. This process of disentanglement can be extremely slow, even in adolescents.

A typical example of the length of this process concerns my work with a child, Alison, who needed three years of three times weekly psychotherapy before she at last recognised that her mother was in some respects mad. Alison was by then nine years old. Before this she had clung to her mother's view that she herself was crazy and so was entirely responsible for provoking her mother's unpredictable and impossible behaviour. Alison's new capacity to conceptualise her relationship with her mother in a more objective manner freed her from feeling enslaved by her mother and enabled her to contemplate going to boarding school with some relief.

The question arises whether child psychotherapists can accelerate the slow course of their work by providing children with help in understanding their families. It is part of the tradition of work at the Anna Freud Clinic to give children such explanations if necessary, in conjunction with traditional analytic work. A good example of this approach is presented in a paper by Hurry and Sandler (1971) in which they described how a four-year-old boy was helped to understand some aspects of his mother's rejection of him and of her mental illness. They emphasised the importance of very careful timing in this work, in order not to provide the child with 'a magical defensive formula' but to free him to achieve some autonomy. The same paper also described the work of helping an 11-year-old girl to disentangle herself from her parents' projections and to resist being cast in the role of family scapegoat.

More recently, and working within a different tradition, using concepts derived from the work of Bion, Emanuel (1984) has described his work with a three-year-old boy who had suffered from 'the primary disappointment' of having parents who had failed to meet 'his innate expectations'. He talked with the boy about his real parents' incapacity and felt that it was essential to have acknowledged how they had failed him in infancy in order to show that as therapist he could bear the pain of knowing about it and therefore that it was bearable and could be understood.

Such interventions can do more than indicate that the unbearable is both knowable and bearable. When well timed they make sense to the child and enable previously unrelated data to be integrated in a new conceptual framework. They can free children from unnecessary feelings of guilt and responsibility and make it more possible to cope with external reality. All these factors help to mitigate the pain and shock with which the child's new perception of his parents may be associated. They also help to mitigate the pain for the child's therapist. Exposing a child to starkly distressing aspects of reality can easily make the therapist feel guilty and responsible. There were certainly many moments in the treatment of both Adam and Sylvia when I wondered if I should have left well alone. It seems that helping a child to recover from trauma is liable to involve the therapist not only in sharing the pain but in suffering grave doubts about whether facing pain so starkly is necessary, and whether the self-protection of turning a blind eye may be preferable. Recognition that suffering such doubts is a feature of the psychotherapeutic work with traumatised children may help to make the work more tolerable.

## References

Balint, M. (1969) 'Trauma and object relationship', *International Journal of Psycho-analysis*, 50: 429–435.

Bowlby, J. (1985) 'The role of childhood experience in cognitive disturbance'. In Mahoney, M.J. and Freeman, A. (eds.) *Cognition and Psychotherapy*. New York: Plenum.

Emanuel, R. (1984) 'Primary disappointment', *Journal of Child Psychotherapy*, 10: 71–88.

Freud, A. (1967) 'Comments on trauma'. In Furst, S. (ed.) *Psychic Trauma*. New York: Basic Books.

Freud, S. (1909) 'Analysis of a phobia in a five-year-old boy', SE 10: 122.

Freud, S. (1920) 'Beyond the pleasure principle', SE 18.

Freud, S. (1926) 'Inhibitions, symptoms and anxiety', SE 20.

Freud, S. (1937) 'Constructions in analysis', SE 22: 267.

Glenn, J. (1984) 'Psychic trauma and masochism', *Journal of American Psychoanalytical Association*, 32: 2.

Greenacre, P. (1953) *Trauma, Growth and Personality*. London: Hogarth.

Hopkins, J. (1977) 'Living under the threat of death. The impact of a congenital illness on an eight-year-old boy', *Journal of Child Psychotherapy*, 4: 5–24.

Hopkins, J. (1984) 'The probable role of trauma in a case of foot and shoe fetishism: aspects of the psychotherapy of a six-year-old girl', *International Review of Psychoanalysis*, 11: 79–91.

Hurry, A. and Sandler, J. (1971) 'Coping with reality: the child's defences against the external world', *British Journal of Medical Psychology*, 44: 379.

Katan, A. (1973) 'Children who were raped', *Psychoanalytic Study of the Child*, 28: 208–224.

Khan, M.M.R. (1972) 'Exorcism of intrusive ego-alien factors in the analytic situation and process. In *The Privacy of the Self*. London: Hogarth (1974).

Rosen, V.H. (1955) 'The reconstruction of a traumatic childhood event in a case of derealization', *Journal of American Psychoanalytical Association*, 3: 211–221.

Tonnesmann, M. (1980) 'Adolescent re-enactment, trauma and reconstruction', *Journal of Child Psychotherapy*, 6: 23–44.

## POSTSCRIPT

In retrospect, this paper gave too much significance to the role of insight and understanding in the resolution of trauma. Although I had to tolerate and contain much negative emotion as my two child patients worked through their traumas, I failed to realise how much this containment itself must have contributed to their recovery. At the time that I wrote the paper, Boston and Szur (1983) had already recently reported that containment reduced the compulsion for repetition in very deprived children. Since then clinical evidence in support of this view has become overwhelming.

Many traumatised children entering psychotherapy are unready and unable to confront their past. They may benefit from spending long periods in which they communicate their inchoate and unprocessed experience through compulsive repetition in the here-and-now. It is the therapist's capacity to tolerate, contain and process these negative experiences without joining the dance of rejection, retaliation, humiliation and helplessness that enables children to move beyond the need for re-enactment and to discover that relationships with adults are less frightening than they had believed. Perhaps Freud (1909) was right to suppose that ghosts of the past can never fully rest until they have been understood, but meanwhile the therapist's capacity for containment can reduce the pressure to repeat the past and so allow new relationships to develop.

*January 2003*

## Postscript references

Boston, M. and Szur, R. (eds.) (1983) *Psychotherapy with Severely Deprived Children*. London: Routledge & Kegan Paul.
Freud, S. (1909) 'Analysis of a phobia in a five-year-old boy', SE 10: 122.

# Part 3

# Mainly applied

# Introduction

The papers in the preceding section vividly illustrate the clinical practice that has always been at the heart of the work of the child psychotherapist. At the same time it has also long been recognised that this approach will only ever reach a small proportion of the child population who might benefit from it, and that for a variety of reasons, there will always be some for whom it is not appropriate.

This does not mean, of course, that psychoanalytic insights, derived from clinical work, might not be applied in a wider setting and thus be of benefit to this larger population. In the papers that follow we can see that an interest in extending the work in this way has been present from the very early days of the profession.[1]

It is striking, however, that what has proved to be particularly valuable in this context are not the findings to have emerged in respect of work with particular clinical groups. Rather, what *has* been applied is the understanding that has been acquired in two main areas. The first of these is the more detailed appreciation of the factors that promote healthy psychological development in the individual; the second, closely linked to this, is our understanding of the elements of the psychoanalytic process that contribute to making this (and, by extension, other human encounters) potentially therapeutic.

Central to the former is the notion that, as Menzies Lyth (1985, this volume) describes,

> Healthy development depends greatly on the availability of appropriate models of individuals, relationships and situations for . . . identification.

She goes on to note that such models realise their importance through the way in which they are internalised: 'development . . . takes place through

---

1 Other early examples of this interest in applied work appear in the 'Colloquium: Hospital Care of the Newborn', *Journal of Child Psychotherapy*, 1981, 7(2).

introjective identification'. She emphasises the contrast between this form of genuine acquisition of resilient internal models and the more spurious form represented by projective identification.

Normally, in ordinary, 'good-enough' development, this process takes place in the context of the infant's transactions with his or her caretakers and leads, in due course, to the infant acquiring what might variously be called a 'good internal object', a particular kind of 'internal working model' or a sense of having a 'secure base'.

When this process has gone awry in some way, it may be possible to address the situation within the setting of a psychoanalytic session, wherein there can be a reworking of these early interactions through the medium of the transference relationship. However, as Menzies Lyth demonstrates, models for identification may also be supplied – and indeed are inevitably present – in the total environment in which the child is developing. Hence the importance, when this is an institution, that its functioning mirrors that which one might expect of a well-functioning parental couple. This may be of paramount importance when the institution represents the total living environment of the child, as in a residential home, but the same principles apply across the whole spectrum of provision for children, and later developments in the area of the kind of organisational consultation that Menzies Lyth offered have reflected this. One such example would be Sprince's consultative work with a social services department about children who are in foster care. As she notes:

> For looked-after children, parental responsibility is often in the hands of a complex organization of carers, including field-workers and their managers as well as foster-families and birth parents.
>
> (Sprince, 2000)

In such an instance it is the whole network that has to be worked with so that its functioning as an 'integrated network' can again provide such a model.

This kind of 'developmental' approach can be extended much further. In Wittenberg's paper (1978, this volume), for instance, we can see how she applies the same basic frame of reference in relation to a large psychotherapy teaching conference, in order to enable effective learning to take place. The setting of the conference provides, in effect, a temporary institution and the same broad principles apply as to the permanent institutions that Menzies Lyth describes.

Thus, in relation to the care needed to provide an appropriate setting, Wittenberg has the same concerns as does Menzies Lyth and there are obvious parallels with both the setting provided by parents for their infant and the clinical setting that the therapist provides:

In terms of our work, it means one has got to provide a reliable setting, reliable time boundaries, keep to an agreed regularity of meetings, prepare clients for separations well in advance.

Wittenberg also shares Menzies Lyth's focus on the key role of introjective processes. She underlines how for real (and lasting) learning to take place particular attention must be paid to how: 'internalisation of the learning experience is powerfully affected by this work of mourning [dealing with the ending of the teaching conference].' Her paper is therefore very concerned with looking at how endings are managed and particularly how the feelings related to loss might undermine the gains that have been made. The importance of these factors has been recognised subsequently across a whole range of other settings (see, for example, Jackson, 2002, in relation to work in a school environment), including that of her own training school, as she notes in her addendum.

Since these early papers child psychotherapists have gone on to develop the application of a psychoanalytic frame of reference in numerous different areas including group work, paediatric liaison, neonatal units, schools, court assessments and so on, although a focus on the impact of group and institutional dynamics has remained central.

There is another area, however, in which there has been a particular growth of interest amongst child psychotherapists and that is in the application of psychoanalytic understanding to the developing parent–infant relationship. Daws's (1985) paper, reprinted here, is a classic in this respect and illustrates how she originally became involved in this work. There are many parallels with the previous two papers in so far as Daws explores how she developed her role as a 'consultant' to the health centre in which she attended the well-baby clinic. Of particular relevance is her role as a container for the anxieties of the staff in the discussions about families that evolved as part of her intervention. This aspect of the work has also been explored subsequently by those who have provided consultation to neonatal units and elsewhere (see for example Cohn, 1994).

However, it has been the clinical work that this paper introduced that has been especially taken up and that has led to the development of a particular style of brief intervention in the form of a 5 or 6 session under-fives counselling model (this is further described elsewhere in Daws, 1989; and in numerous papers in the *Journal of Child Psychotherapy*, for example, Hopkins, 1992; Miller, 1992; Pozzi, 1999). There has also been a more general burgeoning of interest in the whole field of infant mental health that is reflected in the work now being carried out by child psychotherapists from the range of theoretical orientations, in particular in the Parent–Infant Project at the Anna Freud Centre.

As child psychotherapy (in the UK) has become more established within the National Health Service, with all the ensuing pressures that this has brought, there has been a growing wish to further develop applied work, in the broadest sense. This has led to a considerable increase in the range and sophistication of the work undertaken, well illustrated in a recent volume of the *Journal* entirely devoted to the subject (*Journal of Child Psychotherapy* 28(2) 2002). In the pioneering papers that follow we can see the early exemplars of an approach that has gone on to prove immensely valuable and fruitful.

# Chapter 10

# The use of 'here and now' experiences in a teaching conference on psychotherapy as a means of gaining insight into the nature of the helping relationship

*Isca Salzberger-Wittenberg*

Originally published in the *Journal of Child Psychotherapy* (1978) 4(4): 33–50.

> 'If he is indeed wise he does not bid you enter the house of his wisdom but rather leads you to the threshold of your own mind.'
>
> from 'The Teacher' by Kahlil Gibran in *The Prophet*

The question of how to lead others to the threshold of their minds is one that must occupy any teacher in the art of psychotherapy and each one of us has to find his own way of setting about answering it. I have learned most at the Tavistock Clinic, where we have for many years run two basic kinds of seminars for those doing the pre-clinical psychotherapy training: infant observation seminars (first introduced by Dr Ester Bick), and work discussion seminars. For the former, trainees are required to observe infants in their own homes week by week, and to make detailed reports about their observations. This heightens the student's perception of non-verbal communication and draws his attention to primitive object relationships and character development. Most people who participate in such seminars are astounded at the wealth of understanding that can be gained from attention to the minute details of infant behaviour when it is considered within the context of the infant's developing relationships. The work discussion seminar for members of the 'helping professions' (which Mrs Martha Harris initiated) focuses on the student's work situation. Here the emphasis is on the relationship between client and worker, on the manifestations of transference and counter-transference. The student thus begins to look at himself in a relationship, at the reactions aroused in him by his clients and the effect of his own behaviour on the dynamics of the interaction. The seminar-leader's function in both these instances is to help the student to explore and question what is going on, to encourage him to become more aware in a feeling way of the nature of relationships. Thus, the leader starts from where the student is and enables him to think further. As therapeutic work depends so much on an individual's capacity to respond sensitively in an always changing situation it seems particularly important not to foster any sense of dependency on the teacher, but to encourage students to think for themselves. One does not wish to impart a technique so much as to develop a student's capacity to observe, to be aware of his client's and his own feelings, and to think about emotional experiences.

When I was asked in 1973 to run a fortnight's conference on psycho-therapy for a multi-disciplinary professional group in Brisbane, Queensland, it seemed an exciting challenge. I decided to use the models I was familiar with from my teaching at the Tavistock. The programme I decided upon, therefore, consisted of work discussion groups and some infant observation seminars. I was helped by the knowledge that a few psychiatrists had been meeting in Brisbane regularly for a year and a half with a Tavistock-trained child psychotherapist to discuss their detailed observations of mothers and infants. Thus, material for discussion at the conference was available.

When I told the Director of the Tavistock Clinic about the invitation to Australia, he exclaimed, 'What must they be expecting of you if they bring you all that distance in order to teach them!' This proved a most appropriate warning! It is difficult to appreciate what high expectations some people abroad put upon a visitor coming from an internationally renowned institution in Britain. It is indeed easy to be seduced by their fervour and swept into a state of mania. At times I felt as if I was regarded as Moses bringing down God's word from Mount Sinai. In the work discussion and infant observation seminars the group of 50 psychiatrists, psychologists, social workers, teachers of maladjusted children, nurses, clergy and general medical practitioners worked hard. I was impressed by their interest, their willingness to immerse themselves in discussions, their readiness to talk about their own feelings *vis-à-vis* the client and the eagerness with which they took up the ideas I put before them. They were immensely keen to get as much as possible out of this two-week course, and I, in turn, was easily led to give them more and more to abate their apparent thirst for knowledge.

I had requested that the case presentations follow a certain pattern: beginnings of treatment at the beginning of the conference, and situations of separation and endings towards the end. In this way I hoped that the material would to some extent link in with the feelings that the participants might be experiencing at the different stages of the conference and that members might relate what we were talking about to themselves also. Although at times I drew attention to the fact that the feelings we were discussing in terms of the clients also applied to ourselves at that moment, I felt it was inappropriate to make group interpretations. It is, in my opinion, absolutely essential to stick to the set task of a seminar and not overstep the boundary. If one does not, there is a danger of confusion as to whether one is engaged in a work-orientated discussion or a therapy group, or worse still a dangerous mixture of the two.

As the conference progressed I was, however, increasingly perturbed at not being able to diminish the idealisation of myself and the work more effectively. I was equally concerned about the senior clinicians: was the authority invested in me undermining their position in the group? Another disturbing factor was the split between the two membership groups: the morning group considered itself to be my 'good group', while those who attended in the afternoon thought of themselves as 'the baddies' who harboured doubt and showed some hostility. In spite of these qualms I was totally unprepared for the extent of the anger shown at the end of the conference. When it came to the last meeting, the air was thick with hostility. Members were silent most of the time and behaved like deprived children, so angry and so hopeless that they could not even ask for anything either now or in the future. One person, expressing no doubt something for many others, put it succinctly: 'We want a book next time, not a person who goes away and leaves us after a fortnight'. The enormous bouquet of flowers which I received at the close of this meeting seemed like a wreath for my grave. I felt shattered and very depressed. Two other occurrences after the conference gave food for thought: firstly, the psychiatrist who had been responsible for inviting me to Brisbane was the recipient of a flood of hostile attacks. I was burdened with guilt as I had no doubt that these feelings were really meant for me. Secondly, the tensions which had existed amongst the senior group of clinicians erupted and led to a split into two groups, with some members of the rival groups hardly on speaking terms. Thus, although many participants were of the opinion that the conference had been exciting, an eye-opener, and a stimulus to further learning, it was felt by some to have done some harm.

It was incumbent on me, therefore, to think deeply about what had happened and try to learn from my mistakes. I asked myself whether these phenomena could have been prevented. I was the first foreign visitor to spend a whole fortnight teaching in Brisbane, and the event was regarded as a pioneering venture. Was it therefore inevitable that we should have a kind of honeymoon followed by deep disappointment? Was it also unavoidable that new ideas would have a disturbing effect on the established group and cause severe disruption amongst the senior clinicians? Even allowing for both these factors, I questioned whether there were not elements in the structure of the conference or my style that had contributed to a particularly stressful situation for members. After discussion with colleagues, and much further thought, I came to the conclusion that there were a number of things which might have made for unnecessary complications. In terms of structure, I considered it a mistake that every teaching event had been led by me. Thus, all knowledge about psychotherapy might have appeared to be vested in me, and thought to go away with me when I left. The fact that senior clinicians were not given a special position might have erroneously created the impression that I did not recognise their skills and positions of special responsibility. This made the handover more difficult. It was also no doubt a mistake to have a morning and afternoon group who, moreover, never met together; this facilitated splitting along lines typical of groups in institutions. In addition, I became convinced that I had been wrong to assume that transference problems could be dealt with simply by inference via case-material. The infantile hopes aroused by an overseas visitor were so massive that they needed a more direct approach.

It took the Brisbane group a year to recover. Then feelers were put out to see whether I would consider coming for another fortnight's conference in 1975. I was relieved, delighted to be given another chance – frightened, for I knew that this time I would meet the full impact of the hostility which had not been expressed on the previous occasion. I imagined that we would either have a disastrous silently angry conference or hopefully get down to real hard work on a more solid basis. As a result of the lessons learnt in 1973, I decided on a different conference design. I considered it important to:

(a)  work with a staff group drawn from the senior clinicians in Brisbane;
(b)  have plenary meetings which would bring together the total conference membership and staff;
(c)  work openly at aspects of the relationship between conference members and myself, conflicts between members, the relationship between the members and the conference institution, and tensions amongst the staff group.

On the basis of these considerations, I put forward the following conference design:

1.  Daily plenary meetings for the 50 participants led by me.
2.  Daily work-discussion groups: five groups comprising ten people each led by clinicians from Brisbane.
3.  Two staff meetings per day: one for reporting back from work discussion groups and integrating the different parts of the conference; the second to discuss management and staff problems.

A good deal of my pre-conference thinking centred around the plenary meetings. As before, I resisted the invitation to lecture, as my experience had shown me the limited usefulness of formal teaching.

This I had learnt during recent years, particularly in running a course for teachers in primary, secondary and tertiary education. This part-time evening course at the Tavistock (first begun by Roland Harris) is called 'Aspects of Counselling in Education'. It has consisted of lectures and work-discussion groups. While the latter have invariably been found useful, lectures have rarely been very satisfactory. To some extent they meet the students' passive wishes to learn by listening and taking notes but one wonders what on earth they are going to do with such knowledge! At best the subject arouses interest and provides stimulation – at worst one is teaching theory which remains totally undigested. If, on the other hand, one teaches on the basis of clinical material from therapy sessions, it tends to arouse hostility and envy. Some course members then feel that they should be working in a similar way and try to imitate a technique totally inappropriate to their setting and task as educators, and one for which they do not have adequate training. Others object that while they find the clinical material interesting, they do not know how they can apply understanding gained from it to their field of work. In addition, I began after some years to feel that a lecture discussion was not an adequate experience for learning about emotional problems for people not normally involved in therapeutic work, nor in therapy themselves. On one occasion when I was making a few introductory remarks at the beginning of the new course, I became aware of the lack of attention in the group. It struck me that I had just *said* that the course was about the emotional factors involved in the student–teacher relationship, and the student's relationship to an educational institution, yet I was not in fact making use of the emotional experience the students on this course were having at that moment! I therefore stopped and asked members of the course whether they were willing to reflect upon their own feeling-experience as they entered the building, came into a strange room, sat now amongst strangers and thus were faced with a new situation. At first I was afraid that no one would speak, that I had made a big blunder. But once I clarified that I was doing this not in order to analyse the feelings of individuals or intrude upon their privacy, but in order to help us understand the kind of experiences common to all human beings in such situations, comments came thick and fast. Here are some of the points made by members of my teachers group on the first evening we met together; I have grouped the comments under three headings:

1.  *Feelings related to the institution*
    'I feel lost'.
    'I asked the way twice but I still feel in a maze'.
    'I feel confused'.
    'I feel isolated'.
    'I feel it's a strange and frightening place'.
    'This building is cold and impersonal'.

2.  *Feelings related to the leader*
    'I thought you might be cross that I came late'.
    'I felt embarrassed about speaking up just now'.
    'I think that you're judging us to see whether we're good enough to be on this course'.
    'It seems to me that you're a warm and caring person'.
    'Did you put the chairs close together so that we shouldn't feel isolated?'

'I don't know what the rules of this place are; the fact that they're not spelt out makes them more frightening'.

3.   *Feelings related to the peer group*
'As I came in I looked round to see whether I could see a familiar face'.
'I like to sit at the back so that I can survey all the people in front of me'.
'I moved close to my neighbour and smiled at her in order to get some contact with a friendly person'.
'I don't want to sit in the front row in case the others think that I'm trying to be teacher's pet'.
'I feel so ignorant and stupid. I'm sure everyone else here is more knowledgeable'.
'I don't know what we're all talking about, I find it exciting'.

Of course the very act of voicing such thoughts and seeing that one is not the only one to experience such strange and sometimes frightening feelings makes members feel less lonely. As one person put it: 'It was cold when I came in first, but the place feels warmer now'. When we have named some of the anxieties, I tend to point out that these feelings are indeed ubiquitous, but in the normal course of events we do not like to mention or even acknowledge them to ourselves because we consider them to be childish. Although they do arise from our infancy and childhood they remain as part of our emotional equipment throughout adult life. We then look at the helplessness, coldness, lostness, and total dependency at the very beginning of life when we find ourselves in an alien environment. Then we begin to consider how rarely these feelings are taken into account in the management of pupils and students at points of transition: from home to school, from primary school to secondary school, from school to university. So the discussion moves from being in touch with the here-and-now experience of beginning to discussing the nature of beginnings, both tracing them to their roots in infancy and relating them to the work situation in which members of the course are engaged. Thus, we move from present experience to conceptualisation and then to application. Once I had started to use this method I began to see that it was possible to treat subjects like phantasy, transference and counter-transference, separation anxieties and endings in a similar manner. Subject-matter and experience, affective and cognitive learning are thus interlinked; it becomes an alive learning experience, as would seem appropriate for a course on psychodynamic interaction, designed to help members to be more perceptive about themselves and others.

I planned to begin the 1975 Brisbane conference in a way similar to the teachers' course. I was not sure about the subjects for the ensuing days, but thought that if I looked at the themes that came up in the work discussion groups each day, a suitable topic might emerge for the next plenary meeting.

When I arrived in Queensland, I was appalled to find that every member of the two ongoing clinical seminars which had met during the past two years wanted to be on the staff of the conference, yet all but three were committed to carry on with their usual work schedule every afternoon. This meant that only the mornings were available for the conference. The meeting I called for the eve of the conference was attended by only half of the potential staff group, the other half either refusing to turn out on a Sunday evening, or involved in an encounter group that weekend. We were faced with decisions as to who was to form the staff group, and when sufficient time would be found for staff meetings. Only early mornings had been allowed for the latter but I considered it essential to meet at least twice a day. My plan was to have a feed-back from the leaders of each work discussion group and on the basis of this prepare the plenary for the following morning. I made it clear that it was an unmanageable task for me to be filled up with the material from five work discussion groups, digest this and come up with a topic for the plenary immediately following the staff meeting. The staff that were present declared categorically that it was not possible to find another free hour at lunch time or later. At first we got nowhere. Then I decided to be absolutely firm and issued an ultimatum: either they found time for a second meeting with me or else, much as I wished to involve the Brisbane staff, I would have no option but, as last time, take the conference events on my own. I explained that I could not be responsible for containing a membership of 50 unless the staff worked closely together. I knew already that we had a staff group that had been in great conflict with one another over the past two years. I felt it to be utterly irresponsible to conduct a conference with a staff thus divided and without sufficient time to work at the existing tensions. With some reluctance, ten members agreed to re-arrange their programme so as to make themselves available at lunch-time; one, who could give part of the lunch-times only, became the administrator of the conference. I asked the ten staff to pair themselves into co-leaders. It was suggested that they select as partner someone they felt happy to work with. The result was that we had four congenial heterosexual leader pairs – leaving two men of very differing orientation, one a behaviourist. We had been in telephone communication with the absent staff members on Sunday evening but not surprisingly there was still a great deal of unresolved conflict at our meeting early on Monday morning. However, it was agreed that all staff would be present at the plenary meetings, and that we would start with two plenary meetings on the first morning: one to deal with feelings about beginnings, and the second one for a case presentation and discussion. I felt this would give more of an opportunity for the membership to become welded together as a group and that the second meeting would also provide a model for the work discussion seminar leaders.

So we entered upon our first plenary. This was not, however, simply a beginners group for about half the membership had attended the 1973 conference. Right from the start a great deal of the anger and disappointment about the ending of the first conference was brought into the meeting by the old-timers. Indeed, their feelings of fury and their anxiety about what they were letting themselves in for was such that it was quite alarming to the newcomers. I wondered aloud whether this was partially an attempt by 'older siblings' to frighten the new ones away. Also it seemed people were considering whether it would be worthwhile taking the risk of involving themselves at all. I put it as a possibility that if we faced feelings about the end from the beginning and worked at them, it might come less as a shock than it had done on the last occasion. I was asked by the members how I had felt at the end of the last conference and how it felt to be back. I thought it was appropriate for me to share that my experience was one of having depression dumped into me but I was glad to have another chance to see if we could not learn from experience. This openness in sharing my experience was *not* a kind of confession meant to placate the membership; I answered such questions sometimes when I thought it helped the learning process. The case brought to the second meeting of the morning was that of a newly qualified teacher who had lost her voice during the first week of her first job. In her interview with the psychiatrist she repeatedly asked whether he could hear her. It was very clear that no one had heard her before, i.e. heard her distress and understood her problem and she had actually had to lose her voice to show others how frightened she was of facing the responsibility of being in charge of a group of children.

On the second day, the feelings in the plenary centred round members' passivity, dependency and idealisation in relation to myself. I spoke about these and went on to the subject of containment, explaining W.R. Bion's concept of projected distress as either a communication of emotional pain or as a method of dumping excessive distress; the need for the therapist/helper/mother to hold this distress, to be able to digest it mentally/emotionally and by action or words show that she understands the particular nature of the pain, and thus hands it back in a modified form which enables the child/patient to reintroject it rather than be overwhelmed by it. While we talked, there was some restlessness and members expressed concern about the groups they would be joining for the work discussion. Interest in the plenary was evaporating and I felt somewhat rejected.

After the coffee-break, the five small groups assembled in separate rooms. During most of this time a baby could be heard crying heart-rendingly. I knew it to be the eight-month-old daughter of one of the conference members. She seemed quite inconsolable but the young girl who was minding the baby did not wish to call the mother back from her work discussion group as she felt that this would prove her own inadequacy as a baby-minder. The staff group met after lunch and each co-leader pair reported on the cases brought and the ensuing discussion. Thus we all shared information about the separate parts of the conference and could comment and reflect upon them together. I wrote down as much as possible and spent the rest of the day going over my notes, trying to sort and re-sort and digest the themes that seemed to be uppermost in the conference members' minds. Hopefully I would find amongst this mass of material a suitable topic for the next day's plenary! This proved a vain hope. There were any number of important themes and a selection had to be made. However, certain ones stood out in my mind, and when I jotted them down I perceived some connection between them. Looking over them, it became evident to me that members of the conference were bringing topics that were of concern to them not only in their work, but were also a response to feelings stirred up by the conference: thus they were a reflection of their here and now experience. I could not escape noticing the transference elements. With this realisation, a new concept began to emerge: the themes could be seen as the different parts which, taken as a whole, formed the associations to the events of the conference. It might therefore be helpful to bring them together in the plenary, showing the links between them.

When I met the staff group the following morning, I told them about my findings and my intention to relate the concerns of members as portrayed in the work discussion material both to their current conference experience and to their relationships with their clients in similar situations.

One of the functions of the morning staff group was thus a report back on the themes I had picked out. Another was to make management decisions on the basis of what we were learning. (On the second day, for example, we decided that lunch should be provided for members so that they had a chance to meet socially and work through some of the issues raised during the morning.) The third function was to help the staff to think about the anxieties they might be carrying for the membership and, equally important, to face some of the tensions that existed within the staff group, so that these were contained as far as possible. This work is in my view of particular importance, for unless the staff are working well together and aware of the difficulties that exist between them, they are likely to burden members unnecessarily. This seems to me as dangerous as it is in an analytic situation if the analyst's problems intrude upon the session, interfere with his concentration, or worse still, are projected onto the patient. In a conference of this kind, staff have a great responsibility for members who are, hopefully, undergoing a new and intense emotional experience and are therefore in a vulnerable state. The staff also have to be prepared for a great deal of the members' anxieties to be projected onto them, which in turn may touch off problems of their own. A lot of work has to be devoted to understanding who, at any particular moment, is carrying a particular anxiety on behalf of other staff or membership. Our staff group developed quite remarkably well from rather poor beginnings because we all felt very responsibly involved. I was amazed at the frankness that existed between us, my behaviour and attitudes, of course, being as much under scrutiny as any other staff member's. It was impressive how this work was carried through without too much personal hurt, in the spirit of exploration and devotion to the task of understanding and helping each other to function at maximum capacity.

To illustrate the new style of plenary meetings, I shall attempt to give a summary of what happened on the third day, i.e. the plenary at which I first began to use the themes from the work discussion groups. I introduced the meeting by saying: 'This conference is about learning from experience, and the staff have decided that it would aid learning to give a feedback of the themes from the work discussion group. There is of course the problem of how to select the underlying concerns. I must take responsibility for the choice. The following themes [which I then wrote up on the blackboard] are the ones that came together in my mind when I considered the reports I received from the work discussion group leaders:

1.  Adoption and fostering (four out of five groups discussed a case of this kind).
2.  Mothers damaging babies by being uncaring and neglectful.
3.  Nurses being asked to hold patients in the absence of the therapist.
4.  Mothers damaged by babies (an example of a mother getting breast cancer).
5.  How can one be a professional adult 'containing' person if one also has baby needs?
6.  Feelings of inadequacy, especially amongst the non-medicals.
7.  What support is available for those who have to do the containing?'

I then went on to say something like the following: 'The nature of the topics suggests to me that it isn't accidental that adoption and fostering should play such an important part, but is related to the members' experience of the breaking up of the large group into smaller ones and being handed over to other leaders. This appears to have evoked in conference members feelings of being given away, so to speak, for adoption or fostering (Theme 1). Am I then felt to be like the uncaring, neglectful kind of mother, one who just picks members up only to put them down again, hurting them unnecessarily and undermining their trust in a reliable, caring mother (Theme 2)? Yesterday's experience of parting may have brought back memories for some of you of being left two years ago, and also brought forward thoughts in all of us about the end of this conference. Is it perhaps, asking too much in asking you to involve yourself, be open to new experiences and thus take risks in the knowledge that this course will only last for such a short time?

'I failed yesterday to pick up the members' anger and grief at separation. When in the latter part of the plenary interest turned to the small groups, I felt somewhat rejected. Instead of recognising that I was asked to contain the members' pain at being dropped and rejected, I ignored the subject. Thus I failed in the very task I was talking about: namely, understanding the feelings evoked in the worker as a kind of communication from the client, something like: "These feelings are too much for me to bear so I'm making you feel them". We discussed yesterday how one needs to hold this projected distress for one's client (or group), digest it internally and then verbalise it or behave in a way which conveys that one can stand such pain. This makes it possible for the client (or baby) to reintroject it in a modified, less overwhelming way. Something rather terrible happened yesterday because of our failure to contain the grief at parting. A baby was crying heart-rendingly, for its absent mother. It seems to me, therefore, that what we did was to put our own pain at separation into a little baby – we projected it there. Not only did we put it there, we left it there and disowned it; nearly every conference member heard that baby cry and yet no one did anything about it. The person who was put in the position of having to manage this difficult situation was a 17-year-old girl, the baby minder. This reminds me of another theme on the board, i.e. using nurses to hold the clients' anxiety (Theme 3). It is indeed often the auxiliary staff, e.g. a nurse, receptionist or the dinner-lady or janitor who has to hold the anxiety which the therapist, doctor or teacher has not been able to understand or is unwilling to deal with.'

At this point the mother of the baby said that she had not actually heard her baby cry, while other members commented that they had heard the baby but felt it was the mother' s job to do something about it. I commented that it was easier for the group to be disapproving of the mother, one of the members, than to be critical of me who took a mother/ leadership role in this conference. I also felt that what had happened was largely my responsibility. The question of not hearing linked to the case we had discussed, the young teacher whose distress was not heard by anyone. I had failed to pay attention, 'hear' the crying baby-part of the members, and had not provided a holding situation for them, and so the pain had to be further projected. This brought us to another theme on the board (Theme 5), namely the difficulty of professional workers in acting as containers and managing themselves when their own child needs are not met. We talked about a mother's need for father when she is looking after a demanding young infant, and fathers who support and mother the mother. Equally, professionals need the support of colleagues to help them carry the emotional burdens and the demands made on them by their clients (Theme 7). The mother in this conference who had brought her baby along wanted to be allowed to have her needs looked after by someone else. The baby-minder in turn, had felt inadequate and because of this, had not dared to ask for help or call the mother when she was needed (Theme 6).

I then came to the subject which appeared to me to underlie all the other issues: inconsolable grief at parting. It raised the question of what enables one to separate, or, alternatively makes separation excessively painful. This was something we needed to consider at every separation; at the end of each interview, at the end of the week, at holiday times and eventually when ending the relationship. Going back to the early developmental phase we could ask: how is it possible for the baby to experience himself as separate from mother for however brief a time and sustain such absence without becoming unbearably distressed? Briefly, I outlined that, firstly, there had to be repeated good experiences which enabled the baby to feel that the mother would meet his needs, and was reliably available at moments of stress. On the basis of many good experiences the baby comes to internalise a helpful, reliable mother who holds him in distress, that is to say, he establishes in his inner world an internally sustaining situation. Secondly, the anger with a mother not constantly externally available must not be so great as to immediately destroy her in his mind. This has partly to do with endowment, the balance between the capacity for love as opposed to the strength of destructive impulses. It also has to do with the baby's experiencing a mother strong enough to stand angry attacks and survive. In terms of our work, it means one has got to provide a reliable setting, reliable time boundaries, keep to an agreed regularity of meetings, prepare clients for separations well in advance. We must be able to acknowledge and contain hostility while we are still present and in this way help the client to differentiate between ordinary anger and total destruction of the good object out of frustration and envy. When a mother is not reliable, the baby cannot build up a belief in someone good who will meet his needs; if the mother is fragile and frightened of *any* aggression, this increases the baby's phantasy that his anger is unmanageable. A terrible situation arises when reality appears to confirm the baby's phantasy that mother has been bitten up or destroyed by his greed. This can happen if mother withdraws, gets seriously depressed or ill over long periods, or, worse still, dies. Such events make it extremely difficult if not impossible for the baby to differentiate between psychic and external reality, between omnipotently destructive phantasies and a mother in actuality overwhelmed and destroyed by him.

At this point the conference member whose baby had been crying told us that her daughter had been biting her breasts ferociously during the last three weeks; she was in the process of weaning her. I said this might explain why the baby had been so inconsolable. She might have feared that she had destroyed mother's breast by her biting or else that mother was stopping breast-feeds, rejecting her because she had been such a biting baby (Theme 4). Such anxieties arise regularly and in a particularly intense way during weaning when the baby may need a great deal of reassurance that mother is in fact alive, undamaged, and continuing to love him. One of the group remarked that he feared to be critical of me because he might lose me, I might return to England and not come back. Thus, members themselves linked 'biting' remarks to the infant's biting teeth, seeing adult derivatives of infantile anxieties. Their inhibition in relation to me was due to their fear that I could not or would not stand their attacks. I wondered whether their anxieties were heightened by the fact that I had no external protecting or restoring father from London with me; were the staff group not felt to give me enough support? I also commented on the angry outburst of one conference member yesterday. She had had the courage to tell us in the plenary session that she had not experienced any hostility towards me when I left two years ago, but suddenly on my return felt in such a state of fury with me that she could hardly get herself to the conference room. It seemed pertinent that she could experience her hostile feelings only once I had safely returned. Apparently I had to be preserved from so much internal destruction in my absence and only when there was a way of checking that I was alive and strong enough to survive could she allow herself to be furious. We discussed similar situations which we meet with in our clinical practice. Sometimes clients are unable to think about us in the holiday, not because they don't care but because they are afraid that if they were to become aware of missing us the attack would be such, or the despair so great that it would be unbearable. It is only when we have safely returned that they can experience the pain which they previously had denied for fear of losing their object by their damaging destructiveness.

This then was the method that I found made most sense to follow every day: I put up a list of the topics from the work discussion groups which had struck me as particularly relevant and I interpreted how they might reflect the membership's current experience, elucidating what we could learn from this for our work with clients. I spoke without any notes and this freed me to work on the themes on the blackboard and keep in touch with the response of the members, incorporating new ideas as they arose spontaneously. It evolved into a lively interchange between the membership and myself and between the members of the group. It is difficult to recapture this fully from the notes I made after each plenary session. But each day brought interesting new ideas which represented a dynamic development and much questioning. Let me quote some of Wednesday's topics: 'If you are receptive, you let yourself in for a lot of pain'; 'Is it really necessary to have psychic pain?'; 'Are we not harming patients by putting them in touch with painful feelings?'; 'Are all these feelings you mention being pushed into us?'; 'Where does responsibility lie – is it all phantasy?'; 'If one doesn't agree with the leaders, is one going to be shouted down?'. I took it as a sign of growing trust that such doubts and awareness of the risks involved in our task, could be voiced.

On Friday we had a review meeting which brought up many comments about the staff group. Members were angry with doctors because they arrived in expensive limousines; they wondered whether the staff got better lunches than the members, how often did staff meet and what were they doing together? Clearly we were into feelings about the staff/parents' weekend. This enabled us to talk about the angry, jealous, envious reactions that clients have in relation to the worker at every separation, such as at weekends and holiday times. There was also a good deal of material about abortions which in terms of the conference I took up as the aborting of the learning produced during the week. This in effect was our joint conference baby, and one that was still very vulnerable and could so easily be lost or killed off during the weekend.

Just as we were about to disperse after the staff meeting on Friday, one of the psychiatrists received news that a patient of hers (in mental hospital) had run away and committed suicide. Some of the colleagues discussed the case together and this no doubt was a support to the psychiatrist. When the staff met again on Monday morning I said that thoughts about the suicide would no doubt be around in the conference. Not only was the consultant psychiatrist a member of our staff group, but three nurses and one occupational therapist from the same mental hospital were members of the conference. Naturally, the psychiatrist was at first reluctant that I should discuss the matter in the plenary. However, when I outlined the way I intended to handle it, I was able to convince her not only that it was essential to bring the subject up, but also that she personally was less likely to get hurt if it was discussed than if we tried to ignore it.

Friday's work discussion themes seemed long out-of-date by Monday morning, and I saw no point in going back to them. So I opened the plenary by inviting the members to say what they felt about starting the second half of the conference. A general practitioner was the first person to speak. He said: 'Well anyway, we have survived the weekend, it's good to be back!' The psychiatrist interrupted: 'Not everybody has survived, one of my patients committed suicide'. We spent most of the rest of the morning talking about the feelings evoked in us by a suicide. The nurses expressed their worry that attendance at the conference had resulted in their hospital's being short-staffed; hence they felt partly responsible for the suicide. Matron had, however, reassured them that there were plenty of staff about at the time the patient ran away. We discussed the inevitable feelings of responsibility and guilt. We recognised not only the need to assess very carefully in each case to what extent a suicide could be avoided, but also the omnipotent assumption that we could in all instances save or rescue people from disaster. *All* we have to offer is understanding to the best of our ability, and emotional containment, sometimes backed up by physical containment in an institution. But we cannot ultimately be responsible for someone else's actions. There was evidence in a particular case where the suicide had represented a murderous attack on the parental couple. This could then be related to the infantile jealous feelings about mother and father, particularly intense at weekends and holiday times. This can result in an internal (and sometimes external) destruction of the couple. Or, we may find that the client holds himself hostage, conveying that if we leave him he will become self-destructive. We learnt that a patient of one of the other psychiatrists had slashed his wrists over the weekend, and because the psychiatrist felt so guilty about the extra burden that our conference (held at his hospital) imposed on his patients he had stitched up the wrists himself. Thereupon the patient had again slashed his wrists, forcing the psychiatrist to recognise that his stepping out of his therapeutic role had only increased acting out. He tried instead to talk to the patient about his motives for behaving in this way. There was a great deal of material about murder and suicide and I made some attempt to explain the basis of such violent acts in envy and jealousy, persecutory anxiety or persecutory guilt.

Towards the end of the morning one of the non-medicals said: 'We have been talking a lot about how we envy the doctors, and last week we wanted to slash the tyres of their big cars. I now see that they do have to bear the brunt of responsibility when it comes to death and suicide. Perhaps after all they should have a higher financial reward and some advantages'. So we got some recognition that envy of other's/mother's possession (or father's) such as breasts (or the penis) is counteracted when the child/adult becomes aware that riches are linked to responsibility. Turning to the psychiatrist who had lost his patient, one of the nurses said, 'I was very worried about you over the weekend, thinking what a strain you must be under'. After a moment's silence, the psychiatrist replied that he had felt very uptight till now, coping by putting on a brave front; he had been very much on the defensive, fearing to be blamed by the group. Now that he was experiencing other people's concern he could for the first time 'unfreeze', feel sad and sorrowful. Thus the Monday morning meeting ended on a very moving and reparative note.

In view of the recurring themes of absent or non-supporting fathers, it seemed appropriate that we should have a male chairman for the second week's plenary meetings. I thought it particularly important for me to be seen to have male support at this stage of the conference so that members would feel more able to voice the full extent of their anger at my leaving. The staff group had discussed at some length the function of the chairman in this kind of plenary meeting, at which I needed to interact freely with the members. We had come to the conclusion that his role was to be sensitive to the membership and stop me if I was going too fast or failing to pick up some important point. Together we were able to be more aware of my mistakes. For instance, during Wednesday's plenary he quietly pointed out that I was slipping into a lecturing style and becoming too theoretical. I then noticed that a lot of notebooks had suddenly appeared, and members were writing down much of what I was saying. When I began to think about it, I recognised that the change in my technique was in response to the members' demand that I should give them a survey of psychoanalytic theory and so create the impression that they had something concrete to take away with them at the end of the conference. I then said we could see how difficult it was to resist acting like a puppet, doing what we were asked to do, rather than consider the feelings that prompted our actions. In addition, my guilt about leaving probably made me want to be very 'giving'. We talked about the need to stop whenever we find we step out of role and to examine carefully why this has occurred. On another occasion, I made an interpretation to an individual member and again it seemed that this was my response to tremendous pressure, this time to be the therapist instead of remaining a teacher. Openly discussing my mistakes and reflecting on why they happened thus added to the learning experience of all of us. It demonstrated in a concrete and convincing way the power of the transference and counter-transference, how in this particular instance we were all trying to avoid looking at the limitations of this conference and the pain of ending.

There were many ways in which members tried to avoid facing the end. Themes during the second week had to do with stealing, 'using medicines for the wrong purposes', sex without responsibility, having children in order to feel loved, and devaluing good experiences. I pointed out that unless members were able to face the feelings of anger and loss now in relation to me, the peer group, the staff and the whole conference event, they would be left to cope with them afterwards on their own. They might also find themselves angrily 'aborting the conference baby, the learning', or else feel so guilty about their secretive, stealing way of acquiring knowledge that they could not utilise what they had in fact gained during our time together. On the other hand, idealisation, regarding the work we had done as if it were a kind of analytic bible, needed to be avoided; members needed to see what use it was to them or, alternatively, whether it was an approach which did not suit their personality or work setting. By the Wednesday of the second week most people were very aware, in touch with feelings of loss and mourning and the atmosphere became heavy with depression. One member exclaimed: 'Now that I'm actually, aware of the end, I'm frightened to death'. Some members recalled earlier losses and deaths and we had a moving, sad and worrying time.

When I listened to the reports from the Thursday work discussion groups, my heart sank: cases of murder, suicide and abortion were the order of the day. There were sadder feelings around too, signified by such questions as: 'How can one bear loneliness?'; 'How can rich, seeing people understand the poor, the blind?'; 'Does the person leaving you, or the mother when she gives her children for adoption, feel grieved at parting?'; (there was an example of a mother who had seemed to show no interest, but had written after eighteen months to ask for a photograph of her child). After a great deal of heart-searching and examining my counter-transference, I came to the conclusion that I was to be so worried that I would be unable to bring the conference to an end. Although there was no doubt a great deal of violence around, I thought that these subjects coming up so forcibly at this moment did not necessarily indicate that there was a real danger that members would act out. Rather it reminded me of the patient who, at the moment of saying goodbye projects a great deal of worry into the therapist, or tries to blackmail one into staying by holding the child-part of himself hostage. It dawned on me that these dreadful themes were a way of filling me up with such anxiety, that I would be unable to leave, or if I did go, burden me with such worry. that my mind would not be free to turn towards home. Regarding the themes as a way of projecting worry and hopelessness into me made it possible for members to work hard on *their* worry about what they might do to the work we had done together, murdering, aborting it and using it destructively in relation to myself and to the other staff after our parting. We were able to go on to the feeling of loneliness and the wish that I understand it and care. Thus it was possible to bring the Friday plenary to a conclusion that felt painful but not cruel or overwhelming.

We had decided that we would stay together for the second part of the last morning, in order to consider the transition back to work and to review the conference. Members talked about what they had gained and how difficult it was to know just what had been learned. They were worried about their ability to hold onto their learning after the conference. They also wondered what they were going to tell their colleagues back home. Were they going to show off with what they had got and make others envious? Would that not be asking for the work to be attacked by others? What in any case could one say about a conference which had been so much an emotional experience? Someone had the courage to say that it was also a relief to end, as one could not go on at such a pitch of intensity for much longer. It was good to look to the future. We had already been given a demonstration of how conference learning could be used constructively, for after our Monday plenary the four nurses and occupational therapists had gone back to their hospital and called a meeting of all non-medical staff and encouraged them to talk about their reaction to the suicide. The staff who had never shared such anxieties before felt it to be so worthwhile that they instituted regular meetings. This report gave some hope to other members that they too might find it possible to utilise their learning at an appropriate moment, and initiate some new way of dealing with their work problems or helping their colleagues. The conference ended on a positive note, very different from that of two years before. It seemed a satisfying, integrating experience for most.

Two days before the end, the conference administrator had announced that there would be a follow-up meeting for members and the staff group a fortnight hence. This was to review the conference in retrospect and discuss future plans. Thus the conference end held within it hope for the future. It was agreed that as I could not be present, a transcript would be sent to me. I was delighted to hear that this meeting eventually led to the founding of the Brisbane Psychotherapy Association, whose task is to organise regular meetings and arrange future conferences.

For me personally, parting was not so easy. I had had professionally one of the most exciting fortnights of my life. It was a thrilling experience to see the unconscious at work in a conference group; the dynamic impact of allowing the freedom for themes to arise (as opposed to imposing an artificial curriculum) brought a conviction about unconscious processes such as I have only experienced in clinical work. Moreover, it had given me the opportunity and privilege to evolve something new, bringing together different aspects of my past experience and welding them into a personal style. The elements from past learning which I drew on were: clinical experience with patients, a theoretical analytical framework, work with groups, and group relations conferences. Some of the psychoanalytical concepts which I applied in my teaching method include the following:

1.   The setting – using one's mind to be receptive to the members' anxieties and contain them.
2.   Strict boundaries in terms of time, space and task.
3.   Starting from the here-and-now.
4.   Studying the nature of the transference and countertransference.
5.   Taking hold of emotional pain and verbalising it.
6.   The notion that one cannot understand others without first understanding oneself.
7.   Regarding the whole experience as a joint exploration with no prior knowledge as to where it will lead (I knew as little about how the conference would develop as members did).
8.   When a mistake is made (such as a change in one's technique) trying to understand why this has occurred, and talking about it.

## Summary

I have since found that the style I have adopted is helpful for teaching in a large group. This provides enough distance and space to make it possible for members to choose at any moment to what extent they wish to feel personally involved, to disagree, identify or hide behind statements made by others. I have not used this approach with a group of less than 24, for in a smaller group I would fear the danger of being drawn into a more therapeutic role. I have been struck by the fact that the loss of personal identity and fear of mass power so typical of large groups have been strikingly absent. I think this has to do with my particular style. In the first place I refrain from making group interpretations but talk about feelings in each individual and this tends to heighten the members' personal sense of responsibility. I did not set out with this purpose in mind but am very glad that this is the effect. It seems to me that while I respond to individuals in the group I tend to stress the common elements of human experience and conflict. Therefore members feel personally addressed yet not singled out individually; experience is shared yet no 'en masse' feeling is promoted. Another factor is the mix of affective and cognitive learning, with the constant shift of attention from emotional and personal experience to thinking about one's work and adult self. As a leader I tend to move freely between the two, hoping to achieve some balance between them. Too much emphasis within a teaching event on the emotional experience of members could lead to the encouragement of too infantile a transference, while discussion of the work situations without reference to the here and now situation only tends to encourage intellectual thinking, empty of emotionality. A short intensive course or conference provides the leaders and members with an ongoing experience – allowing links to be made from one event to the other – something which is more difficult when there are weekly meetings. A fortnight's conference allows the weekend to be used for work on separations and preparation for parting at the end of the event.

The experience in Australia helped me to integrate personal, individual analytic, group and teaching aspects of myself. I am immensely grateful to all those I taught for their comments and reactions which have led me to think more carefully about what I was doing and what was happening in our relationship. They have helped to lead us to the threshold of our minds – to teach and learn in a way that appeared to lead to mutual growth.

## POSTSCRIPT

I have used the style described in part of this paper, namely drawing on work-discussion group themes to understand the here and now feelings of the members on a few other occasions. It seems to me to be appropriate only when leading a big, multidisciplinary group for an intensive conference over a number of days.

What I have learnt is to pay great attention to the transference which arises in the learning–teaching relationship. It has become part of my style of teaching to engage the group in thinking and verbalising how they feel at the beginning of the course, breaks, ending, about the staff, the group, the institution and the various events which happen within the course, such as absences, losses etc. Having gathered their comments, we then go on to relate this to their work situation, both their own experience and that of those they are responsible for: clients, pupils, other staff etc. I have found that getting in touch with their own emotional experience in the 'here and now' affects the members of the group deeply; it is something that is not easily forgotten and often leads to a more profound understanding of the infantile and mature aspects of relationships.

I have also found over and over again how rarely the painful emotions of ending are paid attention to. I feel it is of particular importance to prepare for and think through the feelings aroused as internalisation of the learning experience is powerfully affected by this work of mourning. I was fortunate in eventually being able to persuade the Professional Committee of the Tavistock to set up an 'ending event' to allow clinical students and staff the opportunity to reflect on the end of training and leaving the clinic, and am happy that this has now become part of what the clinic offers.

*February 2003*

Chapter 11

# The development of the self in children in institutions

*Isabel Menzies Lyth*

Originally published in the *Journal of Child Psychotherapy* (1985) 11(2): 49–64.

## Introduction

The theoretical basis for the thinking in this paper centres on a particular aspect of the development of the self, development that takes place through introjective identification. Healthy development depends greatly on the availability of appropriate models of individuals, relationships and situations for such identification. These models may be found in the adults who care for the children, their relationship with the children and with each other, and the setting for care. Healthy development may also require the management of the child's identification with inappropriate models, for example with other children in institutions for delinquent or maladjusted children.

Institutionalised children are likely to find their most significant models for identification within the institution itself, both in the institution as a whole and its sub-systems and in individual staff members and children. This leads to the concept of the institution as a therapeutic milieu whose primary task may be defined as providing conditions for healthy development and/or providing therapy for damaged children. Thus all the child's experiences in the institution contribute positively or negatively to his development, not only those more narrowly defined as education, individual or group therapy or child care. Indeed it has been the author's experience that the benefits of such provisions may well be counteracted by more general features of the institution.

This formulation would then lead one to take a very wide view of the institution in considering its effectiveness in carrying out its primary task. One would include its whole way of functioning; its management structure, including its division into sub-systems and how those relate to each other; the nature of authority and how that is operated; the social defence system built into the institution; its culture and traditions. In line with the theme of this paper, one would consider these in the context of how far they facilitate the provision of healthy models for identification, or alternatively inhibit the provision of such models.

Although one regards the whole institution as the model, in practice, of course, the impact of the institution on its child clients is mediated to a considerable extent through its staff members who are the individual models for identification. While it is true that they will have their own individual personalities with strengths and weaknesses as models, it is also true that the way they deploy their personalities within the institution will depend on features inherent in the institution, the opportunities it gives staff for mature functioning or the limits it puts on this. The author has discussed elsewhere the severe limits that a traditionally organised nursing service imposes on the mature functioning of both trained and student nurses (Menzies, 1970).

Thus, in considering the adults as models, one would give attention to maximising the opportunity for them to deploy their capacities effectively and to be seen by the children to do so. Indeed, one may go further; experience has shown that in a well-managed institution for children, the adults as well as the children actually gain in ego strength and mature in other ways. The adults thus provide better models.

The author's interest in the importance of the whole institution as a therapeutic milieu has developed over many years of working in two institutions for disturbed children where her formal role was that of management consultant and her task was to work with staff in keeping under continuous review the way the institution as a whole was functioning in relation to the primary task. The role involved both a considerable understanding of the way institutions function and a psychoanalytically based understanding of child development. Similarly, in a collaborative study with the Royal National Orthopaedic Hospital designed to improve the care of young children making long stays and to mitigate the long term effects of hospitalisation, it was found necessary to pay considerable attention to the way the cot unit for young children was managed and related itself to the management of the hospital as a factor affecting the quality of child care.

Against this background, it would appear possible that views about the development of children in institutions have been unduly pessimistic. So many of the early investigations were done in institutions whose whole organisation was inappropriate for healthy child development. For example, the bad effects of hospitalisation on young children were demonstrated first in hospitals with inadequate maternal visiting and multiple indiscriminate caretaking by a large number of nurses which effectively prevented attachment between a child and his caretakers. The same has been true on the whole for children in day and residential nurseries. In fact, these institutions deviated much more from a good model of care than is realistically necessary as also from the kind of setting a good ordinary family provides for a child to grow up in. More recent work provides some grounds for a more optimistic view of the developmental potential of children's institutions. They can be operated very differently from, for example, the old-fashioned hospital and can come much closer to the good ordinary family.

The section that follows discusses in some detail ways in which institutions can be organised or reorganised so as to provide improved models for the child's identification and for his development and it gives examples of work in institutions. I will comment on various aspects of this: ego development, super-ego development, the development of a firm sense of identity and of authority and responsibility for the self, attachment possibilities, the growth of a capacity for insight and confrontation with problems.

## The potential of the institution as a model for identification

### I   Delegation and its relation to staff's attitudes and behaviour

It is in general good management practice to delegate tasks and responsibilities to the lowest level at which they can be competently carried and to the point at which decision-making is most effective. This is of particular importance in children's institutions since such delegation downwards increases the opportunity for staff to behave in an effective and authoritative way, to demonstrate capacity for carrying responsibility for themselves and their tasks and to make realistic decisions, all of which are aspects of a good model.

But this has not traditionally been the practice in many children's institutions; the functions, responsibilities, and decision-making are centralised at a high management level, with a consequent diminution of the responsibility, authority and effectiveness of the staff more directly in contact with the children. In my consultancy with an approved school (a residential school for delinquent boys), I became involved in working with staff to change the management structure and functioning in one such area. The setting was traditional, with a matron who dispensed food in kind to the housemothers who provided meals for the staff and boys in the houses where the boys lived. There were all sorts of deficiencies and inefficiencies in the system, both practically in its effects on food provision and psychosocially, in its effect on the behaviour of staff providing food and the models they presented to boys. The food allowance was not very generous and there were constant complaints about its inadequacy; boys indeed were not very well fed. But the effect of the reality of the food allowance was compounded by the fact that, since the responsibility for food provision and decision-making lay with the matron, there was a notable tendency for the housemothers to disclaim their responsibility and authority; for example, to blame the matron if things went wrong, rather than feel an obligation to cope with them themselves.

A small example illustrates this point. Two boys went for a walk one evening and came back hungry. The housemother gave them two of the eggs she had been given for the breakfast next morning, thus leaving herself two short. She was disconcerted and angry when the matron would not – could not – give her more. Matron was blamed instead of the house-mother's taking responsibility for her own actions. The model presented to the children was one of irresponsibility and of blaming the other.

The system gradually changed. Ultimately the housemothers were given the money to buy the food themselves. With it they were explicitly given the responsibility and authority for the efficient use of the money. The matron gave up her authority and responsibility for direct food provision and instead became an advisor and supporter of the housemothers if they wished to use her in that way. The former central foodstore became a shop where the housemothers could spend their money if they wished but they had no obligations to do so if they preferred to shop elsewhere.

In time there were a number of very positive effects of this change. The housemothers visibly grew in authority and stature as they faced and accepted the new challenge and, for the most part, very effectively took over the task of food provision. The task itself was more realistically and effectively performed. One heard less and less about scarcity and the boys were actually better fed. Most importantly, the confrontation with scarcity and complaints about ineffective provision now became a face-to-face matter between the housemother, her colleagues in the house and the boys. The boys were thus given an important learning experience for life in the world outside, that is in learning to deal with scarce resources themselves, not just to complain about them. Initiative and ingenuity were freed. The resources of the estate itself, such as fruit, were better used and gardening by staff and boys developed on a considerable scale to augment food. The therapeutic effects of the change in the staff models presented and in the participation of the boys in the new system can hardly be exaggerated.

There was another important consequence in the matter of ego develop-ment and defences. As the author has described elsewhere (Menzies, 1970), members of an institution must incorporate and operate to a considerable extent the defences developed in the social system of the institution. Here a thoroughly paranoid defence system had developed around the provision of food. The matron was regarded as a 'mean bitch'; if only she were more generous everything would be all right. Responsibility on the part of the housemothers was converted into blame against the matron and the boys were collusively drawn into the system. This defence was primitive and anti-maturational, but gradually disappeared as the new system developed to be replaced by a more adaptive system of acknowledged responsibility and confrontation with reality.

The implications for staff as super-ego models may also be evident in the carrying of more mature authority for oneself and one's own behaviour and the replacement of blame of the other by more realistic assessment of oneself and one's own performance.

This is but one example of a series of similar changes that gradually changed the provision by staff of ego and super-ego and defensive models, the importance of which can hardly be over-stressed for children whose personality development is immature or already damaged or both. The ego and super-ego strength of staff was both fostered by the changes and given more opportunity to be effectively demonstrated to the children. They in turn were also involved more effectively in control over their own circumstances and given less opportunity to regard themselves as helpless and non-responsible victims of uncontrollable circumstances. It was seen as essential to carry out these other changes so as to achieve consistency and avoid presenting the children with conflicting and confusing models.

Effective delegation implies more than taking responsibility and authority for oneself, however; it implies also that the individual can accept and respect the authority of superiors and be effectively accountable to them and that he can take authority effectively for his subordinates and hold them in turn accountable for their performance. This is again important in the provision of models for children whose relationship with authority is immature and possibly already disturbed. Thus authority channels must be clear; staff must know to whom they are responsible and for what, and for whom they are responsible and for what.

It seems a fault in many children's institutions that they do not handle authority effectively. There may be too much permissiveness, people being allowed or encouraged to follow their own bent with insufficient accountability, guidance or discipline. If this does not work (and it frequently does not, leading to excessive acting out by both staff and children) it may be replaced in time by an excessively rigid and punitive regime. Both are detrimental to child development. The 'super-ego' of the institution needs to be authoritative and responsible, though not authoritarian; firm and kindly, but not sloppily permissive.

## II   Institutional boundaries and the development of identity

An aspect of healthy development in the individual is the establishment of a firm boundary for the self and others across which realistic and effective relationships and transactions can take place and within which a sense of one's own identity can be established. Young children and the damaged children in many institutions have not developed effective boundary control or a firm identity within it, and need help from the institution in doing this. How then can the institution provide models of effective boundary control? The institution as a whole must control its external boundaries and regulate transactions across them so as to protect and facilitate the maintenance of the therapeutic milieu. This function will not be considered in detail since it is less likely to impinge directly on the children than the management of boundaries within the institution. Any institution is divided into sub-systems some of which perform different tasks, as with the education and living sub-systems in a residential school. Some of them do the same tasks for different clients, e.g. a number of houses in the living area. The way these sub-systems control their boundaries and conduct transactions across them is of great importance for the development of the children's personal boundaries.

A danger in children's institutions seems to be that the boundaries are too laxly controlled and too permeable, and that there is too much intrusion into the sub-system from outside and into the individuals within it. There seems to be something about living in an institution that predisposes people to feel that it is all right to have everything open and public and to claim right of entry to almost everywhere at almost any time. Nothing could be more different from the ordinary family home which tends jealously to guard its boundaries, regulating entry and exit and, particularly, protecting its children both from unwarranted intrusions and from excessive freedom to go out across the boundaries. And nothing could be less helpful to the development of children in institutions.

Problems appear particularly in the living space of the children, their homes effectively while they are in the institution. It seems important therefore that these present a model of effective boundary control, with realistically controlled entry and exit by permission of the people in the sub-system, notably the staff, not an open front door through which people wander in and out at will. To put it differently, the members of the sub-system need to take authority for movement in and out.

This was an important aspect of the work in the cot unit in the Royal National Orthopaedic Hospital where, at first, the boundaries were much too open. The unit opened directly into the hospital grounds and people walking there seemed to feel free to drop in and visit children *en passant*, often with very kindly intentions of entertaining and encouraging the children. Further, the cot unit provided the most convenient means of access to the unit for latency children, and people en route for that often stopped to spend time with the young children. The physical boundary between the cot unit and that for latency children was open and there was a good deal of visiting by older children and their families. Altogether the situation seemed highly inappropriate for the healthy development of the children. Individual children were too often 'intruded into' by strange even if kindly adults. Relationships between children, mothers and unit staff could be disrupted by the visitors as could the ongoing work of the unit. So the external door was closed to all except members of the unit. Unit staff and visiting families had the authority and responsibility to control or prevent unauthorised entry. At first an invisible notice saying 'No Admission Except on Business' was hung in the space between the two units and again staff and visiting adults helped to control the boundary. Later, a partition was built that effectively separated the two units and made boundary control much easier. The benefits of this boundary control to the ongoing life of the unit and to the child patients were inestimable.

But there remained the problem of the large number of people from outside the unit who had legitimate business there, surgeons, the paediatrician, pathology staff, physiotherapists, and so on. Their crossing of the boundary also needed to be monitored to mitigate possible detrimental effects to the children's boundaries. Small children have not developed effective control of such contacts with people who may be strangers and who may do unpleasant, frightening or painful things to them, such as taking blood samples or putting them on traction. The normal way that such contacts are mediated for the child is through a loving and familiar adult who can comfort the child and negotiate on his behalf. It became the rule that such visitors approach the child through his mother if present, or through his assigned nurse, or both. Sometimes the visitor would be asked not to approach the child for the moment if the intervention could be postponed and if the adult caretaker judged the moment inappropriate, for instance if a child was already upset or asleep. The adults both protected the child's boundaries and presented models of boundary control.

Similarly, the transactions across the boundaries outwards which involved children were carefully monitored. Work was done with other hospital wards and departments to ensure consistency in the principles of care between their work and that of the cot unit. There was explicit agreement about where mothers or other family adults could accompany children and so on.

Effective control over boundaries can have another positive effect on the development of identity. It gives a stronger sense of belonging to what is inside, of there being something comprehensible to identify with, of there being 'my place', or 'our place', where 'I' belong and where 'we' belong together. Children cannot get identity from or identify with a whole large institution. They get their identity through secure containment in a small part of it first, and only through that with the whole.

This raises the related issue of the desirable size of what is contained within the boundary if it is to be comprehensible to the child. Too often, it seems, the basic unit is too big. For example, a hospital ward of say 20 beds is too big for the small child, both physically and psycho-socially. He cannot 'comprehend' it and risks getting lost and confused. The physical space does not contain him securely within its boundaries and the number of staff is such as to risk multiple indiscriminate caretaking, a care system which is inimical to the establishment of a secure identity since it makes it difficult for the child to become familiar with the identity of the other and to have his own identity consistently reflected back to him by the other

(Menzies, 1975). The cot unit was fortunate in being a 12-bedded unit usually less than full which could be staffed by a staff nurse, three nursery nurses and a nursery teacher during school hours. It was physically quite small and secluded once the partition was built.

An effectively bounded small unit is likely to facilitate the development of an easily identifiable and relatively integrated group within the unit with the staff as its permanent core. This was important in providing support to children and families in the distressing circumstances of long stay in an orthopaedic hospital and in helping to keep anxiety at tolerable levels. This in turn helped prevent the development of inappropriate and anti-maturational defences. In institutions for disturbed children it may also be important in facilitating therapeutic work with the children within the unit through using the dynamics of the group. In a sense it makes escape from appropriate confrontation with realities inside the unit more difficult and facilitates the process of learning from them.

There are boundaries of a more subtle kind that are also significant in providing models for children, notably the boundaries of authority and responsibility. For example, the authority for running the unit needs to be firmly located in its head and his authority not undermined by people from outside, such as his superior, directly intervening inside it. The authority and responsibility for managing the cot unit was delegated firmly to the staff nurse, and the ward sister did not cross that boundary although she still held ultimate responsibility and kept in close touch with the work there. The ward sister sustained this although she found it personally depriving and frustrating to be thus distanced from the young children. Similarly when the head delegates some tasks to his staff the authority needs to be clear and he should not transgress the boundary by direct intervention.

Problems can arise in institutions if the same people work at different times in different sub-systems when their authority and the authority under which they operate can become unclear. For example, teachers in an approved school sometimes work in the living area outside school hours. If they continue to think of themselves as 'teachers' and under the authority of the headmaster, they are confusing an authority boundary as the headmaster has no management responsibility for the living system. The headmaster in an approved school much concerned for the welfare of his teachers had to learn – painfully – not to think and talk of 'my staff', when they were working in the living area and similarly the heads of the houses had to learn to think of the 'teachers' as 'their staff' and take authority over them effectively. These may again seem strange preoccupations for people concerned with the care of children in institutions but they do seem appropriate since confusion or inadequate definition of authority boundaries can confuse staff about who or what they are and threaten their own sense of identity and what they identify with. This confusion will subtly convey itself through their attitudes and behaviour to the children with detrimental effects on their sense of identity and their development.

The final point on this topic concerns the protection of the boundaries of the self and the management of transactions across them with particular reference to the processes of projection and introjection and their effect on the sense of self. Excessive projection can and does change in a major way the apparent identities of both the projector and the recipient if he cannot control what he takes in. Both can feel unreal and strange to themselves and both can act strangely and inappropriately. Similarly, inappropriate introjections can create a false identity and an unstable sense of self. It seems to be a crucial responsibility of the staff in children's institutions to control their own boundaries so as to manage the effects of both projection and introjection and hold them within realistic and therapeutic limits. In so doing they will help the children to control their projections and introjections and strengthen the development of a true and stable identity. Young children and disturbed children are likely to project massively into caretakers. Indeed it is to some extent a normal method of communication telling the other what the child is feeling or what for the moment he cannot tolerate in himself. For example, the apparent 'consciencelessness' of a delinquent child can result from the splitting and projection of a harsh and primitive super-ego which is unbearable to the child. The deprived inadequately mothered child may violently project into the caretakers an idealised mother figure with the demand that the caretaker be that mother and compensate for all his deprivations. The danger for the caretaker and so for the child is that the projections may be so compelling that the caretaker acts on them instead of taking them as communications. His personal boundaries are breached, his identity temporarily changed and the transaction ineffectively controlled.

The staff of approved schools for example may act on the projected primitive super-ego and treat the children in a rigid and punitive way which is anti-therapeutic. It represents an acting out by staff with children instead of a therapeutic confrontation with the problem. Or staff can respond to the demands for compensation for early deprivation by an overgratifying regime which is equally anti-therapeutic since it evades confrontation and real work with the problem.

Similarly staff must be alert to the introjections and false identifications which children use in their desperate search for a self and a sense of identity. These may lead for example to false career ambitions in pseudo-identification with idols or identification with delinquent gangs. Or they may lead to apparent and sudden but false improvement based on pseudo-identification with the staff or the principles of the institution.

Inappropriate projections and introjections between children and staff are by no means the only problems. One must also take note of projections and introjections between staff and staff, between children and children and between sub-systems. For example, it is fairly common to find in institutions a situation where all sub-systems but one are said to be in a good state but that one is in a mess. Frequently this is less a reality than the results of inter-group projections, sub-systems projecting their 'bad' into the one and encapsulating the 'good' in themselves. All such phenomena are of course anti-developmental and anti-therapeutic, and real progress can only be made in so far as people and sub-systems can take back what belongs to them, discard what does not and work with the external and internal reality of their situations.

This has always seemed to me one of the most difficult tasks confronting the staff of children's institutions and one for which they need much help and support. This emphasises the need for the staff to be a close and supportive group able to confront together the projection and introjection systems and to help rescue each other when one or more of them are caught. It requires a culture of honesty and mutual confrontation which is by no means easy to achieve. It requires also a certain permanency and long-standing relationship between the staff, notoriously difficult to achieve in children's institutions which tend to have a high labour turnover.

A consultant from outside the group who can view the situation with a 'semi-detached' eye may be a great help here in understanding with staff the nature of the projections and introjections and helping to re-establish the basic identity of both the staff group and the individuals with it.

### III   Institutional provision for the development of the capacity for relationships

The theoretical basis for the discussion here lies in the work of John Bowlby (1969) and many co-workers. Briefly, the capacity to develop lasting and meaningful relationships develops in accordance with the opportunity the child, especially the very young child, has to form secure attachments. The good ordinary family gives an excellent opportunity where the young child is likely to form a focal intense attachment, usually (though not always) with his mother. He forms other important although less intense attachments with others including his father, siblings, other relatives and friends, his attachment circle extending as he grows older. Moreover the people in his circle of attachment also have attachments to each other which are important to him for identification. He not only loves his mother as he experiences her but identifies with his father loving his mother and extends his 'concept' of the male loving the female. For the most part, although not always, institutions have dismally failed to replicate that pattern. The multiple indiscriminate caretaking system in which all staff indiscriminately care for all children effectively prevents child/adult attachment. This has been traditional in hospitals and can also be seen in day and residential institutions for physically healthy children.

The Robertsons' film *John* (Robertson, 1969a and b) shows how multiple indiscriminate caretaking effectively defeats John's efforts to attach himself to one nurse. Further it has been my experience that multiple indiscriminate caretaking also tends to inhibit attachments between staff so that there is a dearth of attachment models for the children. The situation is of course often compounded by staff turnover, hospital wards being staffed largely by transitory student nurses, and day and residential nurseries tending to have high labour turnover.

I am indebted to my colleague, Alastair Bain (Bain & Barnett, 1980) for a dramatic observation of the child's identification with an inadequate model of relationships in a day nursery and its perpetuation in his later relationships. The observation concerns what he calls 'the discontinuity of care provided even by a single caretaker which occurs when a nursery has to care for a number of children.' He writes, 'Their (the children's) intense needs for individual attention tend to mean that they do not allow the nurse to pay attention to any one child for any length of time; other children will pull at her skirt, want to sit up on her lap, push the child who is receiving attention away.' One can see this very clearly in *John*. He goes on, 'during the periods between moments of attention, the young child experiences his fellows as also receiving moments of attention . . . He will also experience as the predominant pattern of relationships between adult and child, a series of discontinuities of attention, a nurse momentarily directing her attention from one child to another . . . He and his moment are just part of a series of disconnected episodes.'

The follow-up of these children showed them to have identified with and to be operating on that model, the model of episodic and discontinuous attention, forming in turn a series of episodic and discontinuous relationships with their world shown through fleeting superficial attachments and also in episodic discontinuous play activities and later in difficulty in sustaining continuous attention at school. I have come to call this the 'butterfly phenomenon', the child flitting rather aimlessly from person to person or activity to activity.

Fortunately institutions do not have to be like that. It is possible to eliminate multiple indiscriminate caretaking and get closer to the family model. Dividing the institution into small units with firm boundaries as described above provides something more like a family setting even if it is still somewhat larger. Within that setting attachments between staff and children form more easily. Further even with an institutional setting it is possible to provide something nearer to a focal caretaker by assigning children to a single staff member for special care and attention. What this would include varies according to circumstances and needs. In the hospital the assigned nurse took special care of the child and his family, helping the mother care for the child when she was present, doing most of the general care herself if the mother was absent. She escorted him to theatre or to post-operative care, if the mother was not allowed to be present. She comforted him in distress, talking to him if he was verbal and especially talking through problems. For example, a child was overheard having an imaginary conversation with his absent mother on a toy telephone and saying, 'Mummy, I know I've been a naughty boy and that's why you don't come to see me.' The nurse picked that up and worked with the child about it. In residential settings there may be the importance of bedtime for deprived children, of outings like dental or medical visits, playing together, working with distress and problems, having a special relationship with the child and his family together if he is still in contact with his family.

Workers can never equal the mother's almost total availability to the young child since staff have limited working hours, but experience has shown that deep and meaningful attachments can be formed between the child and the assigned caretaker. For example, in the Royal National Orthopaedic Hospital, a small boy came from overseas whose pregnant mother with a large family of other children could not accompany him, and whose father could rarely visit. The assigned nurse developed a closely attached relationship with him (her other assigned children having mothers present). She not only did general care, but talked to him about his family, of which the boy had photographs, thus establishing some continuity. She also helped prepare him for going home to find a new baby by talking, by doll play and by relating to babies, of whom there were always some in the unit. It was very moving to watch them together. Parting when it came was very painful for both, but for both the rewards were enormous. In particular the child's capacity for attachment was sustained.

The gaps in the availability of the focal caretaker are difficult for the child but not impossible to handle. In small firmly bounded units children do form subsidiary attachments to other adults and indeed to each other and the caretaking need not become indiscriminate. The cot unit had explicit re-assignment plans when the assigned nurse was off-duty. Further, with older children in residential settings, adults can and indeed must also relate in an attached way to groups of children engaging in enjoyable activities with the group or handling the group in a state of distress or crisis.

In addition, the small bounded group gives a good setting for the adults to form meaningful relationships with each other. This not only again provides good models of attachments behaviour but also facilitates re-assignment when necessary. The child tends to accept the second adult more easily and to use him better if he has seen him in a good relationship with the first. In the hospital, for instance, when a child was admitted and accompanied by his mother, the nurse would frequently have relatively little to do with the child at first, but concentrated on building her relationships with the mother. The good relationship they established undoubtedly helped the child accept the nurse if and when the mother had to leave, and begin to form an attachment to her.

My references to transitory staff and high labour turnover may seem to suggest that attachments are always under threat from adults leaving. But in fact, we found that in units operated as described, there would be a dramatic fall in staff turnover. The Royal National Orthopaedic Hospital was fortunate that the cot unit was staffed by nursery nurses who were permanent staff and not by transitory student nurses. But in a profession, nursery nursing, that notoriously has an enormously high labour turnover, there was almost no labour turnover during the study and as the care method developed all three nursery nurses stayed over three years, an inestimable benefit for long-stay and repeat-stay children. The work had in fact become more challenging and rewarding and the attachment to the children increased the nurses' wish and sense of responsibility to stay with the children.

The work is not only more rewarding, however, it is also more stressful. Multiple indiscriminate caretaking can in fact be seen as a defence for staff against making meaningful and deep contact with any one child and his family, a contact which frees the child's expressiveness and brings the caretaker more fully into contact with his distress and problems as well as his joys. It can be quite shattering temporarily for staff to move from multiple indiscriminate caretaking to case assignment, a move which may include the disruption of concepts about what a child is like. One staff nurse said, 'I have had to unlearn everything I thought I knew about children since you (the author) have been here.' Too often staff think of the healthy normal child as one who is 'settled', calm, accepting of everyone who approaches him, relatively unprotesting about what is done to him. They need to learn that in the abnormal circumstances of the hospital, the 'normal' child is likely to be frightened or miserable quite a lot of the time, to protest at interventions, to object to the presence of strangers and to be apparently more difficult, certainly a more distressing child for adults to work with.

Again the staff may need help with this, help that can come from a strong attached staff group who support and care for each other, from senior staff, or from an outside consultant. In a sense one may say that the staff need to experience the same concern and support for their stresses that they are expected to provide for children and families, a consistency in the method of care.

I will conclude this section by trying to draw together some of the points I have made within a rather different theoretical framework. Bion (1967) has described the importance for the infant's development of his mother's capacity for reverie, i.e. how she takes in his communications, contains and ponders over them intuitively but not necessarily consciously, and responds to them in a meaningful way. It is particularly important in relation to fear and distress, that the mother can take in his projections and return them to the infant in a more realistic and tolerable version. The function of reverie is important also for staff in children's institutions. It can be reverie in the individual staff member or it can be something analogous to reverie in group situations, staff talking things through in an intuitive way together. The communications on which staff must work are often massive and very disturbing and staff in turn need support of the kind I have mentioned. Like the ordinary devoted mother (Winnicott, 1958) they need themselves to be contained in a system of meaningful attachments if they are to contain the children effectively. They need firmly bounded situations in which to work and they need the support of being able to talk things through in quieter circumstances away from the core of the children's distress and problems.

### IV   The developmental effect of the institution's social defence system

The author has described elsewhere the development and operation of the social defence system in institutions (Menzies, 1970). The institution develops by collusive interaction among its members a system of defences which appear in the structure, the mode of functioning and the culture of the institution. Continued membership of the institution tends to involve acceptance and operation of the accepted social defence system, at least while present in the institution. However, the social defence system is sustained and operated by individuals; notably staff members, and this plays a part in their effectiveness as models for identification. There appears to be a need for constant vigilance if the defence system operated in the institution is to be sustained at a mature level and indeed to be adaptive rather than defensive, for it will be under constant threat. It will be under threat because the stress and disturbance present in the children will predispose staff to use massive defences against confronting the disturbance in a painful although potentially therapeutic way. I have referred to multiple indiscriminate caretaking as one such defence. It can be associated with massive denial of the meaning of the children's communications, with a manic defence that denies it seriousness, with rigid punitive regimes which try to control disturbance rather than working it through. I also described above a paranoid defence system connected with the evasion of a difficult responsibility.

The children may be a threat in another way in that they in turn tend to operate massive and primitive defences against their distress which are in turn not only individual but also tend to become socialised as the children relate to each other in various group situations. This may have a powerful effect on staff who are usually outnumbered by children as the children try to force staff to enter into collusion with their social defence system. Hard work, courage and suffering are often needed if staff are to resist these pressures and sustain more mature defences as a model and as a facilitation of confronting and working through problems.

In the world of approved schools and institutions for delinquents such phenomena are known as sub-cultures in which problems such as homosexuality or violence are acted out away from staff or, sadly, sometimes with staff, and are recognised to be inimical to the therapeutic culture of the institution.

Work done on a consultancy visit to an approved school may illustrate this. I was told first by professional staff that there was great discontent among the domestic staff in the living units. They felt they could not achieve a high enough standard of work and were not getting job satisfaction. I was at first unclear what I was supposed to do about this. But gradually I felt I was beginning to understand. I heard a lot about violence among boys of which there had recently been more than usual and some of it very destructive. More than usually violent boys were said to have been admitted recently or were about to be admitted to the school. The professional staff were not only afraid of the boys' violence, but were anxious also about the impulses to counterviolence they felt in themselves. Up to that point, they had not felt able to confront the violence adequately as a problem to be worked at. Instead they had developed an anti-therapeutic and sub-cultural method of trying to prevent it, by gratification and appeasement. They hoped, not necessarily consciously, that if they provided a very high standard of care in living units, they could in effect keep the boys quiet. Professional staff then put subtle pressures on domestic workers to provide a quite unrealistic living standard, a pressure which the domestic workers in turn accepted and tried to put into operation. In reality they could not and consequently suffered painful feelings of inadequacy and failure. We disentangled this in the course of a long day's discussion during which professional staff faced their fears of violence more openly, realised that developing a sub-culture of dependency to counter a sub-culture of violence was not likely in fact to deal with the violence or to be therapeutic and so became more able to work with the violence directly. The domestic workers were relieved of the projections into and pressures on them and could once again apply themselves to a realistically defined task from which they got satisfaction.[1]

Such sub-cultures are perhaps less likely to appear in institutions which have the features I have suggested as more appropriate for the development of the healthy self in the children, e.g. with authoritative responsible staff,

---

1 What I have described as sub-cultures of violence and dependency are closely linked with Bion's formulation of basic assumptions of fight/flight and dependency as observed in small groups (Bion, 1961). The point Bion makes about the basic assumptions is that they are characterised by psychotic phenomena, are evasive of reality instead of confronting it, and they do not evidence a belief in work as a means of carrying out tasks or in the time and suffering needed to do so. So they are anti-therapeutic.

well-defined delegation, small fairly bounded units, effective opportunities for reverie. But no institution is likely to avoid them fully; hence my comment about the need for constant vigilance, possibly again with the help of a consultant.

## Conclusion

I hope I have succeeded in justifying my optimistic view that institutions for children can be developed in such a way as to provide more effectively for the development of a healthy self than has too often been the case in the past and, unfortunately, is still too often the case in the present. Changes in the desired direction can and have been achieved in institutions, although often at the cost of considerable turmoil, doubt and uncertainty among staff while they are being made.

The effect of such developments on children has been encouraging. At the Royal National Orthopaedic Hospital, no children who had been hospitalised under the new care system showed the typical signs of institutionalisation or of any serious damage to their development. There were problems but none serious, nor of a kind that could not be contained in the families and worked with there. Some of the children indeed seemed to have gained rather than lost ground. We acknowledge with respect and gratitude the major contribution many mothers made to this result, but it was also evident in unmothered children. I have already mentioned one small boy from overseas who actually developed well, but perhaps the most dramatic example was another small boy of foreign parents who were in this country but who very rarely visited. When the mother did come, she could not really make a relationship with him, but only carried out a few simple tasks usually designed to make him look more like a boy from his own country. This was almost meaningless. On admission at nearly four years old, he had no language, neither his own or English, and had most violent temper tantrums, so that for example, due notice had to be given of interventions, so that he could be given tranquillisers in advance. Everyone except the author diagnosed him as mentally defective. The author diagnosed him as psychotic, not only on the direct evidence he presented, but also from his history.

He had been driven from pillar to post, from foster home to residential nursery, day nursery and round and round again. He had passed much time in inadequate children's institutions with no attachment, no containment, no good models. During his 13 months in hospital (the longest continuous stay of any child), he was devotedly cared for by his assigned nurse and the nursery teacher especially, but also by other staff in the small close attachment circle of the unit. When he left he had an age-appropriate English vocabulary, had completely lost his temper tantrums, and had begun to use toys and other methods to work over in a constructive way his hospital experience. A fortunate coincidence for him was that the staff nurse had to resign her post for family reasons and decided to foster children as a means of working at home. She took the boy home with her, thus sustaining an important attachment. He then continued to develop well and settled well into a normal school.

The results in the desperately damaged boys in the approved school do not usually match up to that level, but it is notable that there is in general much less acting out in the school, fewer abscondings, less violence and much more constructive activity than one usually finds in such institutions. The results are also above average in terms of life performance in general and, in particular, in fewer of the repeated delinquencies that take so many such boys later into other institutions, like borstals, prisons or mental hospitals.

Much remains to be done, however, to convert other children's institutions into places more suitable for children to grow up in, in a healthy way. Since powerful pressures are now evident in our society to put children into institutions, there appears to be an urgent and serious need to improve the institutions if children are to be given the best opportunities for development and the 'vicious circle' effect of early institutionalisation prevented, such as delinquency, mental illness, or repeated institutionalisation.

## References

Bain, A. and Barnett, L. (1980) 'The design of a day care system in a nursery setting for children under five.' (Report to the Department of Health and Social Security. London. Unpublished.)

Bion, W.R. (1961) *Experiences in Groups*. London: Tavistock.

Bion, W.R. (1967) *Second Thoughts*. London: Heinemann.

Bowlby, J. (1969) *Attachment and Loss: Vol. 1 Attachment*. London: Hogarth.

Menzies, I.E.P. (1970) 'The functioning of social systems as a defence against anxiety'. London: Tavistock Pamphlet No. 3.

Menzies, I.E.P. (1975) 'Thoughts on the maternal role in contemporary society', *Journal of Child Psychotherapy*, 4(1).

Robertson, J. (1969a) [Film] 'John, 17 months: for nine days in a residential nursery'. 16 mm sound. (England: Concord Films Council. USA: New York University Film Library.)

Robertson, J. (1969b) *Guide to the Film* John. England: Concord Film Council.

Winnicott, D.W. (1958) *Collected Papers*. London: Tavistock.

Chapter 12

# Standing next to the weighing scales[1,2]

*Dilys Daws*

Originally published in the *Journal of Child Psychotherapy*
(1985) 11(2): 77–85.

I have been working for several years in the baby clinic of a general practice
in a health centre. One day weekly there are baby clinics, morning and
afternoon, each taken by two of the GPs and the four health visitors
attached to the practice. A nurse attends to give immunisations. I now go
weekly to the morning clinics. I have contact with the other doctors in the
practice and at times work closely with the practice's social worker who is a
qualified psychotherapist.

I originally started to work at this baby clinic with a thesis that many
mothers of new babies may have difficulties arising from their own personalities and from previous relationships, which become reflected in their
dealings with the baby, or in disturbed behaviour of some kind in the baby.
Mothers who had had no serious difficulties at other periods of their lives
might have been thrown off balance by the experience of pregnancy, childbirth, and caring for a very new baby. I hoped that brief psychotherapeutic
work of a combined interpretative and supportive nature could relieve some
of these problems. Work could be directly with the mother, or mother and
father, or by supporting the doctor or health visitor already involved with
the family. The majority of babies are routinely brought for clinic visits by
their mothers and I believe this influences the nature of my referrals. I see
more mothers and babies together than mothers and fathers and babies.
Usually this seems an appropriate way of working, at other times it may be
symptomatic of a marital or family problem.[3] In the several years I have
worked in the baby clinic I have felt my ambition to carry out short-term
pieces of work has been justified.

1  My title echoes Dr Hyla Hoiden's phrase 'propping up the filing cabinet', coined in similar
   circumstances.
2  This paper was given at a Scientific Meeting of the Association of Child Psychotherapists on
   22nd October 1985.
3  Because the majority of patients are women, I shall use 'she' and 'her' to denote them. The
   majority of doctors in this practice are men and I shall use 'he' and 'him' to denote them.

The issues that have arisen over these years are of two main kinds. One is the nature of the clinical work undertaken. (Much of this presents as sleep problems and I give an account of this work in the companion paper which follows.)[4] The second is the process of being a consultant to an institution other than one's own. I use the term 'consultant' charily: it is not intended as a confusion with the medical use of the term.

As a 'consultant' from outside, the most crucial issue is *where to put oneself*. At first I thought this to be a personal, idiosyncratic problem; it took time to generalise it. An outside professional can be useful in bringing specific skills and knowledge to an institution. Is being an outside consultant or, more baldly, an outsider, of value in itself? Having outsiders around can make a group feel uncomfortable. *Being* an outsider in such a group is uncomfortable. From our potty-training days on we strive to be acceptable members of a social group. Elenore Smith Bowen has described in *Return to Laughter* (published by Gollancz, 1954) how lonely and difficult it is to be an anthropologist living in a primitive culture. While one is occupied in questioning the natives on the details of their kinship patterns, all is well. When night draws in and the anthropologist hears laughter from the nearby huts, she feels excluded and wonders if she is the subject of the laughter. It is apparent, however, that her usefulness as an anthropologist remains only if she continues to study kinship – if she settles in to become a part of the culture, her scientific value is endangered.

How does this analogy apply to the child psychotherapist in a baby clinic of a general practice?

When I started work at this practice, Dr Alexis Brook, who had introduced me to it, offered to support me with monthly discussions on my work there. These were very valuable at first in my newness and tentativeness. Then I began to feel disloyal to the practice, talking about my contacts there 'behind their backs', so to speak. I regret now that I did not voice these feelings to Alexis Brook, I might have learned much sooner what being a 'consultant' is about. As it was, I strove for a feeling of 'belonging' in my once-weekly visits to the practice. In my defence I may say that the atmosphere there is warm and welcoming, appreciated by staff and patients alike.

At this time I sought to do a great deal of clinical work, feeling myself to be a useful member of the primary health care team, seeing the parents and babies thought to be in particular need by their GP or health visitor. Two problems then emerged. The busier I was, the less visible. If I was really energetic and really co-operative, I could see four families, or mothers and babies, in four hours. I would end up bemused, details of feeding and

4 Daws, D. (1985) 'Sleep problems in babies and young children', *Journal of Child Psychotherapy*, 11(2): 87–95. Not reproduced here [ed.].

sleeping patterns, or parents' relationships with their own parents, hopelessly confused. It would be galling to emerge from this to find a health visitor saying, 'I haven't seen you all morning. I didn't know you were here.' It seemed that visibility was an attribute in itself. Secondly, whenever I got a referral, it was rarely soon enough. I would see parents with an eight-month-old baby who had slept badly since birth. They had been patients of the practice for those eight months. I had been visiting for those eight months. Why had I not seen them earlier?

I began to realise that talking about patients was as important as being shut away seeing a few, and that much of my usefulness was in sharing ideas about the problems of mothers and babies with my colleagues; furthermore, that the timing of good referrals was partly dependent on the timing of informal discussions with me. I realised I must be visible, available and receptive.

I first learnt how to stand next to the weighing-scales during vacant hours when a patient had cancelled an appointment. Gradually I realised it might be the optimal place to be. It is the focal point of the baby clinic: near the reception desk; near the chairs where mothers sit and chat, holding their babies, or watching their small children play on the floor; where the health visitors welcome each mother and assess how much or how little help she is asking for that day; where the doctors come out to greet patients or chase up information.

Bringing the baby to be weighed is the focus for the baby clinic. Parents can visit with no other ostensible reason than to weigh the baby. This alone validates the visit while enabling the mother or father to make use of a contact with the health visitor, or make friends with other parents. The moment of weighing the baby can symbolically represent, rationally or not, the total state of development of the baby. A gain of weight can confirm for a mother that her feeding and care have done the baby good; a loss of weight may set the alarm bells going for all concerned. The value of these measurements is not as irrefutable evidence, but as an illustration of what sensitive health care workers have already divined as going on between each mother and baby. Standing by the weighing scales is thus an effective way of eavesdropping on the progress of every baby who attends the clinic.

It takes as much skill to stand next to a weighing machine as it does not to talk during a psychotherapy session. My patients sometimes complain of my silence and I think, 'Me, silent? I've been thinking hard all the time.' The skill of thinking on behalf of the patient is only evident if one says in words one's thoughts; if one talks too much, reflective thought has no time to grow.

Standing doing nothing equally requires skill if it is not to be puzzling and persecuting to the people around. It is legitimised in a busy clinic because members of all professions stand at times looking around, sometimes assessing what to do next, sometimes talking to each other. I could be any of these, standing receptively to watch what is going on, or immediately available for discussion. If I am too self-contained, it must seem that my observations are for some unexplained private use; if I am too efficiently outgoing, mothers hand me their baby books to check them into the clinic.

By watching I gain what for me is invaluable – seeing a whole range of mothers and babies interact. Weekly, my store of impressions of normality and pathology is reinforced so that when someone is referred to me with a problem, I have a background of knowing where this might fit in with what usually happens between mothers and babies. I get the chance to talk informally, at times of less stress, to mothers I have previously worked with, and see how the baby has developed, without further problems needing to be a reason for our meeting. This is a luxury we rarely have in a child guidance clinic.

Most important, by being physically present at the routine baby clinic, I hope to be available for those responsible for the babies to be able to cross-check their own impressions of whether things are going well or badly for a particular baby and its parents. A meeting at the end of the baby clinic briefly reviews each attendance. By having been around I am a more credible part of this discussion. I do not believe that I am the only holder of a psychodynamic viewpoint. We would do well to acknowledge, as members of the psychotherapy professions, that we came to these professions because psychoanalytic thinking is embedded in present-day culture – the culture did not arise because of us. Our contribution is to keep it in circulation in spite of our own as well as our colleagues' many resistances. In the baby clinic, my colleagues have specific medical and nursing skills; they also have a basic underlying psychodynamic approach to their patients. My task is in reinforcing this approach in my colleagues, not in allowing it to be attributed only to me.

I have described myself as centrally placed in the baby clinic – can I persist in calling myself an outsider? I hope so. I hope I do not stop questioning the shared assumptions of the baby clinic. The very acceptance of many disturbed and disturbing people, something that this practice does so well, in itself creates problems. It can lead to a forgetting that some of their behaviours or their problems might be changed; my role is sometimes to highlight this. An outsider who does not have the responsibility for the management and continuance of the baby clinic can listen out for the reverberances that these patients cause in the workers who try to help them. These reverbances are a useful diagnostic tool if they can be recognised as such.

One problem in this kind of consultative work is in the process of continuity. Because I have visited the practice for a long time, and feel at home there, I expect that the staff know me and are used to working with me. I forget that with each new partner or health visitor, or changeover of trainee doctor, I must do more than get to know them in personal terms. I must also let them know what I feel is my function in the practice.

The need for this often becomes evident the first time they attempt to make a referral to me, and I hedge over taking it. In the discussion over whether I should see a particular patient, each of us is forced to spell out our assumptions of what benefit might or might not accrue to the patient if I saw him or her. Talking about the principle behind a referral goes deeper than simply asking what the problems and background of the patient are. It includes looking at what the present and future relationship of referrer (i.e. doctor or health visitor), patient and psychotherapist, will be. Individual work that I do with a patient is a direct extension of work done already by the referrer. A good referral comes usually from someone in whom the patient has already entrusted confidences, or who at least has shown a crack in the face of their rejection of help. Work done by me will connect back into the routine contact the mother has with the baby clinic. Some referrals are made from long, close contact with the patient. The referral letters from one woman senior partner contain as much information and insight about the patient as I am likely to acquire in several weeks of hourly sessions. Where the doctor–patient relationship has achieved so much, the contacts with me may need to be validated for the patient with frequent visits to the GP about physical symptoms. At other times, I suspect that the urgency of a patient's demands makes the worker feel that for me to see a patient would rescue both worker and patient alike.

In spite of all my reservations, I do accept many referrals and perhaps have learnt not to disappear from sight while seeing patients. To that end I always mention the referrer to new patients, with the implication that I will discuss their progress with him or her. In only a few cases has confidentiality that excluded the doctor or health visitor been necessary for confidence to be placed in me.

In the context of a group general practice, doctors and others see themselves as part of a team intervening at different moments over a period of years. Some patients will faithfully attend one doctor, except in emergencies, but often the transference is shared by the practice as a whole, or some members in it, with the actual named doctor of that patient. The transference to me personally has a variety of meanings to different patients. This depends partly on how casually or how formally the referral has been set up. In an atmosphere of informal goodwill, it may seem stuffy to insist on use of surnames, formal referral letters and deferred appointments, but I believe that a professional distance still has value. I rarely see a patient the same day, even if I happen to be free. When I do, I often feel that there has not been the same therapeutic impact in the consultation as one in which the patient has had time to prepare herself, time to work out the balance of vulnerability and defences which will enable her to use this session as more than an emergency outpouring of her troubles.

Although my particular interest is in the problems of new babies, children under the school age of five are the province of this clinic. Problems of all this age range of children are discussed with me. I am more chary of taking on children over five. It often makes sense to see parents for a consultation on a puzzling stage of development in their child. Such brief informal work has obvious supportive and informative use and may help prevent problems increasing. It can, however, leave a child and family with less flexibility in the possibility of other treatment. Granted some families might come once or twice to their own doctor's surgery who would never manage the formality of clinic appointments. Some brief interpretative work might be an opportunity they would never otherwise have. With other cases I feel that seeing me first complicates an eventual referral. I have neither the brief, nor the time, to run a miniature child guidance clinic, but I can also see how irritating this position might be to the GPs. Many emotional and behavioural problems of children over five are brought to them in the course of their surgeries. There is not the easy supportive forum of the baby clinic for the doctor to discuss these older children. He can offer either more time at the end of his own surgery or a formal outside referral to a child guidance clinic.

One main issue about a referral is whether it is more helpful for me to see the patient myself, or to use the approach from the concerned colleague as a chance to discuss together the problems involved. Often a doctor or health visitor needs simply a fresh view of their patient's problems, not a fresh person to see them.

Next is the issue of whether to take a referral as being meant for oneself, or as an assessment to refer on to another agency, usually of course a child guidance clinic. Referring patients from an institution one is involved in to another such is unsurpassable as an opportunity to be seen to be wrong in two places at once. In each situation the intermediary is seen as an intrinsic member of the other team. By definition, one institution seems to misunderstand how to make a proper referral, and the other to misunderstand what to do with one.

Setting this aside, a too quick assumption that patients should be passed on seems to dismay the referring doctor. One who makes many excellent referrals to me had a couple of recent ones that I had then passed on to our child guidance clinic recommended for intensive therapy. He said he had not thought of them as being so disturbed. One of the strengths of an experienced GP is that he has seen a lot of children grow up and seen families tolerate a lot of disturbed behaviour. It may not be helpful if he feels that I as a psychotherapist panic every time I meet a child showing some disturbance and head them off away from the practice.

Doctors are used to making many referrals of patients. Good doctors are used to discussing the referral with the patients in such a way that the patient feels the referral to be an extension of the doctor's own care, not a rejection of the patient, nor as a giving up in despair by the doctor. What doctors are not so used to doing is discussing a referral at length with the colleague to whom they are making it. I feel that this is one of my main functions in the practice. It is also the hardest to manage and the hardest to explain.

Discussing the case makes obvious sense as an opportunity for me to be given information about the patient, about the problem, and some of the background. All I need to do is ask for more details, enquire why the referral is being made at this particular moment, express my interest, and my intention of keeping the referrer informed. This may be a successful interchange. Some brief psychotherapy has been economically set up, convenient for the patients, and quite often successful enough. Why not settle for as many such cases as I can pick up?

It seems as though struggling with the reason for a referral still makes sense, not only to evaluate whether I could help this particular patient, but also in terms of a need to make the work done with the patient as known as possible to the referrer. I can see busy doctors trying to hide their impatience. They are torn daily by their need to deal with medical emergencies and get through a long list of appointments, and their awareness that some patients need time to talk about their problems. They have to juggle these two kinds of needs and feel that what I can offer is the luxury of time to a few selected patients. By contrast, I feel that much of my value to the practice is in reporting back my conclusions on how referral symptoms connect with family relationships. It takes time to relate this convincingly and the doctor may think he is not saving much time if he listens to it. I am not the only one who can make such connections – I was only invited to work in this practice because of the awareness already there. But if the doctor does listen to my conclusions, he will be supported in increasingly seeing such connections when families tell him of their problems. Additional insight brings additional responsibilities. The more he recognises problems, the more he will feel the need to listen, and to worry. His work will increase beyond bearing, either in time or accumulated anxiety.

Contained in this is one answer to my earlier question, 'Why do I so often get a referral "too late"?' Perhaps it is impossible for doctors and health visitors to receive the full impact of the pathology of every patient they see. In fact, the baby clinic is a 'well-baby' clinic, and much of the work is in supporting normality and healthy development. In order for such a clinic to survive, there must be a basic assumption that the anxieties brought constantly are being by definition met and dealt with by the routine activities of the clinic.

Mothers, and fathers, particularly with first babies, may have an infinite dread that they are unable and unworthy to look after a baby properly and that the proof of this will be that the baby does not survive. For many of these, the weekly confirmation that their baby *has* survived, even that it is doing well, becomes a validation for the mother by her health visitor and doctor that she is being a good-enough mother. Something that perhaps was not worked out with the mother's own mother, the permission to be a good mother, becomes worked out through this weekly interchange. The workers in the baby clinic have to stand this projected anxiety weekly and survive for the parents until the next week. Sharing the anxiety can protect the worker; passing it on in the form of a referral can break the experience of the baby clinic as a bulwark of continuing mothering.

Similarly, doctors know that patients use a consultation with them as a focus for cumulative anxiety about their child. How does a doctor distinguish between a consultation where anxiety is communicated and satisfactorily contained for the patient within that consultation, from one where the signal is to use outside help? The feelings stirred up in the doctor do not always help to distinguish. Consultations that leave the doctor feeling anxious and helpless may have been highly successful from the point of view of a patient who goes off relieved of a burden. The doctor's efforts to produce additional help for the patient may mystify someone who already feels much better. Conversely, other patients are unable to say how bad things really are – they protect themselves and workers alike with a facade of well-turned-out babies. Doctors and health visitors have to do sensitive detective work to prise out the agonies of broken nights or other difficulties in relationships between babies and parents.

In a careful baby clinic the end-of-clinic meeting reviews every attendance, and worries about each baby and family seen are spoken and noted. These meetings inform the workers involved and this information is then an enriched background to every contact each member of the team has with that family. The meeting also enables the workers to share the experience of aroused anxiety that has accumulated during the three hours or more of the baby clinic. It serves as a process of working through that enables the workers to go home no longer invaded by a total experience of anxieties communicated and absorbed, but not openly interpreted as in a psychotherapy session. The positive use to these meetings is thus obvious. Should we, however, worry about whether their use as a resolution of anxiety for the workers mediates against a continuity of action on behalf of the patient?

The converse problem for health-care workers is in the giving up of their omnipotence. Health visitors have an obligation to visit all new babies and it is rarely that they are refused access to the home for this visit. After this, unless there is grave cause for concern about how a baby is being treated, visits by families to the clinic, or by workers to the home, are conducted on the basis that families are voluntarily using professional services set up for their benefit. Professionals have to wait to be consulted, and they have to think carefully of what they are being asked to do. Like good grandparents, they do not use their own experience to take over parenting from the parents: perhaps they provide a model of availability and receptivity to the parents' anxieties, which enables the parents to do the same for their babies.

What I hope to have done in this paper is to have spelled out the complexity of being a 'consultant', i.e. an outsider in an institution, involved at the point where anxiety can effectively be aroused or allayed. The process of being involved in the referral of patients means being involved with the referrer at a moment of working out which is in the best interests of both patients and of the workers.

The unexpressed underlying theme might be what happens to all this anxiety when it touches the consultant weekly. Being an outsider enables the consultant to be free of shared defences and thus free to pick out anxieties. This same outside position means he does not have continued responsibility for the institution and can perhaps leave the anxieties behind on going home. Paradoxically, the most effective resolution for me of the anxieties aroused is in the clinical work I undertake at the baby clinic. Work with albeit a few selected patients can represent a working through of the cumulative mass of problems raised at the clinics.

I believe that I, as an outsider, help my insider colleagues continually to look at the assumptions on which their clinic is run. Perhaps what all such clinics need is not necessarily an outside person, but the flexibility to put themselves from time to time *outside* their institution in order to question how useful it really is to the patients who come to it.

## Acknowledgement

With thanks to the James Wigg Practice at the Kentish Town Health Centre for giving me standing room.

# References to introductory material

Alvarez, A. (1992) *Live Company*. London & New York: Tavistock/Routledge.

Alvarez, A. (1996) 'Addressing the element of deficit in children with autism: psychotherapy which is both psychoanalytically and developmentally informed', *Clinical Child Psychology and Psychiatry*, 1(4): 525–537.

Barrows, P. (2001) 'The aims of child psychotherapy', *Clinical Child Psychology and Psychiatry*, 6(3): 371–385.

Bick, E. (1941) 'Child analysis today'. In Williams, M.H. (ed.) *Collected Papers of Martha Harris and Esther Bick*. Strath Tay: Clunie Press.

Boston, M. (1967) 'Some effects of external circumstances on the inner experience of two child patients', *Journal of Child Psychotherapy*, 2(1): 28–32.

Boston, M. (1972) 'Psychotherapy with a boy from a children's home', *Journal of Child Psychotherapy*, 3(2): 53–67.

Boston, M. and Szur, R. (1983) *Psychotherapy with Severely Deprived Children*. London: Routledge & Kegan Paul.

Cohn, N. (1994) 'Attending to emotional issues on a special care baby unit'. In Obholzer, A. and Zagier Roberts, V. (eds.) *The Unconscious at Work*. London & New York: Routledge.

Daws, D. (1989) *Through the Night*. London: Free Association.

Daws, D. and Boston, M. (eds.) (1988) *The Child Psychotherapist and Problems of Young People*. London: Karnac.

Gaensbauer, T.J. (2002) 'Representations of trauma in infancy: Clinical and theoretical implications for the understanding of early memory', *Infant Mental Health Journal*, 23(3): 259–277.

Harris, M. (1971) 'The place of once-weekly treatment in the work of an analytically trained child psychotherapist', *Journal of Child Psychotherapy*, 3(1): 31–39.

Hopkins, J. (1992) 'Infant–parent psychotherapy', *Journal of Child Psychotherapy*, 18(1): 5–18.

Hopkins, J. (2000) 'Overcoming a child's resistance to late adoption: how one new attachment can facilitate another', *Journal of Child Psychotherapy*, 26(3): 335–347.

Hurry, A. (1998) 'Psychoanalysis and developmental therapy'. In Hurry, A. (ed.) *Psychoanalysis and Developmental Therapy*. London: Karnac.

Jackson, E. (2002) 'Mental health in schools: what about the staff? Thinking about the impact of work discussion groups for staff in school settings', *Journal of Child Psychotherapy*, 28(2): 129–146.

Klein, H.S. (1980) 'Autistic phenomena in neurotic patients', *International Journal of Psychoanalysis*, 61(3): 395–402.

Klein, M. (1946) 'Notes on some schizoid mechanisms'. In *Envy and Gratitude and Other Works*. London: Hogarth (1975).

Klein, M. (1952) 'Some theoretical conclusions regarding the emotional life of the infant'. In *Envy and Gratitude and Other Works*. London: Hogarth (1975).

Klein, M. (1955a) 'On identification'. In *Envy and Gratitude and Other Works*. London: Hogarth (1975).

Klein, M. (1955b) 'The psycho-analytic play technique: its history and significance'. In *Envy and Gratitude and Other Works*. London: Hogarth (1975).

Lanyado, M. (2001) 'The symbolism of the story of Lot and his wife: the function of the 'present relationship' and non-interpretative aspects of the therapeutic relationship in facilitating change', *Journal of Child Psychotherapy*, 27(1): 19–33.

Lanyado, M. and Horne, A. (eds.) (1999) *The Handbook of Child and Adolescent Psychotherapy*: Psychoanalytic Approaches. London & New York: Routledge.

Likierman, M. and Urban, E. (1999) 'The roots of child and adolescent psycho-therapy in psychoanalysis'. In Lanyado, M. and Horne, A. (eds.) *The Handbook of Child and Adolescent Psychotherapy: Psychoanalytic Approaches*. London & New York: Routledge.

Lubbe. T. (1998) 'Projective identification fifty years on: a personal view', *Journal of Child Psychotherapy*, 24(3): 367–391.

Meltzer, D. (1967) *The Psychoanalytic Process*. London: Heinemann.

Miller, L. (1992) 'The relation of infant observation to clinical practice in an under-fives counselling service', *Journal of Child Psychotherapy*, 18(1): 19–32.

Mitrani, J.L. (1996) *A Framework for the Imaginary*. Northvale, NJ: Aronson.

Mitrani, J.L. (2001) *Ordinary People and Extra-Ordinary Protections*. Hove: Routledge.

O'Shaughnessy, E. (1981) 'A commemorative essay on W.R. Bion's theory of thinking', *Journal of Child Psychotherapy*, 7(2): 181–192. In Spillius, E.B. (ed.) *Melanie Klein Today*, Vol. 2. London & New York: Routledge (1988).

Perry, B.D., Pollard, R., Blakely, T., Baker, W. and Vigilante, D. (1995) 'Childhood trauma, the neurobiology of adaptation and 'use-dependent' development of the brain: How 'states' become 'traits', *Infant Mental Health Journal*, 16(4): 271–291.

Pozzi, M.E. (1999) 'Psychodynamic counselling with under-5s and their families', *Journal of Child Psychotherapy*, 25(1): 51–70.

Reid, S. (1990) 'The importance of beauty in the psychoanalytic experience', *Journal of Child Psychotherapy*, 16(1): 29–52.

Reid, S. (1999) 'Autism and trauma: autistic post-traumatic developmental disorder'. In Alvarez, A. and Reid, S. *Autism and Personality*. London & New York: Routledge.

Rustin, M. and Quagliata, E. (2000) *Assessment in Child Psychotherapy*. London: Duckworth.

Sandler, J. (ed.) (1989) *Projection, Identification, Projective Identification*. London: Karnac.

Schore, A.N. (2001) 'The effects of early relational trauma on right brain development, affect regulation, and infant mental health', *Infant Mental Health Journal*, 22(1–2): 201–269.

Spillius, E.B. (1994) 'Developments in Kleinian thought: Overview and personal view', *Psychoanalytic Inquiry*, 14(3): 324–365.

Sprince, J. (2000) 'Towards an integrated network', *Journal of Child Psychotherapy*, 26(3): 413–431.

Strachey, J. (1934) 'The nature of the therapeutic action of psychoanalysis', *International Journal of Psycho-Analysis*, 15: 127–59.

Szur, R.T. and Miller, S. (1991) *Extending Horizons. Psychoanalytic psychotherapy with children, adolescents and families.* London & New York: Karnac.

Tustin, F. (1994) 'The perpetuation of an error', *Journal of Child Psychotherapy*, 20(1): 3–23.

## Some key papers available in other works/collections

Alvarez, A. (1988) 'Beyond the unpleasure principle', *Journal of Child Psychotherapy*, 14(2): 1–13. In Szur, R. and Miller, S. (eds.) *Extending Horizons. Psychoanalytic psychotherapy with children, adolescents and families.* London & New York: Karnac (1991).

Furman, E. (1981) 'Treatment-via-the-parent: a case of bereavement', *Journal of Child Psychotherapy*, 7(1): 89–103. In Szur, R. and Miller, S. (eds.) *Extending Horizons. Psychoanalytic psychotherapy with children, adolescents and families.* London & New York: Karnac (1991).

Harris, M. (1965) 'Depression and the depressive position in an adolescent boy', *Journal of Child Psychotherapy*, 1(3): 33–40. In Spillius, E.B. (ed.) *Melanie Klein Today*, Vol. 2. London & New York: Routledge (1988).

Menzies, I.E.P. (1975) 'Thoughts on the maternal role in contemporary society', *Journal of Child Psychotherapy*, 4(1): 5–14. In *Containing Anxiety in Institutions.* London: Free Association (1988).

O'Shaughnessy, E. (1981) 'A commemorative essay on W.R. Bion's theory of thinking', *Journal of Child Psychotherapy*, 7(2): 181–192. In Spillius, E.B. (ed.) *Melanie Klein Today*, Vol. 2. London & New York: Routledge (1988).

# Author index

# Subject index